CANTERBURY PILGRIMS
AND THEIR WAYS

BY THE SAME AUTHOR
R. L. S.
EDINBURGH AND THE LOTHIANS

In Collaboration with T. F. HENDERSON
SCOTLAND OF TO-DAY

CANTERBURY PILGRIMS
AND THEIR WAYS

BY
FRANCIS WATT

FOLCROFT LIBRARY EDITIONS / 1973

Library of Congress Cataloging in Publication Data

Watt, Francis, 1849-1927.
   Canterbury pilgrims and their ways.

   Reprint of the 1917 ed. publisehd by Dodd, Mead,
New York.
   1. Canterbury, Eng.--Description. 2. Pilgrims and
pilgrimages--Canterbury, Eng. 3. Thomas à Becket,
Saint, Abp. of Canterbury, 1118?-1170. I. Title.
DA690.C3W3 1973   914.22'3   73-4912
ISBN 0-8414-9353-7 (lib. bdg.)

Manufactured in the United States of America.

CANTERBURY PILGRIMS
AND THEIR WAYS

BY
FRANCIS WATT

WITH A FRONTISPIECE IN COLOUR
AND TWELVE ILLUSTRATIONS IN MONOTONE

NEW YORK
DODD, MEAD AND CO.
1917

CONTENTS

CHAPTER I

A Medieval Tragedy

Page

Importance of the Canterbury Pilgrimage—The Personality of St. Thomas—His Early Years—A Gay Courtier—Archdeacon and Chancellor—Archbishop of Canterbury—A Sudden Change—Conflict with the King—Exile of the Archbishop—His Return—Extreme Measures—The King and the Knights—The Knights and the Archbishop—The Last Scene in the Cathedral—St. Thomas of Canterbury 1

CHAPTER II

After the Murder

Horror of the Deed—Details that heightened It—After History of the Murderers—The King and the Crime—His Penance at Canterbury—Its Supposed Results—Desolation and Reconsecration of the Cathedral—Canonisation of St. Thomas—The Beginning of the Miracles . . . 15

CHAPTER III

The Miracles

The Question of Miracles—Necessary to the Cult of St. Thomas—The Chief Chroniclers—Wonders after Death—The Blood of the Martyr—The Well of St. Thomas—Miracles at the Tomb—Victory over a Demon—Two Canterbury Cases—The Milk of the Church—A Dire Alternative—The Dead raised to Life—The Monks and the Doctors—The Perquisites of Saintship—Domestic Wonders—Petty Cash—Miracles and the Animal Creation—Unfortunate Supplicants—A Condemned Criminal—A Rascal Shepherd—The Fame of St. Thomas 24

CHAPTER IV

The Honours, the Relics and the Shrine

St. Thomas a peculiarly English Saint—Memorials of Him in Old London—His Honours in Scotland—Relics of Him in England and Abroad—True and False Relics—Holy Places at Canterbury—The Feast of the Translation of the Relics—A Memorable Tuesday—The Shrine in Trinity Chapel—Gifts to the Tomb—A Splendid Diamond—How the Shrine was Guarded—Pious Frauds—The End of the Business—The Shrine Despoiled—Alleged Trial of Bishop Becket—A Modern Discovery—Queen Mary and Cardinal Pole 35

CHAPTER V

Pilgrims and Pilgrimages

The Pilgrim Through the Ages—Wonders of an Unknown World—Meaning of the Pilgrimage—The Greater and Lesser Pilgrimage—Derived Words—Various Classes of Pilgrims—Equipment of the Pilgrim—Provision made by the Pious—Some Royal Pilgrimages—The Return of the Pilgrim—The End of the Matter—Modern Revivals—Sir Walter Raleigh's Allegory 47

CHAPTER VI

The Main Route. The Start—London to St. Thomas à Waterings

Two Men of Letters—A Pair of Fallacies—The Capital—The Real Starting Point—How it Looked in Medieval Times—Old London Bridge—Legend of the Ferryman—How the Bridge was Kept Up—Chapel of St. Thomas—Memories of the Old Bridge—Southwark in Ancient Times—"The Tabard"—Harry Bailly, the Host—Fact and Fiction about Him—Southwark Memorials of St. Thomas—Out in the Country—Old Time Fares—St. Thomas à Waterings—Memories of the Place . . . 56

CHAPTER VII

Chaucer

What We know of Him—Facts of His Life—Varied Occupations and Fortunes—Adventures at Home and Abroad—Death and Burial—Curious Incidents in His Career—Portraits of Him, Literary and Otherwise—Fondness for Books and for Nature—Comments on Women—Ironical Humour—Broad Touches—Character of Harry Bailly—"The

CONTENTS

Tavern Sentiment"—An Objective Poet—*The Canterbury Tales*—Idea of the Work—The Supplementary *Tale of Beryn*—Places Mentioned in the *Tales*—Theory about Harbledown—The French of the Prioress—Chaucer, Spenser and Tennyson 70

CHAPTER VIII

The Main Route (*continued*). On the Way to Dartford

The Main Route—Aspect of the Country—The Fields—The Crops—The Cottages—The Castles—The Old Towns—The Churches—Deptford—The Bridge—The Ravensbourne—Greenwich—Memories of St. Alphege—Blackheath and Blackheath Hill—The Manor of Placentia—Shooter's Hill—Its Evil Reputation—Dartford—Its Connection with the Pilgrimage—Its Religious Houses—Dartford Bridge—The Story of Wat Tyler 85

CHAPTER IX

The Main Route (*continued*). The Twin Paths to Rochester

The Problem of the Ways—How Chaucer Went—Stone Castle and Stone Church—The Watermen of Gravesend and their Charges—Remiss Churchwardens—Milton, Denton, and Chalk—Gad's Hill and its Robbers—A Legal Argument—The Road by Watling Street—Singlewell—Swanscombe and its Legend—Danes' Holes—Religious Houses at Stroud—" Frindsbury Clubs "—Children with Tails—Rochester Bridge and its Chapels—St. William of Perth—His Shrine in the Cathedral—A Pious Innkeeper—Old Time Inns—The Good Works of Bishop Gundulf 98

CHAPTER X

The Main Route (*continued*). Rochester to Ospringe

Rainham Down and its Memories—The Cross at Newington—More Miracles—Crime in Holy Places—Roman Echoes—The Four-Went-Way—Sittingbourne—The Varied Fortunes of Schamel Hermitage—A Princely Alms—A Bid for Patronage—Old Time Feasting—Some Ancient Inns—The Legend of Tong Castle—Bapchild and Radfield—The Strange Story of " Judd's Folly "—Halt at Ospringe 112

CHAPTER XI

The Main Route (concluded). The Last Stage to Canterbury

The *Maison Dieu* at Ospringe—Its Various Fortunes—Religious Houses at Faversham—St. Crispin, St. Crispianus and St. Erasmus—The Poor Nuns of Davington—The Forest of the Blean-Boughton Hill—The First View of Canterbury—The Hospital of St. Nicholas at Harbledown—Its Long History—Erasmus and Dean Colet—Treasures of the Hospital—The Black Prince's Well—" Blue Dick "—His Outrageous Proceedings —On the Threshold 123

CHAPTER XII

The Story of Canterbury

The Place before the People—The Roman City—Its Remains To-day—Early Christians and their Churches—Coming of the Northmen—The Pagan Tribes—Red Ruin—Queen Bertha—Mythical Canterbury—The Ancient Legend of Pope Gregory—The Coming of Augustine—Conversion of Kent—St. Augustine's Abbey and the Priory of Christ Church—Their Rivalries—Archbishop Cuthbert's Device—Victory of Christ Church—Limits of Saxon Canterbury—Famous Archbishops—Old Town Life in Canterbury 136

CHAPTER XIII

The Cathedral

As We Know It—The Saxon Church—Fire and Invasion—Building and Rebuilding—"The Glorious Choir of Conrad"—William of Sens and William the Englishman—Notable Things about the Cathedral—Becket's Crown—The Crypt—The Black Prince's Chantry—His Life and Death—His Burial and Tomb—The Angel Steeple—Christ Church Gate —The Priory of Christchurch 149

CHAPTER XIV

The Pilgrims at the Shrine

Outside the West Gate—The Entrance—Aspects of Old Canterbury—Pilgrims' Hostels—"The Chequers of the Hope"—Mercery Lane and its Wares—Entrance to the Cathedral—Its Then Aspect—A Masterpiece of the Middle Ages—The Pilgrims Round—Old World Treasures—The Shrine of St. Thomas—Its Glories—Tribute of the Pilgrims—The Blood of St. Thomas—His Well—Pilgrim Stories—*The Tale of Beryn*—The Visit of Erasmus—Other Holy Places in the City—The Supremacy of St. Thomas 160

CONTENTS

CHAPTER XV

Sandwich and the Sandwich Road

St. Thomas at Sandwich—Former Importance—Its Decline—The Journey There—"Hearts Delight"—Wingham Church—Chestnut Pillars—An Absurd Memorial—Traditions of Guilton—Ash-next-Sandwich—A Green Level—Richborough Castle through the Ages—Coins and Oysters—A Thunderstorm—The Maze of Sandwich Streets—Hospices and Hospitals—Some Quaint Points from their Records—The Vanished Gates—A Golf Carnival—Houses by the Sea—The Bells of St. Clements—Farewell to Sandwich 175

CHAPTER XVI

The Path of the Knights, Stone Street, Saltwood Castle and Lymne

Picking up Stone Street—Its Character—Its Great Age—Changes on It—Lessons from a Chalk Pit—Villages on the Way—The West Wood—The Prospect of Kent—Saltwood and its Castle—Restorations, their Good and Evil—The Postern Gate—History of the Castle—Its Connection with the Martyrdom—Tradition of Archbishop Courtenay—The Primate Then and Now—The Eloquence of Z. Cousins—On to Lymne—The Great Fragments of Studfall Castle—The Scene from Below—The Church and the House on the Cliff—Their Debt to Studfall Castle—Antiquities and Antiquaries—John Leland, Dr. Stukeley and R. Smith—The "Nun of Kent" 187

CHAPTER XVII

The Winchester Road

"The Pilgrims' Way"—The Old Road—The Course it would Take—Dread of the Forest and the Swamp—Along the Hill Slope—Roman Influence—Heathen and Christian—The Rise of the Pilgrimage—Relative Importance of the Ways—Some Writers on the Subject—Far Fetched Theories 200

CHAPTER XVIII

The Winchester Road (continued)

St. Swithun—The Fame of Winchester—Its Sights and Shows—Its Memorials of St. Thomas—The Banks of the Itchin—Legend of the Tichborne Dole—An Early Adventure of Edward I—Problem of the Hog's Back—Through the Villages—The Pilgrim, the Beggar, and the Robber—St. Catherine's and St. Martha's—From the Wey to the Mole—Reigate and the Heights Above It—The Kent Border . . . 208

CANTERBURY PILGRIMS

CHAPTER XIX

The Winchester Road (*concluded*)

Otford and its Palace—Legends of St. Thomas—The Nightingale Goes and Comes—St. Edith's Well at Kemsing—A Characteristic Piece of the Way—The Wrotham Hills—Solitude of the Byways—The Holy Land of Old Britain—Megalithic Monuments—Addington and Trottiscliffe—The Stones at Coldrum—The Long Line of Trees—Kits Coity House—"A Field of Antiquity"—The Last Stand Against the Invader—Treasure Hunting—Along the Pilgrims' Way—A Night Encampment—The Ford over the Medway—Boxley Abbey and its "Sotellties"—Pennenden Heath—The Wonder of Charing Church—Exquisite Chilham—The Fort in Bigberry Wood—Cutthroat Lane 217

CHAPTER XX

A Note on Other Places and Routes

"All Roads lead to Rome"—Maidstone and Canterbury—Pilgrim Traces—An Old Bridge—The Cult of St. Thomas at Maidstone—The Port of Dover—A Strange Monopoly—The Housing of Pilgrims—The Murder of Thomas de la Hale—Objections to Canonisation—The Chapels in Dover Castle—Stray Memorials of St. Thomas throughout Kent . . 231

CHAPTER XXI

A Pilgrim of To-day—London to Dartford

The Start—Over London Bridge—The White Tower—Southwark Cathedral—"The Moral Gower"—The Boro' High Street—"The Old Tabard"—Talbot Yard—The Old Kent Road—The Pilgrims Revived—"The Thomas à Becket"—"Admirals All"—Blackheath Hill—A Wayside Well—Some Quaint Names and Old Houses—Dartford . . . 236

CHAPTER XXII

A Pilgrim of To-day (*continued*). Dartford to Rochester

The Church at Dartford—The Priests Chamber—A Pleasant Retreat—Houses by the River—The Parting of the Ways—A Roadside Adventure—Beautiful Stone Church—Epitaphs, Quaint and Otherwise—Prospect of the Thames—Churches on the Route—Roadside Inns—Up Gad's Hill—The Dickens Country—Dartford Brent again—A Genuine Bit of Watling Street—The Noontide Halt—Round by Singlewell—Wisdom, if You Wait—The Well of St. Thomas—Swanscombe Church—Clappernapper's Hole at Last—The Story of its Ruin—Junction of the Roads . 245

CONTENTS

CHAPTER XXIII

A Pilgrim of To-day (*continued*). Rochester to Sittingbourne

The Suburbs of Rochester—The New Bridge—Provident City Fathers—The Town Wall—Rochester Cathedral—Desolate Shrines and Beautiful Gardens—The Grim Old Castle—A Bunch of Hospitals—Chatham Hill—Memories of Latter Day Saints—Rainham and Newington—On the Road at Night—Time's Whirligig at Schamel—The Modern Growth of Legends—Sittingbourne High Street 256

CHAPTER XXIV

A Pilgrim of To-day (*concluded*). On to Canterbury

Roadside Inquiries—The Intelligent Rustic—Queen's Court at Ospringe—A Quiet Nook—Brenley Corner—Another Parting of the Ways—A Village Parliament—A Woodland Ramble—Roads, Ancient and Modern—By the Waters of the Stour—Back to Brenley Corner—Up Boughton Hill—At Harbledown—The Prospect of Canterbury—Through the West Gate 264

CHAPTER XXV

To-day at Canterbury

The Best of the City—The Old World Charm—Medieval Remains—Gates, Vanished and Existing—The Cathedral—Its Overpowering Effect—The Service Therein—The Regular Round—Talks with a Verger—Memories of St. Thomas—Old Time Customs—St. Augustine's, Past and Present—St. Pancras' and St. Martin's—The Lesser Churches and their Yards—The Greyfriars and the Blackfriars—Modern and Ancient Creeds—St. John's Hospital—Ivy Lane—In the Museums—The West Gate again—Farewell to Canterbury 272

INDEX 285

LIST OF ILLUSTRATIONS

CANTERBURY CATHEDRAL FROM THE SOUTH-WEST . *Frontispiece*
    From a Water-colour Drawing by WALTER DEXTER, R.B.A.

                                                                               Page

THE MARTYRDOM, CANTERBURY CATHEDRAL 12
    From a Drawing by B. C. BOULTER.

THE SHRINE OF ST. THOMAS OF CANTERBURY . . . 40
    Cottonian MS., Tib. E. viii, f. 269.

PORTRAIT OF CHAUCER 74
    Painted by order of his pupil Thomas Hoccleve, in a copy of the latter's *Regiment of Princes*.

ROCHESTER FROM ACROSS THE MEDWAY 108
    From a Photograph by F. FRITH & CO., LTD.

HARBLEDOWN HOSPITAL OF ST. NICHOLAS, NEAR CANTERBURY 128
    From an Engraving by COOK after the Drawing by NELSON (1766).

CHRIST CHURCH GATE, CANTERBURY CATHEDRAL . . . 164
    From a Drawing by B. C. BOULTER.

RELIQUARY DEPICTING THE MURDER AND ENTOMBMENT OF
    ST. THOMAS OF CANTERBURY 168
    Limoges. 1200 A.D. in the British Museum.

RICHBOROUGH CASTLE 182
    From a Photograph by J. VALENTINE & SONS, LTD.

	Page
Kits Coity House	200
From a Photograph by the Photochrom Company, Ltd.	
Old Palace, Maidstone	232
From a Photograph by De'Ath & Dunk, *Maidstone.*	
Rochester Castle	260
From a Photograph by the London Photographic Company.	
Canterbury from the North-west	272
From a Photograph by the Photochrom Company, Ltd.	

CANTERBURY PILGRIMS
AND THEIR WAYS

CANTERBURY CATHEDRAL FROM THE SOUTH-WEST

CANTERBURY PILGRIMS AND THEIR WAYS

CHAPTER I

A MEDIEVAL TRAGEDY

Importance of the Canterbury Pilgrimage—The Personality of St. Thomas—His Early Years—A Gay Courtier—Archdeacon and Chancellor—Archbishop of Canterbury—A Sudden Change—Conflict with the King—Exile of the Archbishop—His Return—Extreme Measures—The King and the Knights—The Knights and the Archbishop—The Last Scene in the Cathedral—St. Thomas of Canterbury.

THIS book is an account of the Pilgrimage to the Shrine of St. Thomas of Canterbury in old times as well as to-day. I have added some words on important towns and notable places on the route in their ancient and modern aspects, with special insistence on the venerable and sacred city of Canterbury. I also speak of the chief ways and the life of the wayfarers. The Pilgrimage lasted from 1170, the date of the murder of St. Thomas, to 1538, when the Shrine was destroyed by the Commissioners of Henry VIII. It was one of the most marked features of English medieval life, also it has for us this peculiar value, as we trace it we get nearer to the reality of this bygone world than we do in any other record. The Pilgrimage marked the whole country, and touched Canterbury with the glamour of a Holy City. The murder had important bearings on the relations of Church and State in England. The course of her history must have lain in other directions had it not taken place. As we look back many of the details that made this murder of tremendous importance appear as chance incidents; partly they were, but behind is the imposing personality of Thomas himself. First then it is necessary to inquire what manner of man this was.

The materials are only too abundant. There are thirty narratives of his death, some of them by eye-witnesses, also about a dozen lives of him were written within ten years. As was to be expected in many points the narratives are inconsistent. The eye-witnesses to a crime of to-day differ widely yet honestly in their accounts; it was so then, but the main facts are not in dispute, and it is only with these we are here concerned. Historians, as was to be expected, are not at one as to his character and motives. Even where the facts are tolerably certain they are differently explained. Yet his character is not difficult to grasp. There was nothing of the modern man about him; he had a strong individuality, but was a true product of his age. The lines are clear and well-marked. If he was sometimes inconsistent, that is merely to say he was human.

Thomas Becket or à Becket was born at London in or about 1118, and he was murdered in the last days of 1170. His place of birth is now occupied by the Mercers Chapel in Cheapside. His father was Gilbert Becket or à Becket, his mother was probably called Matilda. Of the pair a picturesque legend was long current. Gilbert, it was said, was a knight and crusader. As he fought before Jerusalem, he was taken prisoner by the Saracens and committed for safe keeping to the custody of a powerful Emir. This Emir had a beautiful daughter who, falling in love with the captive, assisted his escape. She followed him; her knowledge of English was limited for she knew but two words, "London" and "Gilbert"; by constantly repeating the first she got there, and had not long practised the second, when she encountered Gilbert in the street. She was easily convinced of the error of the Saracen faith, was baptised, and married. The future Archbishop was the result of the union. You easily believe this legend was a favourite theme for the balladist. In fact Gilbert's parents were of Norman origin. If evidence were wanting of this it is supplied by the character of Thomas himself. In the extent of his views, his gift of finesse and management, there was nothing of the dull-witted Saxon about him, but at that date a man of his type was not Norman or Saxon but English.

His father was in fairly easy circumstances, able to give his son a good education, first at Merton Priory, then at London, finally at Paris. In 1140 he returned home to find family affairs altered for the worse. He had to do something, so betook himself actively to city life in various minor capacities. He was tall and handsome, sufficiently learned, and able to make the best of his learning; he was quick and active, in every respect an adroit man of the world, one bound to succeed.

About 1143 he entered the household of Theobald, Archbishop of Canterbury, who made him his intimate friend and trusted confidant. He accompanied his patron to Rome, but withdrew for a year to study canon law at Bologna and Auxerre. Though as yet only in minor orders he had many preferments. In 1154 he was made Archdeacon of Canterbury, an important and lucrative office. In 1155 Henry II appointed him Chancellor of England. The bright, gay, learned, clever, politic man of affairs fascinated the King as he had fascinated the Archbishop. They were hand and glove together, hunted, sported, feasted, joked in company. One famous story is how in riding through the streets of London the King roughly tore off Thomas's cloak to throw to a beggar, a joke which passed well enough from a King! More than all they worked together. Henry was bent on vast reforms; he had to set the kingdom right after the absolute chaos of the previous reign. He worked well, for it was from his schemes that to-day's method of government as well as legal systems developed. No doubt the schemes were the King's own, but he was assisted in important details by his Chancellor both in planning and working out. Becket also acted as itinerant Justice and as Ambassador. He accompanied his sovereign on his expedition to Toulouse in 1159: here he showed himself as eager in the fight as in more peaceful pursuits.

When he progressed as the King's representative, he was accompanied by a gorgeous train of attendants; also his lavish expenditure was a subject of wondering or envious comment. The vast sums that Henry required were partly raised by increased taxation of Church property; his Chancellor was naturally active in finding the money; thus Thomas became unpopular with the clergy. He seemed more man of the world than priest, the pattern of a courtly ecclesiastic; but there was an inner life little known or noted by the gay courtly throng. He spent hours in private prayer, and it is thought practised secret austerities. He was chaste amongst dissolute surroundings, he was truthful where falsehood was common.

In April, 1161, the See of Canterbury became vacant; so it remained for more than a year. It was Theobald's last and earnest wish that Thomas should succeed him; the King was like-minded. He thought that now with his aid he would be able to carry out easily all his schemes. Becket did not show undue eagerness. The splendid prize must have attracted, but he felt that there would be trouble with the King who was bent on submitting the clergy to the secular courts. He certainly did make some representation to that effect to the monarch, but perhaps he did not make it with sufficient clearness, at any rate the stubborn and determined nature of his master made light of difficulties. In May, 1162, at Henry's instigation, he was elected. On 2 June he was ordained priest in Canterbury Cathedral, and on the 3rd he was consecrated there as Archbishop.

Against the wish of the King, Becket gave up the Chancellorship. The gay courtier became an ascetic priest; he feasted beggars daily and washed their feet with his own hands; his charity to the poor was boundless; more than all he showed himself a determined upholder of the privileges of the Church. Then came the Constitutions of Clarendon at Wiltshire in January, 1164. Henry and his Council decreed that clerks after they were convicted and degraded in their own courts were to be handed over to his courts to be dealt with. The King was to have a voice in the election of bishops and his chief tenants were not to be excommunicated without his consent—such were the chief measures. Thomas found it difficult to break at once with old associations. First he gave a dubious assent to the measures, then he withdrew this. Even his fellow-bishops advised him to submit. The Pope, Alexander III, did not at first give an effective support for he had difficulties of his own, but Thomas did not yield. Henry was furious, called him to account for his past administration, charged him indeed with embezzlement. He was insulted and mocked, and like to be ruined, but he gave in no whit, though the illness under which he suffered showed the strain put upon him. On 2 November, 1164, he fled the Kingdom, and six years of exile began. Before the end of the year Henry confiscated the property of the See and banished his relatives, friends, and servants.

We need not follow the details of the struggle. Becket had the King of France and the Pope finally and entirely on his side, also no doubt the mass of the clergy, though even his friends were wearied or appalled at his stubbornness. Henry was supported by many of the English bishops, moreover he was the "man in possession". He desired to have his eldest son Henry crowned in his lifetime as King, and this he procured to be done by the Archbishop of York, though the act was a violation of the rights of the See of Canterbury. To Becket's fervid imagination the deed seemed a crime. With the help of the Pope he was able to issue two extreme measures. He could excommunicate the King, he could lay an interdict on the kingdom, by which last he would deprive the land of all religious ordinance. An existence without such was to the men of the time unthinkable; those were extreme steps, but Henry was made aware that the Archbishop was prepared to take them. He met his former Chancellor at Fréteval where a sort of reconciliation was patched up; it permitted Thomas to return to England and resume his position as Archbishop of Canterbury. On 1 December, 1170, he landed at Sandwich. In the front of the boat his cross was prominently displayed. He had been absent six years. He was conducted to Canterbury by a huge concourse of people. All came out to meet him, kneeling at the roadside to ask his blessing; his was, beyond doubt, the popular side. It is not unfair to suggest that there was an obvious reason for this. His lavish hospitality must have acted as immediate stimulus to the mob.

It is difficult in many ways to judge between the King and the Prelate. The ideals of those days are not ours. The modern man would give his vote for Henry. The penance, the scourging, and the hair-shirt, for such things he imposed on himself, are more like to excite a derisive smile from the most than to compel admiration. Henry was trying to organise his Kingdom. It seemed just that clerks should be under the jurisdiction of the ordinary Courts, whilst whether York or Canterbury performed a coronation rite might seem of little moment. Henry was a reformer. No doubt he was an honest reformer though he scarce recognised the existence of the people, save as subjects of the Crown, as pawns in the royal games he was playing. If he thought of them at all, he believed he was acting for their good, nor did Thomas regard the people except as faithful sons of the Church. He was filled with no abstract enthusiasm of humanity, but he honestly believed that the Church had a divine mission and that he was set there to help in that mission.

When Becket reached Canterbury he was received with every expression of popular joy. He preached from the text, "Here have we no lasting city but we seek one to come" (Heb. XIII. 14). He saw clearly his peril. He found, as was natural, all in confusion. In special the Brocs of Saltwood near Hythe had done him grievous wrong. They had seized a vessel laden with wine which the King had sent him as a present; they had hunted his deer with his own hounds through his own woods; finally on Christmas Eve they cut off the tails of his sumpter mule and one of his horses. These were petty but peculiarly irritating insults. With all his asceticism, Thomas was a judge of, and had a relish for good wine and fine horses. Probably he had a lingering interest in the chase though he no longer practised it; moreover we know to the last his stalls held a superb steed carefully fed and groomed. As for the tail of the mule the legend will meet us again at Strood. The trick seems that of a schoolboy, but it was characteristic of the medieval temperament. Moreover Saltwood was his own castle which the De Brocs had seized.

The Archbishop made a journey to London on the way to Winchester to visit the young King whom he thought to persuade or overawe. He failed, and had to return, yet he was received with such popular demonstrations that it was clearer than ever that the people were wholly with him. He plainly showed that he had abated nothing of his pretensions. If the Church was to be set against the State then the State must yield; he was not a man to compromise, yet Henry could not yield without disgrace. It was "the fell opposed points of mighty opposites" and the solution time must bring boded itself forth as tragic. "Archbishop, 'ware the knife!" cried a voice from the crowd as he approached London Bridge. He had received letters warning him that his life was in danger, also timid friends must have made the theme familiar; he recognised the danger very clearly, but he was moved no whit: his strong resolute nature compels our admiration.

Henry was at Bayeux in Normandy, where he had abundant information as to Becket's acts. He was not a patient man, also the words of those about him increased his anger. There would be no peace, they suggested, whilst Thomas lived. The King maddened with worry and anger burst forth in a bitter tirade. "What cowards have I about me," he thundered as he glared round the hall, "that none will deliver me from this troublesome low-born priest?" Four of his hearers, Reginald Fitzurse, Sir Hugh de Morville, Sir William de Tracy and Sir Richard le Breton, determined to force Becket to submission. It had been intended to send them with others to negotiate with the Archbishop; things had gone beyond that now. With perhaps no clearly defined purpose they set off for England by separate ways and met together at De Broc's Castle at Saltwood, thirteen miles from Canterbury, a place, as we have seen, Becket's own, yet in the possession of his enemies. Thomas held on his course. On Christmas Day he preached in the chapter-house on the text,

A MEDIEVAL TRAGEDY

" Peace to men of good will "; he commemorated the Holy Men of Canterbury. One martyr they had already, this was Alphege killed by the Danes: his tomb was there by the High Altar, possibly there would soon be another. His hearers were in a passion of excitement. He wept though not from fear, and they wept with him. " To whom will you leave us ? " they said, and then he held as it were a commination service in which those who had wronged the Church or himself were solemnly cursed. As he pronounced each name he extinguished a candle and threw it to the ground amid the awestruck silence of his people.

It is impossible for human nature to remain without reaction on such high levels. When service was over the feast of Christmas Day was celebrated in the hall. You fancy there was more gaiety than usual, but Thomas said things, and did acts, that showed he was obsessed by the idea of his martyrdom. The days to the 29th passed at Canterbury without noteworthy incident though there were continual warnings of danger. Becket continued his ominous sayings as he would not outlive the year which had so short a space to run, and that those were to escape who desired it.

The four knights had arrived at Saltwood on the 28th. The King when he heard of their departure made some feeble attempt to recall them, but it must have been half-hearted. At any rate it did not succeed. In the midnight hours of the 28th they conferred together in darkness as if they dare not look one another in the face. Apparently they agreed to terrify Becket into submission and, if they failed, to slay him, but they cannot have meant events should have taken the course they afterwards did for such would be to plan injury to their master. In fact the tragedy was managed, you might say stage managed, by their victim, not by themselves.

On the morning of 29 December they set off towards

Canterbury accompanied by De Broc. They took the old Roman way from the ancient Roman sea-port of Lymne (*Portus Limanus*) to Canterbury. The road still exists. I have to speak of it later on. The knights with their escort went to St. Augustine's Abbey outside the walls where they were entertained by Abbot Clarembald, an enemy of Becket's. They then marched through the city to the Archbishop's palace. It was four in the afternoon. Dinner was just over. Thomas had passed the day as usual in devotion and ascetic practices, but at table he had drunk more wine than usual to the surprise of his cup-bearer. "Who has much blood to lose," said he, "must drink much." He had now withdrawn to his room and was sitting on the bed talking to his friends when the knights were announced. "Let them come in;" they entered, and sat down in silence on the floor. Becket at first gave them no notice. They were somewhat abashed, angry, yet not daring to break silence. Finally Thomas said some word of salutation, whereupon they stammered out that they had a message from the King, would he hear it in private or in public? "As you wish," said Thomas with ironical courtesy. They professed that it must be as *he* wished, and they wrangled over the point for a minute till finally the monks half-withdrew, but were called back by Becket when the knights began to speak. For an instant they were alone with him, and had some thought of slaying him then and there with the only available weapon, his own episcopal cross, which lay on the floor, for they had left their arms outside!

The point is of this interest that had they done so they would have deprived their act of its worst feature, for it would have been committed outside the church, but the monks flocked back and they had to deliver their message. He must accompany them to the King's Court and there answer for his misconduct both to his

A MEDIEVAL TRAGEDY

lord and his brother prelates. Thomas flatly refused: he would never let the sea come between himself and his church again, unless he were dragged from it by force. The controversy quickly degenerated into a fierce wrangle, the knights jumped to their feet, gnashed their teeth, waved their arms, and rushed about with angry and threatening aspect. Thomas himself, in a state of great excitement, scornfully referred to their threats, vowed he would do his duty to God and the Church. You believe the Archbishop had far the best of the wordy encounter, superior as they must be in physical force. "This is the hour of the might of darkness," said Thomas. If they could not overawe this audacious priest in talk, they were more than a match for him in deed. They withdrew and under a sycamore tree in the garden threw off their cloaks, then, girding on their swords, attempted to re-enter the hall, but in the meantime the door had been shut and barred. De Broc knew the place very well, so under his guidance they forced an entry at the back, reached the hall, and opened the door to their crew.

In the meantime Thomas, sitting down on his bed, again continued to talk with his friends. The more timid or more prudent urged moderation, perhaps some show of submission, but their head saw his way clear before him. "I am prepared to die." Whilst they talked the noise of breaking and crashing outside showed that the knights had forced their way and were instant on their victim. The monks almost dragged Becket out of the palace through the cloisters towards the cathedral. Even in the hurry he insisted that his cross-staff should, as was usual and proper, be carried before him. A locked door was in their way, but it flew open. With some difficulty they hurried him along, till at last they reached the door to the south of the north transept where Becket was induced to enter. They urged him to hide somewhere in the great church, but he refused; then they forced him up one or two steps towards the choir.

It was about five o'clock on the winter evening, so must have been dark save for the dim light of a few candles. The door had been closed behind him, but there was loud knocking from those who wished to take refuge with their brethren in the church. Becket ordered his folk to open.

> Why, these are our own monks who follow'd us,
> And will you bolt them out, and have them slain?
> Undo the doors: the church is not a castle.
> Knock and it shall be open'd. Are you deaf?
> What, have I lost authority among you?
> Stand by, make way!

So the door was again unbarred; the fugitives entered with the knights at their heels. The monks scattered in all directions; only three were left with their head, chief of them Edward Grim, the Saxon monk and, as was presently proved, the most faithful follower. Perhaps the knights were checked for a moment by the solemn hush in the great building, if so they soon recovered and loudly called for the Archbishop, that "traitor to the King". Becket at first kept silence, then he spoke.

> No traitor to the King, but Priest of God,
> Primate of England, I am he ye seek.

Forthwith he descended to the transept which has ever since borne the name of "The Martyrdom". He was in episcopal dress and again the intruders shrank back from the majestic figure, but they soon gathered round him as he stood by the central pillar; they called on him to submit, they shouted he was their prisoner, and De Morville, milder than the others, suggested flight. Tennyson always closely following the words gives the answer in his *Becket*.

> I will not.
> I am readier to be slain, than thou to slay.
> Hugh, I know well thou hast but half a heart
> To bathe the sacred pavement with my blood,
> God pardon thee and these, but God's full curse
> Shatter you all to pieces if ye harm
> One of my flock!

THE MARTYRDOM, CANTERBURY CATHEDRAL.

A MEDIEVAL TRAGEDY

He refused to go with them or to comply with any of their demands.

Even to their maddened minds some dim sense was present of the cruelty, the terrible nature of a deed of violence in a church, so they tried to drag him forth, but he was a powerful man and with Grim's help was able to resist. Some fierce words next passed between the stubborn opponents. Fitzurse advanced with his sword drawn. "You pimp," said the Archbishop, "you owe me fealty, how dare you touch me." The other, moved to still more passion, aimed a stroke which merely knocked off the Archbishop's cap; the blow at least brought their victim to a sense of his own dignity; he struggled no more; he covered his eyes with his hands, commended his soul and the cause of the Church to God and to his Saints, among whom St. Alphege was specially mentioned. Another stroke wounded him in the head and broke the arm of the faithful Grim raised to protect his master. Even he, the last friend, then moved off and the victim was left alone.

Succeeding blows forced him to his knees, a final thrust struck off the scalp, and he fell dead or mortally wounded to the pavement, but in such seemly fashion that the cloak he wore was not disarranged. To conclude, one of the band set his foot on the dead man's neck, and with his sword brutally scattered the brains on the pavement. "Let us go," he said, "the traitor is dead, he will trouble us no more." Then they rushed forth shouting wild cries of triumph; they proceeded to sack the palace and seize a great mass of the Archbishop's papers, then they mounted the best horses in the stable and dashed from the town.

Immediately after the murder, a terrific storm broke over Canterbury city, the rain fell in a deluge, the stately building rocked and echoed to the thunder. For a succession of vivid instants the lightning made all clear as at noonday. When it at length passed, an Aurora Borealis gleamed in the sky and shed a fitful and ghostly light o'er the terrified town. All men, such was the belief of the age, saw an immediate relation between the storm, the light, and the murder.

In the first confusion the cathedral was crowded with the folk of the place, but it was presently cleared and the body was left alone for a while. It was soon known that the assailants had fled. The monks collected round the corpse. They were struck by the majestic calm of the face, the head had been bound up, but one streak of blood marked the features. The body was carried to the high altar. Almost from the first the monks recognised that the Church had another martyr, already they were acclaiming St. Thomas, and their grief was passing into an ecstasy of admiration. Already they had collected all the debris, as it were, connected with the murder. Already the populace were carrying away what they could snatch as relics. Then as they handled the body it was known to all for the first time that he wore a coarse hair-shirt beneath the splendid robes of the Archbishop, and as they stripped him for burial, they discovered the hair-shirt was swarming with vermin: on the body were the marks of the scourge. In a fever of awe-struck feeling they laid him in the crypt in a sarcophagus of marble for there could be no burial, indeed no proper sacred office, until the cathedral had been cleansed from the guilt of sacrilege. Slowly the world, as it were, swung back to its place; the commonplace events of the day flowed on, but profoundly modified by what had happened on that eventful night, Tuesday, 29 December, 1170, to be known for centuries afterwards as the day of St. Thomas.

CHAPTER II

AFTER THE MURDER

Horror of the Deed—Details that Heightened It—After History of the Murderers—The King and the Crime—His Penance at Canterbury—Its supposed Results—Desolation and Reconsecration of the Cathedral—Canonisation of St. Thomas—The Beginning of the Miracles.

THE actors in a great historic crime invariably show an imperfect appreciation of the results. They lack imagination, they are not able to project their thoughts into the future, and anticipate the state of things that will result; also their minds are distorted by passion; they do not do what they intended; the development of their plan is taken out of their control; they are mere puppets in the hand of fate. The murder of Becket, terrible in itself, was set about with every circumstance of impressive horror that could affect the minds of men of his own time. It was the murder of a priest, and since he was Archbishop of Canterbury, of the priest most highly placed in all England. It was in a church and that the principal church in England. Further, he fell because he was fighting for the rights of the Church, and that was the same thing to the mass of the people as the cause of religion and God. Then the central figure had acted in the most heroic manner; he proclaimed again and again his willingness to die for the sacred cause, and himself unarmed confronted with armed assailants, he had shown perfect courage and perfect dignity. As the details of the tragedy were noised abroad, pity was lost in awe, admiration, and devotion. Before he was formally canonised he was acclaimed

Saint and Martyr by English Church and English people alike.

It might well have been otherwise; the knights might have dragged him out, or they might have slain him before he entered the sacred building; his courage might have failed; he might have tendered an unavailing submission or even begged for mercy, then indeed the act had still remained a great crime, but it had been robbed of those poignant and affecting details which appealed so strongly to the imagination. This is only part. More common-place, nay mercenary, motives acted powerfully for the glorification of Thomas. It was the direct interest of the Church, even its direct pecuniary interest, to make everything it could of the martyrdom, it was a valuable asset in its conflict with the State; through it the secular spirit always strong in England against priestly pretensions was held in check for centuries.

Much was written about the murder in the years that followed, also everybody who wrote was an ecclesiastic. It was as if all the newspapers of a nation were subsidised in the interest of one party. The simile is not exact, for in those days nobody could read but the priests themselves, and that to a limited extent; at least all the educated class were partisans of Thomas, they were in touch with the people to whom they talked, and with whom they lived. We need not assume that the clergy were consciously self-seeking and selfish. From the Pope downwards they truly believed that their cause and their interests were those of religion and truth. To some extent they were, and it is just those half-truths that are most effective in a world of mixed motives. Hence the universal interest not merely in England but throughout the Christian world excited by this tragedy, hence the celebrity of St. Thomas and the widespread devotion paid to his memory.

The after history of the murderers presents points of interest and problems, which when all has been said, it is hard to solve. Medieval times are removed from us by other things than years. We often fail to understand why men acted as they did; they seem to us like children, delighted with simple and absurd things, credulous and curious, easily enraged, and easily pacified, showing their emotions by puerile action, cruel or benevolent on impulse. Far other is our impression of an earlier period, of the Roman era, for instance; there is no difficulty in appreciating the actions of Cicero or Cæsar. We can find a reason for everything they did. It is not so with a man like Henry II. We can only guess why he treated the murderers in the way he did. One would have thought he would have hunted them down, if only for the sake of appearances, but in fact some of them, at any rate, were afterwards at Court and in favour, whilst no effective steps were taken to punish. At first the knights were brutally glad, nay they boasted to each other. De Broc remained in possession of the palace at Canterbury for some little time. Thence he issued threats to the monks, the others rode back to Saltwood in the night. Almost immediately afterwards they betook themselves to Knaresborough Castle on the summit of a hill by the river Nidd, seventeen miles north-west of York; here, as garrison or captives, they remained for a year. The monkish chronicles have many legends telling of their remorse and of the dismal ends to which each of them at last came.

It is difficult to get at the exact truth; medieval chronicles are plentiful enough, but they are marked by strange gaps. The minor characters stand out one moment in bold relief, then they pass into darkness or are lost in legend. It was said that when they threw their coats of mail and weapons on a table, the table turned over as if unwilling to bear the accursed weight. Dogs refused to eat of their crumbs, they lost all sense of taste and smell, they were objects of popular horror and execration, marked with a mark more deadly than that of Cain, the very safety of their lives dependent on the horror which hedged them round. At length they made a pilgrimage to Rome to beseech penance and pardon for their sacrilege from Pope Alexander III. He directed them to proceed to the Holy Land and do battle for its recovery from the Saracens. Here three of them died and were buried with an inscription which showed forth their guilty story, but Tracy, supposed their ring-leader, was not permitted to make this expiation. His ship was ever driven back whence it had set out, by contrary winds. This fate it was averred clung to his descendants, who were subject to the peculiar enmity of the elements.

>The Tracys
>Have always the wind in their faces.

The knights seem to us stupid as well as violent; they had done the worst possible service to their master; horror and remorse must speedily have taken the place of savage glee. It is significant that though they had set out to do (as they believed) the King's will, having accomplished in some sort their end, they did not return to Court, but betook themselves to a comparatively remote part of the kingdom. They were certainly not hunted down or even molested by King or people. There was some theory that just as a priest who killed a man ought not to be tried by a secular court, so neither ought a man who killed a priest; such was the view of the Church if not of the State. Notwithstanding all the trouble that fell on Henry, he may have felt at the bottom of his heart that Thomas, who had been so troublesome, was at last out of the way and that services so zealous, even though mistaken, did not call for direct punishment. The murderers, of course, were excommunicated, but that was all. Whether their remorse was mainly dread for the safety of their skins in this world and their souls in the next, may remain an open question. Their portraits were handed down preserved to popular hatred in church windows and psalters and frescoes.

The King was still in Normandy when the news arrived. He at least had imagination and ability enough to recognise what a terrible business the murder was for him. He spent days, nay weeks, in seclusion uttering loud cries of lamentation and horror. He kept on declaring that he had no hand in it, nay that his only crime was that he had not loved Thomas enough. Again you ask how much this was policy and how much remorse. He lent all his energy to evade the threatened consequences. He had many enemies, chief among them the French King, who were doing all they could to bring about his excommunication and ruin. Pope Alexander III was unfriendly, for Henry had not been a dutiful son of the Church. The Pontiff, it was also whispered, was struck with remorse that he had not given a whole-hearted help to Thomas, yet Henry was a foe to be reckoned with when driven to desperation: thus his immediate submission averted the threatened danger of excommunication and interdict. Tedious negotiations followed, for the Church was obviously anxious to make as much out of the matter as possible. Finally at Avranches in Normandy in May, 1172, he did penance and received absolution from the papal legates; he swore he had nothing to do with the death of the Archbishop, he likewise swore fealty to the Pope, he gave up the Constitutions of Clarendon, he promised full satisfaction to the See of Canterbury for the property taken from it, he also intimated a desire to fight against the infidels before the walls of Jerusalem, but this came to nothing; if ever seriously intended, it was given up as impracticable.

All this might be worldly policy in which both the King and Pope were playing a game of statecraft, but two years later Henry did a memorable act which showed that in truth the iron had entered his soul. His remorse was surely genuine, as surely as it was quickened by threatened dangers; his sons had openly risen against him, whilst all England seemed to rise with them. The Scots had crossed the Border under their King, William the Lion, and were devastating the northern provinces with fire and sword as was their wont. His share, however small or even unintentional, in the murder seemed the cause of all his troubles; he determined on an extreme act of penance.

Early in July he landed at Southampton. He withdrew himself entirely from secular affairs and living the while on bread and water sped as speedily as possible on horseback, through Surrey and Kent, following the ancient road, already taking new importance as the Pilgrims' Way. When from the crest of the hill beyond Harbledown, where at the Leper Hospital he had halted to make a gift of forty marks, he caught sight of the Holy City of the Martyrdom, he got down from his horse and tramped on foot, over ground made heavy with recent rains, till he reached the Church of St. Dunstan, outside the West Gate. Here he cast off his royal garments and clad merely in shirt and cloak, he went barefoot over the rough stones that cut his skin to the shedding of blood, as the awe-struck crowd noted. At the church he went straight to the place of Martyrdom and kissed the pavement where Thomas had fallen; he repaired next to the crypt where with every expression of remorse and grief, followed by fervent prayers, he embraced the tomb. The dignified clergy present suitably improved the occasion. It was announced again that the King would undo all he had done against the Church; then came the most impressive passage. The King threw off his outer coat, and knelt down against the tomb; here he was scourged by the Bishops and Prior with five strokes each, and by each monk, and there were eighty of them, with three. It may be that they did not strike viciously, but that is of little moment. The King passed the whole night there without food, without removing from his body the mud or the marks of disorder. He prayed next morning at the various altars at the great church, heard mass by the tomb, drank of the Martyr's well, like every Canterbury pilgrim was supplied with a phial full of water tinctured with some portion, however small, of the Martyr's blood.

This terrible ordeal had a violent reaction, he became feverish and ill, but he had soon good tidings that helped his recovery. The King of Scots had been taken prisoner at Alnwick and the invasion repelled; the ships in which his eldest son was proposing to invade England from Flanders were driven back by weather, the conspiracy against him was for the time being shattered. He as well as the whole nation assumed the turn in his affairs, and the favour now shown him, a direct consequence of his penance.

This was scarce four years after the murder, and meanwhile the fame of the martyr had continually grown so that Canterbury had become a centre of pilgrimage. The townsfolk were not at all likely to forget the event, but it was impressed on their memory in a remarkable way for a year after the event by the state in which of necessity the cathedral, that they had always looked upon with pride as peculiarly theirs, remained. The crime had destroyed the sacred seal of consecration. No proper service could be held within the walls, no bell sounded from the tower to call the people to prayer, the decorations were taken from the altars, and the image of the Christ draped. Nothing could be more impressive than the spectacle of the bare and silent church, no preacher could have told the story to more eloquent effect; the thing must have laid a weight of horror on the souls of clergy and people alike.

The bishops were not all friendly to St. Thomas. The Archbishop of York was notoriously hostile, and this among other reasons may have delayed the act of reconsecration. However, papal legates came to England to inquire into and report on the murder, so through them the reconsecration was brought about. On 21 December, which wanted but a week and a day to the first anniversary of the martyrdom, Mass was celebrated once more in the cathedral by Bartholomew, Bishop of Exeter. The text of the sermon was singularly appropriate, " For the multitude of sorrows that I had in my heart, Thy comforts have refreshed my soul ". With what joy and emotion the townsfolk must have heard the bells ring forth again their glad message, the solemn chant of the Latin service again rolling through the long reach of the nave, the church again decorated and again beautiful!

It has been noted that the Pope was believed to have felt the prick of conscience at the indifferent manner in which he had supported the claims of the living Thomas. The dead Thomas was a power that could neither be ignored nor denied, and His Holiness was presently zealous in his service. That the claims of Thomas were exactly in line with those of the Church and the Papal See was not a fact that could lessen his enthusiasm. All the inquiries he caused to be made in England were favourable. He presently issued letters in which the martyr was set forth as a saint, and prayers were allowed to be addressed to him as such. These letters were read at a Council at Westminster in 1173, whereupon those bishops who had opposed him in life acknowledged their error, so that henceforth the English Church adopted him without one dissentient voice. His formal canonisation on 21 February, 1173, merely gave official and formal sanction to the verdict of the whole Catholic world. It was inevitable that the day of the feast of Thomas of Canterbury should be 29 December, the anniversary of his murder. The story of the great penance of King Henry which took place the year after has already been told; if it could not increase the sanctity of the martyr at least it must have added enthusiasm to the devotion with which he was regarded. By this time a number of miracles, attested by what that age believed to be indisputable witnesses and cogent evidence, were on record. Even in a few years those miracles were so numerous that it became impossible to describe them all. They are obviously closely connected with the pilgrims and the shrine; they are full of interesting details; they illustrate the thought and life of the time in a striking manner. I must speak of them in a chapter by themselves.

CHAPTER III

THE MIRACLES

The Question of Miracles—Necessary to the Cult of St. Thomas—The Chief Chroniclers—Wonders after Death—The Blood of the Martyr—The Well of St. Thomas—Miracles at the Tomb—Victory over a Demon—Two Canterbury Cases—The Milk of the Church—A Dire Alternative—The Dead raised to Life—The Monks and the Doctors—The Perquisites of Saintship—Domestic Wonders—Petty Cash—Miracles and the Animal Creation—Unfortunate Supplicants—A Condemned Criminal—A Rascal Shepherd—The Fame of St. Thomas.

IT is not necessary or desirable to discuss here the general question of miracles. According to Hume you cannot prove a miracle because the evidence against it consisting in the teaching of experience as to the invariable regularity of natural law must always be greater than the evidence for it. According to the believers in wellnigh every form of religion, supernatural interference with those very laws is a well-attested fact. Within the Christian faith the Protestant theory is that miracles were permitted during the life of Christ, also until the close of the apostolic age. The Catholic Church on the other hand asserts the existence of miracles right on to our own time. During the period when Thomas was regarded as a saint by all England, miracles wrought by his intercession were a common article of faith, they were even necessary, since without them he had not been saint at all. Though a credulous and not at all critical period, the possibility of sham or mistaken miracles was always recognised, thus the presented cases were submitted to some sort of proof, not enough to satisfy a scientific inquirer, but sufficient to show that the beliefs were honest, and rested upon genuine facts. The early miracles were systematically noted by direction of the Chapter of Canterbury Cathedral. The chief records are those of the monk Benedict, afterwards Abbot of Peterborough, and of William of Canterbury, though there are numerous cases from other and later sources. Some are mere coincidences as of a dream turning out true ; others are instances of faith-healing, of what we would call to-day Christian Science; others again, might be put down to distorted or feverish imagination. Under the strain of exciting experiences young men saw visions, and old men dreamt dreams, and visions and dreams were alike accepted as literal facts.

Two curious notes, so to speak, of the time are in those wonders. Sometimes they were wrought to save the guilty from deserved punishment as if the appeal to St. Thomas brought about the desired result without merit in the subject ; others are of the most childish, even ludicrous description. The age was keenly alive to the comic side of the business, nay was heartily amused thereat, but it accepted the miracle all the same. There seemed nothing incongruous in the Saint mixing himself up with trifling domestic details, or fulfilling the smallest desires of children. I give a selection as illustrative as possible of the miracles of those early years. They began immediately on the death. Before burial the body lifted itself up, made the sign of the cross on itself and on those who stood by, and then fell flat on the pavement. A blind man, formerly of the household, on touching his eyes with the blood that was spread around, recovered his sight. There followed eager longing of the infirm to touch the blood of the Martyr which was forthwith accepted as a sovereign remedy against all ills. A townsman soaked his shirt with the precious fluid, went home, squeezed the linen into some water and gave it to his wife who was afflicted with paralysis; she promptly recovered. These legends and the very nature of the murder turned th direction of devotees to the precious blood. Endlessly diluted, it was supplied to each pilgrim. At first it was carried in wooden or clay vessels, but these were found clumsy to handle as well as liable to break. They were finally superseded by leaden or tin phials.

At first the crypt was closed, for the monks were afraid that the enemies of St. Thomas might attempt to put an end to the veneration of the Martyr by removing the body. So only a few were admitted, and those in secret, but towards the end of Easter week in 1171 all was thrown open. Then, according to Benedict, the scenes at the Pool of Bethesda were continually renewed in the cathedral. In order to provide against malicious or even pious pilfer,—for an over-zealous devotee might hunt more keenly than an enemy after the relics,—the tomb was surrounded by a wall with spaces through which the head could be thrust to kiss the stone. One of the devotees contracting himself in some miraculous fashion bounded through the narrow opening. When within he uncurled himself to his full size like the genius imprisoned in a bottle in the Arabian tale! The monks were in great perplexity, they feared they must break down the wall to get this mad fellow out; presently however he bounded back again in like marvellous fashion.

Stephen, a knight of Hoyland, suffered from a nightly oppressive suffocation. On hearing of the death of Thomas and doing him reverence he was entirely delivered from his malady but not from the terror of it. The cause was a demon who took the bodily shape of a dwarf, circling round the knight, ever trying to get at him. By invoking the Martyr the dwarf was kept at bay, then finally driven off. Among the wonders of Easter, 1171, was the recovery of a man dumb for five years. He had seen two glorious figures in a vision who ordered him to repair to the Martyr's tomb. On making the pilgrimage he recovered his speech though imperfectly—he had disused it so long. The host with whom he lodged when at Canterbury was sceptical, but he confessed that "over and over again he had made the lad drunk," yet had he never contradicted himself. In *vino veritas*, forsooth!

Here are two Canterbury cases. Edmund of that town was blind in one eye, also was grievously afflicted with a mysterious something in his left side that moved to his great agony. The first effect of the Martyr's blood was to contort him in a fit, then a lump like a gall-stone fell from his mouth, and he rose from the ground fully restored to life and health. Murial, a woman also of the place, drank of the tinctured water and presently was at the point of death. As it was contrary to the custom of the Christian religion that she should die on a feather bed—so we are assured—she was laid on the floor. She threw up cherry stones, plum stones, and acorns, some of which were sprouting, whereupon she immediately recovered.

One Robert, a smith of Thanet, in a vision, was ordered to bathe an afflicted eye with milk. He was in some perplexity until a monk at Canterbury riddled the dream for him. "Was not a martyr's blood the sweetest milk?" queried the ingenious priest. The sick eye was thereupon touched with the precious fluid; thunderclaps sounded in the head of our smith. On the instant he was cured. Robert, a youth from Northampton, was beset in sleep by an appearance that offered him death in nine days or a living death for nine years. It was an evil alternative, but life seemed to him so sweet that he chose the latter. He became grievously sick. Another appearance in the shape of a beautiful man urged a pilgrimage to Canterbury, thereafter prayer at the tomb. Following this counsel he speedily recovered full possession of health.

Even when all hope was abandoned the Martyr's

help was efficacious. Eveard, Chaplain of St. Mary's, Winchester, had a terrible fall downstairs; he lay senseless for a whole week, so that he was accounted dead; his post was given to another and his property divided. His brother, ere abandoning hope, tried the water on him. The dead seemed to speak, " Praise God I shall go to Canterbury," and then lay lifeless as before, so that even the faithful brother departed, but he was scarce gone, when the patient, of a sudden, completely recovered, followed on horseback much astonished at the sensation his appearance created. At least as wonderful was the case of Robert, a youth of Rochester, who fell into the Medway at three p.m. of the afternoon and was only dragged out at the time of vespers. He was blue in the face, and quite senseless. Primitive, even violent, remedies were practised without success. He was hung up by the feet, thereafter rolled about in a tub, but the water in him remained obstinate. His mother had invoked St. Thomas hour after hour, at length she vowed to the Martyr a silver thread as long as her son. The water forthwith gushed from the mouth of the youth, who presently sat up as well as ever.

Another Kentish story is of Gilbert, the six-months-old child of Ralph and Wulviva of Sarre. By the carelessness of his nurse he had lain under water at the bottom of his bath for three hours and to all seeming was long dead. The mother rushed through the village with the child in her arms shrieking so that the women of the place crowded round her. All praying, they invoked the help of St. Thomas, but for some time in vain, till one suggested that a thread should be brought, the babe measured, and a candle of the same length vowed for the shrine. Immediately water issued from the child, then he moved his eyelids, burst out crying, and all was well. Another case, even more remarkable, also tells of the revival of a

THE MIRACLES

child. He was the son of Adam of Oldham, was three years old, was apparently dead and was laid out for burial with closed eyelids and hands across the breast, but some stubborn devotee sprinkled the body with the sacred water, the child stirred, then shifted an arm, gave a great cry, called for its mother and recovered. Another case is of a priest sent for to administer the last sacrament to a dying man. He was so delayed that the man had expired ere his coming. Through the intercession of St. Thomas the departed spirit was called back for a little to its earthly tabernacle, the last rites were performed, then the arrested soul passed peacefully away.

Leprosy, that dread scourge of the Middle Ages, yielded to the might of the Martyr's name, but I need not here quote special cases. In them, as well as in other examples, the Saint was often laid hold on as a desperate remedy. Physicians did their best or worst yet no cure resulted, then, the Saint being invoked, the patient recovered forthwith. Whether it was with a desire to extol their patron or because there was an ancient jealousy or perpetual feud between priest and doctor, the monkish writers scoffed at medical aid; the moral of their stories was neglect the physician, for he is useless when compared with the Saint.

As candles were a frequent gift to the shrine, it became a common practice to measure the sick for a candle; indeed the monks at Canterbury did considerable business in vending wax for the manufacture of tapers, more or less gorgeous.

Presents of money were also made. This practice went on increasing, nay! just as Thomas, when living, had shown zealous care in maintaining the rights of the Church, he now exhibited an equal care in looking after what might be called the perquisites of his Saintship. A curious reason was given for this. During the years of his exile he had incurred considerable debts, and it was suggested that he desired to collect sufficient to discharge them. It was not explained how exactly the creditors were to be benefited; perhaps they were to reap the spiritual advantage of the gifts so bestowed.

There are some genuinely comic touches, which the monkish chroniclers seem not unwilling to introduce, also with these are mixed the most trivial details. Thus a girl at Ramsholt, having mislaid the cheese, feared her mother would whip her for carelessness; at her wits' end she consulted her brother who recommended an application to St. Thomas. The Saint being duly invoked appeared to each separately in a dream; he directed their attention to an old disused churn; the girl had put it there and forgotten all about it.

If the Saint exacted money he was ready to supply it on occasion. A shoemaker of Dover had been so incredibly simple as to pray for the Martyr, but how could a Saint who is not in sin be helped by human prayers? St. Thomas, touched by this mistaken devotion, directed him in a dream to a place under a mill which he might find it worth his while to search. All he found was a rusty denarius, but a sharp friend by biting it with his teeth discovered it to be of gold. It was a coin of the Emperor Diocletian of the value of forty pieces of silver. Still more remarkable was the case of Richard, Chaplain to the Sheriff of Devon. Setting forth on the pilgrimage to Canterbury, he vowed to give alms to each and all who begged in the name of St. Thomas. He presently found himself destitute of small change. Thus he needs must give a denarius to each suppliant and himself be beggared, or break his vow, which was not to be thought of. At the next demand he bravely plunged in his hand and pulled out an obol, the smallest coin in existence. This miracle was continually repeated, St. Thomas more mindful of the pilgrim than the beggar having supplied our friend with an indefinite amount of petty cash!

Dreams were, with Thomas, a favourite mode of revelation. A certain girl fell into a heavy sleep, so heavy indeed, that her friends became alarmed and used violent means to waken her. She was far from grateful. St. Thomas had appeared and was just about to endow her with miraculous powers when she was unreasonably roused. Her pious mother gave three masses and a candle a week to the Saint. She received a message through her daughter that she was to continue the gifts to her last farthing. According to the girl's report the Saint also intimated that the maid-servant must be forthwith dismissed. This rather startling interference with minor domestic details was almost too much, even for the credulity of the time. The mother hesitated but the maid presently went of her own accord, thus solving the difficulty.

Some of the prodigies refer to the lower animals; thus a sucking pig, drowned in a river, was carried down to the house of one Walter of Norwich. Here a pious daughter urged its dedication to St. Thomas, whereupon it speedily revived, nay! it seemed taken into special favour, since it was inspired to hide itself when the other pigs were undergoing a certain disagreeable operation, wherefrom it thus escaped. The story of a gander hard by Canterbury is still more remarkable. It seemed quite dead, its neck twisted, its feathers plucked, but then being dedicated to St. Thomas, even when other geese were cackling round it as if in sorrow, it lifted up its head, squeaked audibly, and was as sound as ever! William, who tells the story, cites as witness the honest countryman who reared the bird even from the egg, the Martyr's tomb to which it was led loudly cackling the while, and finally his reverend brethren of the Cloister by whom the gander was received with acclamation, cooked and eaten!

The hawk from its use in hunting down birds was prominent in those years. Several of the miracles refer to it. Randulph a Fleming tried to lure an errant hawk through eight weary days, but the wary bird eluded his grasp. He vowed a denarius to St. Thomas for help. It came straight to his hand. The monk records that the denarius was duly paid.

Wiscard, the King's falcon, was run through the eye by the bill of a crane on which it had swooped. A vow to St. Thomas resulted in the restoration of the falcon to a sound condition of body. When the King was told the story he thanked the Martyr for saving the favourite companion of his sporting hours. Sometimes the Saint interfered on the side of the hunted. A starling had learned from its mistress to warble an incantation to St. Thomas. Being attacked by a kite, it trilled forth the sacred words. The kite fell dead in an instant whilst the starling flew away unhurt. A clerk falling sick, nothing would serve him but a woodcock; his mistress prayed to St. Thomas, whereupon a hawk chased the desired bird into her bosom. Perhaps this is the same hawk which, being ill, recovered just when an offering, sent on its behalf, reached the tomb at Canterbury.

Thomas was not invariably of an amiable disposition; he was subject to peevish fits. A lame boy, tired with his pilgrimage, fell sound asleep with his head on the tomb. The Martyr forthwith appeared in a vision looking anything but saintly. "Why do you lie on me? You shall certainly not recover; go home, I will do nothing for you," and nothing was done though the lad was long and earnest in his prayers. To another sleeping youth the message was "sin committed before your birth deprives you of recovery".

Perhaps those utterances did not appear to the monkish chroniclers as they do to us, but the instructive simplicity of the following narrative was likely to suggest, one would have thought, even to that time a theory of faith healing. A lad was at the point of death and, in what seemed his last agony, begged piteously for the Martyr's water. Alas, there was none to be had! A friend was so moved that he got water from the nearest spring which he boldly presented to the patient. " Here's the water of the Saint which you require," quoth he. The sick man eagerly drank and forthwith recovered. All repaired to Canterbury to give thanks to St. Thomas; a little inexplicable, unless the theory was that the Martyr was able to inspire common water, given in his name, with health-giving powers. It was a dangerous theory, corrected however by other records which note how useless sham water proved. The real stuff had a miraculous power not always respective of the person who used it, or the cause it was used in. Early in 1177 a pilgrim was passing through Rochester; he could find no place of lodging till he was received under the humble hut of one Gilbert, a baker. That night a great fire destroyed all Rochester save the baker's dwelling, on the roof of which stood the pilgrim with a phial of the water. He presented it at the flames which discreetly withdrew.

Prisoners were freed, not because they were innocent but because they invoked St. Thomas. Girald, a weaver of La Tour Blanche near Perigueux, was condemned for flagrant theft. Before trial he was confined in a cellar. As he prayed to St. Thomas the huge stone at the mouth of the den was rolled away, and he issued forth. The officers having knocked him on the head, thrust him back again, whilst he kept praising St. Thomas. Before his end he besought the sacrament. The eucharist, said the priest, is not for thieves, " Let earth or grass be your sacrament," which indeed they were believed to be in certain cases. Girald was now strung up and soon seemed dead to those who pulled his legs to expedite his end, but he was supported by the voice of the Martyr that all would be well. At eventide his wife was allowed to cut him down. Bounding up again hale and hearty, he dashed into the Chapel of St. Eparchius which was sanctuary, a prudent step though it perhaps implied some distrust of the Martyr. At any rate it was needless; his very judges kissed his limbs and besought pardon, though, what for, does not appear. With somewhat of the reputation of a saint himself, Girald in due course presented himself in Canterbury with as much of the precious halter as he could bring with him. "Virtue went out of it and healed many."

There is no end to the miracles of St. Thomas. By his aid, lost ships turned into port of their own accord, lost anchors were fished up from the depth of the sea upon a waxen anchor being vowed to his shrine and so forth. Let one final story be given. An Essex farmer named Richard was feasting with his friends when his shepherd entered, the proud possessor of a pyx of Canterbury water. The farmer entertained some suspicion of his shepherd's honesty and asked him to put it to the proof. If he were a rascal the pyx would now be dry. It was. The servant tried to brazen it out, but finally confessed that he had cooked the accounts for butter and cheese. "For love of the Saint," the sinner was pardoned. All the neighbourhood was much amused, and in sign of this festive miracle, as it was called, the pyx was hung up in the church to be looked upon somewhat askance, you believe, in all time coming by the peccant shepherd.

These are a fair sample of the miracles of the early years. You must believe them repeated in endless succession to the time of the Reformation. Thomas was a peculiarly English saint. As the monkish chronicler points out, he was once forbidden to go to England or visit his diocese when alive. Himself, now dead, was visited by all England.

CHAPTER IV

THE HONOURS, THE RELICS, AND THE SHRINE

Memorials of St. Thomas in Old London—His Honours in Scotland—Relics of Him in England and Abroad—True and False Relics—Holy Places at Canterbury—The Feast of the Translation of the Relics—A Memorable Tuesday—The Shrine in Trinity Chapel—Gifts to the Tomb—A Splendid Diamond—How the Shrine was Guarded—Pious Frauds—The End of the Business—The Shrine Despoiled—Alleged Trial of Bishop Becket—A Modern Discovery—Queen Mary and Cardinal Pole.

ST. THOMAS though a peculiarly English saint, yet had widespread fame, and was highly honoured abroad. Also he was opposed to the King who was the embodiment of might, not always joined with right, thus such democratic feeling as existed was for him. Eighty-four churches were dedicated to him in England alone. Abroad "there was hardly a country," says Dean Stanley, "which did not possess some church or convent connected with St. Thomas". The citizens of London never forgot that he was one of themselves. The chapel on old London Bridge was dedicated to him, his effigy adorned the seal of the bridge. On his birthplace the Church of St. Thomas of Acon or Acre was erected by his sister Agnes and her husband Thomas Fitztheobald. The name of Acre came from the military order of St. Thomas, founded by King Richard at Acre where there was also a chapel dedicated to him. This order survived in some form or other till 1538, hence Acre was commonly added to the Saint's name. Each new Lord Mayor went from his house to the church where the aldermen were already assembled, thence all repaired to St. Paul's where *de Profundis* was sung hard by the tombs in the churchyard of the Saint's father and mother, thence they processioned again to the church with lighted candles if it was dry weather. Here my Lord Mayor and his fellows made offering of a penny apiece.

At the other end of the scale the devotion was as great. In an era when your suburban path was oft a quagmire, the river was the great highway. The watermen (your cabmen or motormen of the time), as their trim wherries sped past Lambeth Palace, solemnly lifted their caps to the statue of St. Thomas which stood in the niche now significantly vacant. For centuries he was looked upon as the patron saint of the city. In St. Thomas's Hospital we still have a memory of this once great figure, and the frequent occurrence in England of the Christian name of Thomas has been traced to him.

I have stated that coincident with the penance of Henry II, William the Lion, invading England, had been taken prisoner at Alnwick. The Scots monarch had known Thomas at Henry's court, and had felt the influence of his dominating personality. When he regained his liberty immediately on returning to his own kingdom he founded the Abbey of Aberbrothock or Arbroath, in 1178, and dedicated it to St. Thomas. It was one of the wealthiest as well as one of the most beautiful in the north, a fact to which its mouldering remains still bear witness; here William was buried. In a curious fitful way our saint emerges, from time to time, in later centuries in the Catholic world. Thus he appears in a vision to St. Catherine of Bologna (1413-63). He is clad in pontifical robes, he commands her not to wear herself out with prayers and good works, then, giving her his hand to kiss, he vanishes.

During the Middle Ages the very idea of a saint

carried with it that of his relics. These were parts of his body or clothing, or things he had used or touched. The whims, desires, fancies of our own day since they are founded on human nature existed then though in a narrower form, for there was less scope for their development. The zeal for curios, the desire to possess some part of the furniture or belongings of a king or famous man, the rage for collecting pictures, books, manuscripts, all was then absorbed in the passion for relics. This lasted from the fifth to the fifteenth century of our era, and long through the ages the passion grew ever stronger. These relics were not mere objects of curiosity or even reverence, they had a more direct value, since they were able to effect cures, and indeed all manner of miracles. Moreover, whether you believed in them or no, they had such a place in the opinion of mankind that they had great value in money ; an enormous trade was done in them. But the age was credulous and curious, ignorant and superstitious, thus a great mass of spurious relics were in the market.

The thing has been painted for us by the masterhand of Chaucer. The pardoner in the *Prologue* to the *Canterbury Tales* had a pillow-case which he vowed was the veil of Our Lady, he had a part of the seal of St. Peter :—

> He hadde a cros of latoun ful of stones,
> And in a glas he hadde pigges bones.
> But with these reliques, whan that he fond
> A poure persoun dwellyng uppon lond,
> Upon a day he gat him more moneye
> Than that the persoun gat in monthes tweye.

Those preserved in churches were not such barefaced attempts to deceive the public. Some must have been genuine, others cannot have been since they were merely impossible or repetitions of the same thing, and though these last were sometimes accounted for as miraculous, yet even the devout must have seen the possibility of fraud.

As St. Thomas was a famous saint, his relics were numerous, they were widely scattered, they were of the most diverse character. Here is a selection. Carlisle Cathedral had the sword of Hugh de Morville. Another sword was kept in the church at London; portions of the dress were scattered through England. Chester had his girdle, at Alnwick or at Corby, possibly at both, was his cup; his boots and penknife enriched Bury, and drops of his blood were possessed by many churches. The relics were not confined to England. His priestly vestments are still shown in the cathedral at Sens in Normandy. In Verona the church that was dedicated to him possessed one of his teeth. A convent at Florence had a part of his arm, whilst Lisbon again showed forth both his arms. The papal legates of 1172 took back to Rome the blood-stained tunic, part of the brains and a fragment of the pavement of the Martyrdom. These were deposited in the Basilica of St. Maria Maggiore.

Even in the modern world some traces of this veneration for the relics of St. Thomas survive among men of education and culture. Father R. H. Benson assures us that at St. Thomas's Abbey at Erdington there are carefully treasured " Great and precious relics of the Saint's body and that amice which he wore round his neck at holy mass". Here also is the wooden cup from which he drank.

Naturally the great centre of relic worship was at Canterbury. At first there was no regular shrine though various spots were reputed peculiarly sacred from their connection with him. The place where he was murdered was within five years known as the Martyrdom. The stone on which his skull was dashed, also a solid block of masonry by which he fell, remain unchanged. You can still trace the space where the

HONOURS, RELICS AND THE SHRINE

wooden altar, placed there in 1172 and not disturbed till the Reformation, stood. Another place of veneration was the High Altar by which the body of Thomas had rested for some time. There was also the tomb in the crypt, at first the chiefest place, and even after the translation an object of devotion.

So things remain for some years, but on 5 September, 1174, the choir called from its splendour "the glorious choir of Conrad" was burned to ashes. The Canterbury Cathedral had become by then chiefly known as the casket that held the sacred remains of St. Thomas. A great problem in the rebuilding was to give these the best accommodation. Among the northern nations the east end of the church was the Holy of Holies: behind the altar it was common to build the Lady Chapel, but here the extreme eastern part was called Becket's Crown. The windows of this were filled with the most costly stained glass showing forth memorable events in his life. Here in a precious reliquary, fashioned like a head, was kept that part of the crown that had been hewn off, whilst the rest of the skull was preserved in silver in the crypt at the ancient tomb, and there also the hair-shirt and drawers taken from the body at death were hung, in the same manner, it has been said, as the coats of mail of knights were suspended above *their* tombs, of which practice a very famous instance exists in Canterbury Cathedral at the present day, at the grave of the Black Prince,—but this is to anticipate a little, since this state of things probably belongs to the cathedral after the translation in 1220.

Pope Alexander III in his Bull of Canonisation had ordered the relics to be put in some fitting shrine. He contributed two columns of coloured marble from the ruins of ancient Carthage, which columns are still to be seen hard by. The fire, the troubles of the time, prevented this being done immediately, and it was not till 7 July, 1220, that the solemn function took place. It was during the primacy of Stephen Langton. The tomb had ere this become enriched with precious offerings great in number and value. Everything was done to make the occasion memorable. Notice had been given two years before throughout the Christian world. Maintenance had been provided for the expected multitude, not merely in the city itself but on all the ways that led thereto, not merely for the multitude but for their beasts of burden, yet so great was the enormous throng that all could not be housed. The overflow sheltered under tents and when these were crammed, in the open air. Wine was free at the gates; the very gutters ran of it. The enormous sum spent taxed the resources of the wealthy See of Canterbury during a long course of subsequent years.

In the silence of the preceding night the remains were examined and placed in a strong chest securely locked and sealed. On the next day all that was noble in England marched in procession to the church; there also was the legate of the Pope, and a crowd of dignified ecclesiastics. The chest was deposited in the rebuilt Trinity chapel in a shrine fashioned by the most cunning artificers. Again it was a Tuesday, the fated day of Thomas's life as Tennyson puts it in his *Becket* :—

> On a Tuesday was I born, and on a Tuesday
> Baptised; and on a Tuesday did I fly
> Forth from Northampton; on a Tuesday pass'd
> From England into bitter banishment;
> On a Tuesday at Pontigny came to me
> The ghostly warning of my martyrdom;
> On a Tuesday from mine exile I return'd,
> And on a Tuesday——

He had been slain in the same cathedral, and it was now to be known not only as the day of the Martyrdom of St. Thomas but as the feast of the Translation of St. Thomas. The treasures of the tomb were re-

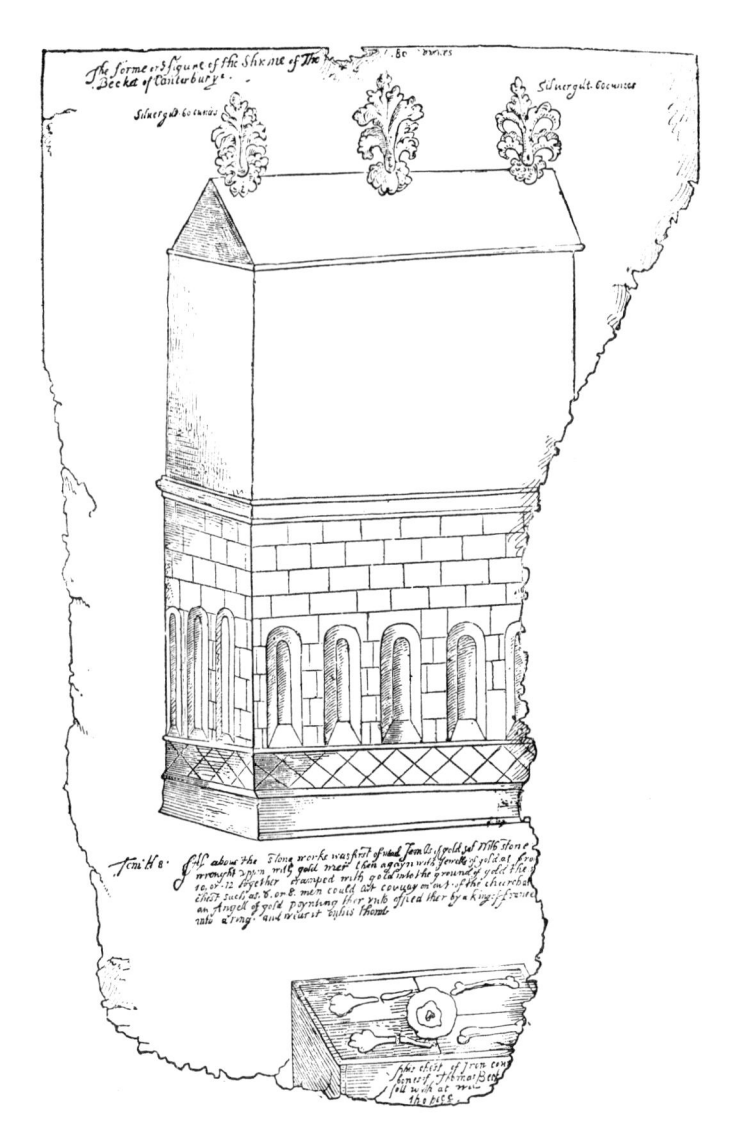

THE SHRINE OF ST. THOMAS OF CANTERBURY
COTTONIAN MS., TIB. E. VIII. F. 269

HONOURS, RELICS AND THE SHRINE 41

moved to the new shrine in the Trinity Chapel though others in time were heaped up in their place.

The store in the chapel was enormously added to in the centuries that followed, so that finally its riches became almost incalculable. Among the gifts a few may be noted. Henry II, after his penance, gave four marks of pure gold and silk hangings and an endowment of £40 per annum. Louis VII, the first French King in England, moved to seek help for a sickly son, gave the Regale, a gem indeed " of purest ray serene," again mentioned in a later chapter. Edward I gave to it the golden crown of Scotland, at length conquered, as he believed. The Barons of the Cinque Ports who, at coronations, carried splendid canopies over the King and Queen, regularly offered up one of those canopies to the Saint. There was a dispute as to the rights of the Archbishop of York. In 1354 it was arranged that York was to have his cross borne before him in the southern province on condition that each Archbishop gave a golden figure of himself with his cross within two months of consecration, and it is recorded that Archbishop Booth in 1452 did this homage. No wonder that Albert, Archbishop of Livonia, said it was the most splendid shrine in all Christendom.

A Venetian pilgrim saw it about 1500. It was covered with pure gold, yet the gold was scarce seen on account of the various precious stones, sapphires, diamonds, rubies, emeralds, which overlaid it. There were also beautiful sculptured gems, agates, onyxes, cornels, so great that it seemed incredible. More marvellous than all was a ruby as big as a thumb-nail. The church was dark, especially hard by the shrine, the sun was near setting in a cloudy sky, yet the ruby blazed with such wondrous power that it made itself plain to all as if it had lain in the hollow of the hand— this was the *regale*. To the Bohemian ambassador who visited Canterbury in 1446, it seemed a carbuncle half the size of a hen's egg. It shone bright at night, he said; perhaps it was another stone, perhaps he was confused with so much splendour.

If the earlier pilgrims were moved to devotion by this gorgeous display, such was not the case with Madame de Montreuil who had attended Mary of Guise to Scotland and took Canterbury on the return journey in August, 1538. The prior offered her St. Thomas's head to kiss three times saying, you imagine, with rising emphasis, "This is the head of St. Thomas"; but she did not kiss nor did she kneel to prayer on the cushion put there for that purpose; her eyes were glued on the splendid shrine—she stared for an hour, it is reported; how she must have longed for a handful of those jewels wherewith to deck herself! Yes, but of devotion there is no trace.

These were unscrupulous if pious early times. The treasures of the shrine were carefully guarded. The place was well provided with monks who stood round during the day. High up in St. Anselm's Tower on the south was a watching chamber with a gallery whence the inmate could look down on the shrine, no doubt always well lighted, and prevent nocturnal marauders. It is said he had the help of a band of ferocious hounds, kept near at hand. To the strange morality of the time it seemed that relic hunting justified the means. Get your relics honestly if you could, but at all events get them. Benedict, already mentioned as recording the miracles of St. Thomas, was made Abbot of Peterborough in 1176. His new charge had a singular dearth of such treasures. He purloined certain flagstones of the Martyrdom wherewith he built two altars, also two vases of blood and part of the clothing. In this strange way did he show his devotion to his dead Saint.

Outside the walls stood St. Augustine's Abbey, the other great religious foundation of Canterbury. At first it was the more important, but was being quite put in the shade by the superior splendour and growth of Christ Church, all of which was due to the fame of St. Thomas and his precious relics. The monk Roger was *Custos Martyrii* or Keeper of the Martyrdom, but who was to keep the Keeper? The Abbacy of St. Augustine's being vacant the authorities there offered it to Roger on condition that he brought with him to his new post a part of St. Thomas's skull. He successfully accomplished this glaring breach of trust and received his reward, nor was he, or anybody else, the least ashamed of this strange transaction.

It was a necessary consequence of the Reformation that the pilgrimage and the shrine and indeed the whole cult of St. Thomas should come for all practical purposes to a sudden stop. The legislation of 1536 against superfluous holidays summarily extinguished the Feast of the Translation of the Relics. On the eve of St. Thomas in 1537 the Archbishop of Canterbury ate flesh openly in the Hall at Lambeth, the first time for over 300 years of the like feasting. And yet there were occasional pilgrims a month before the final scene which was presently enacted.

Henry VIII in many things broke from the past with a certain disdainful contempt, but he seemed to have a special grudge against St. Thomas. He took up the quarrel just where Henry II had stopped at Becket's death; he was "a rebel and traitor to his Prince," and was pursued with what seemed special malignity. Thomas Cromwell was Vicar-General, and under him a royal commission was issued to Dr. John Layton in 1538 to carry out the work of destruction. A strong military guard accompanied him to Canterbury in September, but there seems to have been not even a protest, and certainly no resistance, nor apparently was any attempt made to remove beforehand any of the treasures. Henry had at least the art of making himself dreaded;

also the abounding faith of past ages was gone, gone even from among the monks themselves. All that was done, and even this is conjecture, was to gather together the two pieces of Becket's skull from the old tomb in the crypt and the eastern chapel known as Becket's Crown, and add them to the rest of the bones at the feretory at the shrine.

Stow, though he wrote twenty-five years after, is our best authority for what happened. He dilates on the richness of the shrine; it was covered with plates of gold clamped together with gilt-wire. The gold was covered with jewels, precious stones, great pearls, brooches, images, angels, and bunches of gold rings, ten or twelve in a bunch, and many of the rings set with precious stones. These were collected into two huge coffers, each so heavy that eight men could hardly drag it from the church. The contents were loaded on twenty-six carts which bore them away to Henry's treasury.

Two months later it was ordered that all pictures and images of Becket were to be destroyed, his festivals were not to be observed, and all notes of him in Church books were to be deleted. This was so vigorously carried out that we can trace the gaps even to-day. The bones of the Saint, the object for centuries of such reverence, had ere this been burned and scattered to the winds, nay a picturesque legend as to this haunted Catholic Europe. It was said a court had been held, that Thomas Becket had been summoned thrice to appear and answer to the charge of treason, and on no response being made, he was declared contumacious and a traitor. The treasure at the shrine was forfeited to the King's use, and execution was ordered on his bones by burning. Pope Paul III in his bull *Cum Redemptor Noster* of 17 December, 1538, refers to this trial in the year of the despoiling of the shrine; indeed the statement in the

HONOURS, RELICS AND THE SHRINE 45

bull seems to be the only authority we have for the story. There is no mention of it in English records. It was not in accordance with English procedure or with English modes of thought, and there is no parallel case with which it can be compared or supported (that of Wycliffe at Lutterworth cited by Dean Stanley is in reality very different), but it is easy to believe how our Catholic refugee, foreign or native, himself not clearly understanding the legal forms under which the matter was carried out, would bring a confused story to the Court of Rome which finally took shape in the papal bull.

In January, 1888, the bones of a large-sized man were found in a coffin near the site of the original tomb of St. Thomas in the crypt, and these it was suggested were in fact the remains of the Saint placed there the night before the shrine was destroyed; the feretory being left empty of them or their place supplied with spurious remains. We are told that a Roman Catholic gentleman brought his son whose sight was failing to those remains. Making him kneel down he touched the weak eyes with the orbits of the skull. " If this does not cure him, nothing will" was the not particularly devout remark of the parent. He had found that many oculists had failed with the lad, but there is no record of the after-effect of a proceeding which reads almost like a parody of the old-time pilgrimage and miracles wellnigh as bad as an *Ingoldsby Legend!* The jewels soon melted away from Henry's treasury, whither who can tell?

In 1538, when the shrine was destroyed, Cranmer was Archbishop of Canterbury. He suffered death by burning at Oxford, 25 March, 1556, and that same year Cardinal Pole succeeded him. Mary's reign had still two years to run; they were years of desperate effort to restore the old order. Pole himself at an earlier period had wished for a Reformation but within the Church.

It was not a time when men could hold ambiguous or aloof positions. He threw in his lot finally with the reactionaries; the name of the Martyrs' Field at Canterbury recalls the fact that during this period of set-back, men gave their lives here for the Protestant faith, yet even to him some things must have seemed past mending. It is significant that he made no attempt to re-create the Shrine or the Pilgrimage. He died the day after Mary and was the last Roman Catholic Archbishop of Canterbury.

CHAPTER V

PILGRIMS AND PILGRIMAGES

The Pilgrims through the Ages—Wonders of an Unknown World—Meaning of the Pilgrimage—The Greater and Lesser Pilgrimage—Derived Words—Various Classes of Pilgrims—Equipment of the Pilgrim—Provision made by the Pious—Some Royal Pilgrimages—The Return of the Pilgrim—The End of the Matter—Modern Revivals—Sir Walter Raleigh's Allegory.

THE Pilgrimage was one of the marked and most engaging features of the Middle Ages. The thing then attained proportions not known before or since, but there were pilgrimages from the earliest times, nor have they ceased at our own day, for they result from certain universal principles in the human mind. The Indian goes to the Ganges and the holy city of Benares. The Moslem has missed the great good of life if he has not visited Mecca. The most enlightened of ancient folks had like observances. The Greeks travelled far to see famous shrines of their Gods. Indeed, some have derived the medieval custom of Pilgrimage from the visits in search of health to the shrine of Æsculapius, the antique prototype of all healers. Our heathen forefathers and the Scandinavian nations generally had in their simple and primitive religions no such rite or practice. You note the idea was not merely religious. Cicero at Athens tells us of the pleasure he had in tracing the spots where great men lived and worked. Something of this feeling was present in the religious Pilgrimage. Again, in the Middle Ages the life of man was limited. The desire to visit foreign countries near or far which in our own time has produced the tourist and the globe trotter existed then and could only find scope in a Pilgrimage.

The prospect if less comfortable was more entrancing. It was a dim, wonderful, mysterious world that lay beyond the bounds of your own parish, still more beyond your own country. It was inhabited by strange and wonderful beasts and still more strange and wonderful men. Marvels and miracles were there of everyday occurrence—so it was firmly believed. Still first and most of all the medieval pilgrimage had a pious purpose; it was an act of devotion to visit the tomb of a saint. It was often enjoined as penance that relieved the penitent from the consequences and guilt of sin; it was done in the accomplishment of a vow. A Pilgrimage was even decreed for children in their cradle, so that when these grew up they performed it as a solemn duty. It was an expression of thanks for some ill averted or some good obtained. In special it was a means to be cured of a particular disease. You would leave your malady behind you, it was thought, if you could but once see and touch the sacred shrine. There were reports of so many and such marvellous cures (samples have been given) that the efficacy of the remedy gained universal credence. However exaggerated the reports, there must have been a solid basis of fact, but the fact is largely explained by obvious natural causes. Conditions of medieval life were so unhealthy and insanitary, that by comparison a modern slum might seem a paradise. In the Pilgrimage you had fresh air, wholesome exercise, probably better food than usual, since to entertain you was the duty of everybody; your mind was at rest, nay elated by the consciousness that you were doing a good work. Whatever their shortcoming the Middle Ages were times of intense belief and perfect devotion. Thus faith-healing was a common fact of daily life though it went by the less scientific name of a saintly miracle.

The Christian Pilgrimage was as old as Christianity. In the first ages the martyrs' tombs were visited, as also the sites of famous events in religious history. The custom grew and grew, ever increasing in magnitude and importance. First and greatest was the Pilgrimage to the Holy Land, for there were the very scenes of the gospel story. After that came the Pilgrimage to Rome to visit the shrines of St. Peter and St. Paul; such were the chief objects of what was called the greater Pilgrimage. The lesser comprised visits to local holy places of which each Christian country had a more or less important number. In England by far the greatest was that of St. Thomas of Canterbury, the subject of this book.

These Pilgrimages had important results; they produced the Crusades, for the difficulties of a journey to the Holy Land were increased when it fell into the possession of infidels. That very possession was an insult to Christian feeling and was bitterly resented both by those who had visited Palestine and those to whom the loss was but a traveller's tale. They brought the East in contact with the West, and imparted to each new and quickening ideas. Throughout the Christian world they produced incessant communication and action. The life of the time would have been more stagnant than it was but for them. In truly pious minds they induced high ideals and generous thoughts; at the lowest they must have given every pilgrim greater knowledge and wider culture. Alas! there was another side to the picture. From the King to the beggar every class was found in the Pilgrim ranks. Workmen, it was complained, would assume the part to escape uncongenial tasks, thus laziness and unrest were fostered. In the case of women a visit to Palestine or even Rome could scarcely be undertaken without debauchery. St. Gregory alleged the weaker sex found special temptation in Pilgrimages, whilst St. Jerome urged that heaven is as easy of access from Britain as from Jerusalem. In after years the Reformers of the Church attacked the whole system. Wycliffe, for instance, was a persistent denouncer, and Erasmus had no good to say of them. His friend, Sir Thomas More, on the other hand, defended both Pilgrimages and relics in a dialogue not the least readable of his works. He laid it down as certain that God wishes to be worshipped in particular places, though he professed himself unable to give any reason why this should be so.

The thing so worked itself into the popular imagination that many words in common use were derived from its incidents. A *roamer* was one who visited Rome to venerate the apostles' graves. A *saunterer* had been to the *Sainte Terre* or Holy Land. A *canter* is an abbreviation of a Canterbury gallop, referring to the easy motion of the Pilgrims, and we are assured that in America " What a Canterbury ! " is still the exclamation that condemns an incredible story, because a Canterbury tale was so called from the wild narratives wherewith the Pilgrims entertained themselves and the outer world. The latter two words are a striking testimony to the pre-eminence of the Canterbury Pilgrimage over all others.

Pilgrims have been divided into various classes. The palmer was one who had been at the Holy Land, and was decked with a palm branch as a sign. Chaucer, however, uses the word, as the quotation shows, merely to express a Pilgrim to distant countries. Again he was taken to mean a lifelong Pilgrim who had no fixed place he could call home. He was ever on the move from one shrine to another. It was a condition of his life that he should profess poverty. The more commonplace Pilgrim went, at his own expense, to perform one definite devotion, but these distinctions, as we see, were not universal in practice and no doubt " Pilgrim " was the common word for all.

A Pilgrim had properly a letter from his spiritual or temporal Lord which acted at once as a license to travel, a safeguard against wrong, and a recommendation of him to the pious and charitable. A number usually started together, and they did so upon due religious rites. A service was held, after which the priest accompanied the band at least to the boundary of the parish, after which they must plunge into that dim, unknown world that lay beyond.

In the Middle Ages, every sort or condition of men was known by its dress, which seems to us now vastly picturesque. The Pilgrim was no exception to the rule. You "spotted" him on the instant. At his side hung a bag where he stored his provisions ; in his hand was a staff ; a piece of metal glittered on the knob thereof, whereon was written *Hæc tute dirigat iter!* May this guide thee safely on the way ! At the other end was a point of iron. Nothing was more characteristic of the Pilgrim than this staff. Do we not still talk of the Pilgrim's stave ? It was not always put to pious uses, in a quarrel or crush it oft tested the thickness of the human head. Attempts were made to induce the wanderers to carry crosses and banners instead of staves. This might be all very well for a short procession, but not for prolonged days of travel. They were dressed in a rough coat of grey with a broad belt, like a monk's dress in fact. They had a sack for needments, chiefly food, a gourd for liquor, and a purse rarely well furnished, the whole attire was surmounted by a broad plumed hat. It was not the habit to shave on the journey.

This hat and dress were covered with shells, images painted with divers colours, and as if that was not enough special pilgrim signs were carried, most commonly in returning, appropriate to the shrine which they visited. We have already seen that at Canterbury those signs were usually tin phials made in the image of Saint Thomas, and containing a portion of the so-called blood. In that case it was stamped with the legend *Optimus aegrorum medicus fit Thomas bonorum*—for good people who are sick Thomas is the best doctor. If the implied slur at the faculty seems uncalled for, remember how deficient was the medical science of the day. A diet of beetles or bats was gravely prescribed by court physicians, nay certain remedies were even worse. At Canterbury you could also buy brooches of pewter or lead with quaint images of the Saint upon them, perhaps a head or a figure of him on horseback, or again a Canterbury Bell. These were perforated so that you could conveniently attach them to the cap or some part of the dress or body. If you went on Pilgrimage to St. James of Compostella, you wore a shell or the image of one. Another sign was the head of St. John the Baptist. Very common was a vernicle or image of the Christ after the legend of St. Veronica. You remember that the pardoner in Chaucer had one of these sewn in his cap. These Pilgrims made a strange figure as they passed through towns and villages; they sang songs relating their travels, the miracles of their patron saint, and scriptural subjects. Such were composed by the more ingenious members of the band. Many have come down to us and some at least possess real merit. Too ingenious scholars have seen in these wild notes not merely the origin of plays and miracles but the rudiments of the modern theatre.

To receive Pilgrims and give them alms was the duty of every good Christian. Charlemagne made it a legal obligation throughout his vast empire. The Pilgrim was free from tolls and imposts generally, and even in a lawless time his quasi sacred character was some protection against outrage. On well-defined Pilgrim tracks hospices were founded for their reception by religious orders. There were associations established to assist Pilgrims bound for the East; there were even guide-books especially for the way to Jerusalem. As you easily believe your medieval Murray or Baedeker makes sufficiently quaint reading. Among other curious facts, we gather it took between six and eight weeks to go from Venice to Jerusalem, and the journey there and back cost from £150 to £200 of to-day's money. But these were not beggar Pilgrims. The best-known hospices, indeed they exist down to our own time, were those on the Alps, but they were to be found in every country. The fare and the lodgment were ever of the plainest, but it was a peculiar and grateful act of piety to wash the feet. A direction of St. Columba (560) is reported, "Draw water to wash our guests' feet". Royal Pilgrimages were frequent. Here are one or two examples taken from the English Kings. William the Conqueror and Henry II both visited St. David's shrine in the town of that name. Edward I journeyed to the shrine of St. Richard of Chichester on several occasions, and was present at the translation of the remains on 16 June, 1276. He also made a Pilgrimage to the shrine of St. Thomas of Hereford and attended the translation of the remains on 6 April, 1287. Here he made offerings on divers occasions for his sick falcons, each took the form of a waxen image of the bird in question.

This book is devoted to the story of one set of Pilgrimages and little can be said of others, however remarkable. One of the most famous was in 1064 to the Holy Land under the Archbishop of Mainz and the Bishops of Utrecht and Ratisbon. The pious travellers were well received at Constantinople, and apparently being well supplied with money had a favourable journey till they drew near their destination. Then the imprudent display of wealth incited the cupidity of the Bedouins, by whom they were attacked and robbed. It is said that only 2000 out of 7000 returned to their native land, but this did not discourage their successors. One effect of the Pilgrimage was to define exactly places in the Holy Land connected with the gospel story, not merely in Jerusalem but throughout Palestine, also many localities connected with the Saints. As the appetite of Pilgrims for such things was insatiable, those whose interest it was to supply their wants amplified and particularised their accounts. It was their aim to make things as great and marvellous as possible. This does not apply to religion alone; to-day you are shown at Verona the tomb of Juliet, a stone cist full of visiting cards, and there is also pointed out the very monastery to which Friar Laurence retired after the tragedy that ended in the death of the lovers. In the words of modern commerce, the demand must produce the supply.

On their return the Pilgrims were again received with religious ceremonies and general rejoicing. They were henceforth noteworthy characters looked upon with respect. Something of the wonder and sanctity of the distant shrines at which they had worshipped attached to them for the rest of their life. Those remarks obviously only apply to the more distant journeys. A man cannot have risen much in the esteem of his neighbours because he had made the short and safe journey to Canterbury, nor would such be made the occasion of any religious ceremony. Thousands indeed made Pilgrimage, but they made it in all sorts of ways and under all sorts of conditions. To some it was no more than a pleasant holiday trip, to a few it was the great event of a lifetime.

The Reformation practically made an end of the old-time Pilgrimage, not only without but within the pale of the Catholic Church itself. Our own day has witnessed a revival of the ancient practice, often with healing as its object. The great Catholic Pilgrim town of modern time is Lourdes, and the visions that gave rise to it date from 1858. At the dedication of the church there in 1876 there were present thirty bishops, 3000 priests, and 100,000 Pilgrims, the next year, 1877, the Pilgrims attained the enormous number of 250,000. No doubt many were devout, and it is not for me to discuss whether they were right or wrong. The journey was made under changed conditions, for all the aid that modern science could give was pressed into their service. Perhaps those who went with the same devout faith found a blessed result bodily or spiritual, but how to constitute again that strange, motley, picturesque medieval world of which the Pilgrimage was so remarkable an expression? These things are but pale shadows of what in far-distant and vanished years were living realities. Let me conclude this chapter with Sir Walter Raleigh's graceful lines that give the equipments of the old-time Pilgrim, but touch them to finer issues and read into them a spiritual meaning :—

> Give me my scallop shell of quiet,
> My staff of faith to walk upon,
> My scrap of joy, immortal diet
> My bottle of salvation,
> My gown of glory (hope's true gage),
> And then I'll take my Pilgrimage.

CHAPTER VI

THE MAIN ROUTE. THE START—LONDON TO ST. THOMAS À WATERINGS

Two Men of Letters—A Pair of Fallacies—The Capital—The Real Starting Point—How it Looked in Medieval Times—Old London Bridge—Legend of the Ferryman—How the Bridge was Kept Up—Chapel of St. Thomas—Memories of the Old Bridge—Southwark in Ancient Times—"The Tabard"—Harry Bailly, the Host—Fact and Fiction about Him—Southwark Memorials of St. Thomas—Out in the Country—Old Time Fares—St. Thomas à Waterings—Memories of the Place.

MANY great ones of the earth went the Canterbury Pilgrimage. Their progress made sufficient noise at the time, but that has long passed away. The record remains in history as an incident in their lives, but for us now of little moment. Two men of letters, who were also men of genius, travelled each in his own day to the shrine. One was Erasmus (1466-1536), a scholar, a foreigner, in some sense a reformer. The other is one of the great figures of English literature. In or about 1385, Geoffrey Chaucer made the journey that gave rise to the *Canterbury Tales*. His work will be discussed presently. No fault of his that it is responsible for two misconceptions; one, that the majority of Pilgrims started from the "Tabard" or its neighbourhood, that is from Southwark; the other, that the Pilgrimage was merely a sort of pious picnic. The first calls for attention in this chapter. We are dealing with the road from London to Canterbury, and therefore London, or rather a definite point in London, must be our starting-place. Chaucer himself has said:—

THE MAIN ROUTE

> And specially, from every schirés ende
> Of Engelond, to Caunterbury they wende,
> The holy blisful martir for to seeke,
> That hem hath holpen whan that they were seeke.

The Pilgrims from nearly all England north of the Thames would pass through the capital. There was no bridge farther down or indeed farther up till you came to Kingston. There was an important Ferry at Westminster and various other places, but besides that a bridge is more convenient, there is the question of cross-country routes. Even to-day with all our railway facilities the traveller usually finds it advisable to go straight to London or Paris, and thence to the English or French country places—even though as the crow flies the mileage may be considerably more. The advantage of a main route was greater then than now; the roads of the Middle Ages were mere tracks, but at least the best tracks were those most frequented. Again not merely had the capital an attraction of its own, but remember how close was the connection of St. Thomas with London. The devout Pilgrim, who was the salt of the whole affair, the figure that prevented the thing collapsing as a sham, had many things connected with his Saint to see here. St. Thomas was born in London; there was the chapel on the site of his birthplace; the tombs of his father and mother in the churchyard of St. Paul's; he had been baptised at St. Mary, Colchurch, and all these places would be visited among the sights of the Metropolis. The church was close to the north end of London Bridge, and since all needs must pass over the bridge, here was the true point of departure.

We all know London was a small place then, but do we realise how small? The modern town, London and elsewhere in England, is not merely huge in itself, but it is given to spread and sprawl in a queer ungainly way that only those who travel on foot or bicycle understand. Even within my own memory this has much increased because of our tramways which stretch out like tentacles or feelers along the main roads and at once destroy the rural track. The medieval town, being walled, was compact and definite. London was only the city; there was no smoke for there was no coal; the fog was white and natural. There was a profusion of gardens among the houses which were quaint, wooden, or largely wooden structures, with sloping roofs and overhanging upper stories. They were small, for each man had his own, and people were content with narrow accommodation. The Thames was a clean river well stocked with fish. There were churches and chapels, crosses and shrines, in a profusion that would now seem far in excess of the needs of the population. Such in brief was the city on which the Pilgrim turned his back as he passed on to London Bridge, and that bridge, since all must go over it, seems a fit starting-place for the first stage of the journey. Each of Chaucer's Pilgrims, when we meet them, had already made some progress on the way. Each of them, ere he made the memorable halt at the "Tabard," had crossed the river.

Old London Bridge lasted from 1176 to 1832, nearly seven centuries. It was almost 1000 feet long and had something under twenty piers and arches. It was 40 feet wide. It will be remembered that Becket was murdered in the last days of 1170, so that by the time the bridge was built, the Pilgrimage was in full swing. The first Pilgrims then must have gone over the earlier wooden bridge which lay a little to the east of its successor. St. Thomas himself used it on many occasions, notably during his last visit to London in the days just preceding his Martyrdom. This wooden bridge had been renewed on more than one occasion. In 944 the Thames was first spanned, before that there was a ferry. There was a quaint, even ridiculous legend about the last ferryman, one Audrey or Overs. It must have been one of the most popular of the tales told to the pilgrims, both from its local, its romantic, and its religious interest.

He was a wealthy man for the post was lucrative; also he was of a saving disposition; that is to put it mildly, for a greater skinflint the world never had. His helpers, servants, retainers were, he opined, a troublesome, useless lot; could he starve them for a day they would be none the worse, and he much the better. He hit upon the maddest device. With the help of his daughter Mary he laid himself out, a candle at his head, another at his feet, in short was furnished with all the ghastly apparatus of a corpse. No doubt he looked the part. His servants took him at his look though they could not at his word, but then came the rub! *He* had assumed they would fast to honour his memory, *they*, openly glad at their release, broke into the pantry and the wine cellar so that a riotous feast was soon in progress. Old skinflint had kept a cautious eye on the proceedings, the din and the revelry were too much for him, so he presently appeared on the scene clad in his winding sheet! The mirth suddenly ceased, the servants were half-sobered and altogether frightened at the apparition which they took for Satan in person. One of them seized the butt end of a broken oar, wherewith he caught the ferryman such a blow on the head that he incontinently expired. Legal proceedings followed; the servant was acquitted and the ferryman brought in accessory and cause of his own death! At first no one would give him Christian burial, until the tears of his daughter prevailed on the monks of Bermondsey Abbey to grant him a sepulchre. Their abbot was away at the time. On his return he was mighty indignant. He had the wretch dug up again, and tied on an ass, which was driven forth the premises. The beast wandered on to the place of execution; there it stuck. The omen was accepted, so that the ferryman found rest at last in the common grave of departed criminals.

The tale of sorrow is not ended. The daughter Mary, young, wealthy, and beautiful, had a faithful lover who, hearing of her dire plight, mounted his steed and galloped off to comfort her, but it was the more haste the less speed! The horse stumbled, off he fell, and broke his neck. Mary had nothing now to live for; she gave all her wealth to found the Abbey of St. Mary, Overies, which preserved her name. Hence was derived the Abbey and Church of St. Mary Overie sometime called St. Saviour's, and still in existence as the Southwark Cathedral.

It is not likely that the Pilgrims had a philologist among their numbers, able to point out that St. Mary Overie simply meant St. Mary over the water or as some say on the Bankside.

According to the legend it was this religious house which built the first wooden bridge. As all the intellect of the age, or nearly all, was in the Church, those who planned bridges were usually monks, and not merely did they build bridges but they helped to support them. The brothers of London Bridge roamed far and wide over England to collect alms to be used for the upkeep of the fabric. We are more nearly concerned with Peter of Colchurch's stone structure which was a very wonderful and impressive work. It was closed with gates at either end. It had a portcullis and a drawbridge and it was set off with towers. The south gate was sometimes called Traitors' Gate, for on it was spiked the heads of many people whom we now look upon with respect and reverence. Here was set up the head of Wallace, the Scots patriot—"This man of Belial," as Mathew of Westminster calls him; cheek by jowl with him was the head of another Scots worthy, Simon Fraser to wit. In after times Jack Cade grinned down from one of the spikes, and in the last days of the Pilgrimage, the heads of John Fisher, Bishop and Cardinal, and of Sir Thomas More, Lord Chancellor, were here set up as a sign of the end of the old order of things. These last two heads, it was rumoured, did not blacken or decay, but remained fair and fresh and comely, and whatever your creed you will wish that part of the story true. Fisher's was finally taken down and thrown into the river; the other had a stranger fate. We shall come across it again at the end of our Pilgrimage.

The bridge carried a whole street of houses used for shops and for places of abode. No doubt as shops they were in great demand. The Pilgrims would be tempted to buy things useful for their journey, and things useless also; then there was the chance custom from a hundred other sources. The bridge had a master and wardens, and a house in Tooley Street just off the south end. It needed constant repair, so the rents of the houses on it came in very useful though they were not sufficient, so that other houses and land were set apart for a like purpose. Also taxes were especially laid on the kingdom; more than all there were the tolls collected from those who used the crossing, and these did not finally cease till 1785. On the other hand, kings and queens could not keep their hands from this desirable source of revenue; from time to time they seized the ready cash for themselves.

There was one thing on the bridge itself to which the Pilgrims would pay very special attention, and that was the chapel of St. Thomas. It stood on the centre or Great Pier on the east side. It was 60 feet long and 40 feet high, and the path or street on the bridge went past it at a breadth of 20 feet on the west side. It consisted of two stories, the upper was on a level with the street, the lower or crypt was built in the bridge itself. This crypt was entered from the upper chapel or the street, and there was also a landing-place with stairs so that there was access from the river. The chapel was splendid with white and black marble. It was served by two priests and four clerks, also various chantries were afterwards founded in connection therewith. These gave employment to additional priests. After the dissolution it lost its religious character and was used as a paper warehouse. At high tides the water rose to the level of the crypt, but the paper inside had no touch of damp so strongly was the place built. When pulled down in 1760, it gave the wreckers considerable trouble.

The last of the houses on the bridge were removed the year after; finally in 1832 the old bridge itself was taken away. One gruesome relic of the past was revealed. This was nothing less than the bones and dust of old Peter Colchurch which came to light amid the foundations of the chapel. The old bridge had its wealth of legend later than the Pilgrimage. For instance there is the engaging story of the apprentice Osborne who saved his master's infant daughter by diving into the river from the height of the bridge after her. Virtue and courage were in due time rewarded by marriage and prosperity. The legend is better authenticated than most of its kind, and no doubt this humbler tale is also true.

Mr. Baldwin, the haberdasher, who was born in a house over the chapel dwelt there all his life till at seventy-one he was ordered to the country for a change, and gat him to the rural solitudes of Chislehurst, but he got worse instead of better, for he could not sleep when the sound of the rushing water was absent from his ears, so he needs must hurry home again. Those same rushing waters among the piles of the old bridge were very dangerous to navigation, and the pilgrims must often have crossed themselves devoutly and thanked St. Thomas that they had a bridge to pass over. He was of that way of thinking who first put together the proverb that London Bridge was made for wise men to go over and for fools to go under!

If the Pilgrims were fortunate they would see rare spectacles on the bridge. Thus in 1390 Sir David Lindsay of Glenesk and Lord Wells fought there a duel on horseback in the most approved style of chivalry and after long preparation, or again they might see splendid or remarkable processions because all the great folk who went to London from the south would pass that way. The southern gateway of the bridge was obviously the predestined spot for those cumbersome allegorical pageants, wherein medieval times took so singular a delight. Out of numbers I give but one example for its dramatic contrast. In 1415 Henry V passed over the bridge in the midst of splendid feasting and rejoicing; he was returning from the victory at Agincourt. Seven years afterwards his body was brought over London Bridge for he had died in France and was being carried for burial to Westminster Abbey.

We pass into the High Street of Southwark. What was that street like? The private houses were no doubt as those of London already noted. There was an abundance of churches and chapels, but there were also splendid mansions of the nobles for Southwark was a favourite place of residence, something higher and better than the trading streets of the city. Then great ecclesiastics, Bishops and mitred Abbots such as the Bishop of Winchester and the Abbot of Hyde, had their town residence here. There was also a vast number of inns which are highly commended. From some, parties were made up for the Pilgrimage, at others, travellers going to or returning from the Continent put up. The Inn and the Church are the two most prominent buildings in medieval times, so that Southwark was a typical medieval place. We have the names of many of those inns.

There was the "White Hart," the "Bear," the "King's Head," and more than all the "Tabard," which requires here some special mention. It was not an infrequent name for an old-world inn. In London itself there was one so called in Gracechurch Street, but the genius of Chaucer has so marked the one in Southwark that we think of no other. In letters there is only one "Tabard," but put Chaucer out of your mind altogether, you will still find this house historically remarkable. It was the oldest inn in the borough, and was a favourite resort of Pilgrims. It began in 1306, if not earlier, in the Abbot of Hyde's lodgings, one portion being specially set apart as a hostelry for Pilgrims. A Tabard, otherwise Syrcote or Circot, was a sleeveless jacket, once a common article of dress, so that those who wore it at Oxford, obliged to wear it one would say according to the statutes of their College, were officially called *Taberdarii*, thus "the Taberdars of Queen's College". It came at last to be exclusively reserved for heralds.

The inn was built round three sides of a square with galleries one above the other; these were of wood and were supported by wooden pillars. Within the memory of many still living the "Tabard" presented a venerable aspect. A wooden bridge ran from the inn proper to the galleries. Huge stables were attached out of all proportion to the number of horses that of later years stood there. The doorways were low, so were the windows, both a little crooked under time's rough hand and the ceilings bulged somewhat. The fireplaces and the pantries were of ample proportions. There was a great room in the inn buildings. It was called the "Pilgrims' room," and mine host would assure the curious inquirer it was the very room where the immortal nine-and-twenty had gloried and drank deep on the night ere they started. No doubt he believed it, and they were none the worse for believing it either, but alas! what house could hold out against such rough usage for so many centuries? Even if you traced it back to 1676, long after the Pilgrimage itself had vanished, you must be reminded there was then a great fire in Southwark wherein the "Tabard" blazed as fiercely as its neighbours. True it was rebuilt after the old plan, and as some have fondly believed with part of the old material. Yet fashion or whim procured it another name, for now it was known as the "Talbot". Talbot some say meant a dove, but others of greater authority interpret "a dog with a turned-up tail". Lest memory of its old renown should fail, a part in the middle of the street bore a sign whereon was inscribed, " This is the Inn where Sir Jeffry Chaucer, and the nine and twenty Pilgrims lay in their journey to Canterbury, Anno 1383". Hanging signs are still a familiar feature of country inns. As far back as 1763 it was decreed that such things were too great an obstruction in London. They were all pulled down and this went with the others, but the inscription was repeated over the gateway, where so it remained till 1831 when it was barbarously obliterated.

A certain literary flavour lingered about the old place whether called the "Talbot" or "Tabard". Much of the spacious area was used as warehouses, railway receiving office and whatnot. In 1875 there were some improvements or at any rate changes, in which the whole of the ancient edifice vanished. Many protested, but I think without just reason. True the thing was ancient and interesting, but its claim to be in any sense the "Tabard" of Chaucer's day was preposterous. We shall meet a strange modern continuation or revival when we come to make our strictly up-to-date Pilgrimage to Canterbury.

The landlord of this ancient house in Chaucer's day was the renowned Harry Bailly. It seems impossible to describe him in other than our poet's words:—

> A semely man oure hoost he was withalle
> For to han been a marschal in an halle ;
> A large man he was with eyghen stepe,
> A fairer burgeys was ther noon in Chepe :
> Bold of his speche, and wys and wel i-taught,
> And of manhede him lakkede right naught,
> Eek therto he was right a mery man.

A famous man indeed ! According to some he served as a model for Shakespeare, since mine host of the "Garter" in the *Merry Wives of Windsor* is " obviously derived" from this great original. One questions both the "obviously" and the "derived". Shakespeare was royally magnificent in everything, not least in his literary appropriations, not to give them a grosser name, but you fancy he drew his host from life just as Chaucer did. Harry Bailly was no figment of the poet's brain, but a substantial burgher of the later fourteenth century. He was a supposed descendant too of Henry Fitz Martin to whom Henry III in the fiftieth year of his reign, 1266 to wit, granted the customs of Southwark. He was bailiff of Southwark and thus would be called in the fashion of the time Henry Bailiff or le Bailly. However this may be, we know that our Harry sat in two Parliaments, that of Edward III in 1376, and that of Richard II in 1378, as M.P. for Southwark. He is mentioned in a subsidiary roll of the fourth of Richard II as innkeeper, where he and his wife are assessed at the sum of two shillings. At any rate Chaucer's picture is clear and definite enough, and we know that in the *Tales* he is frequent and prominent.

The "Tabard" Inn stood right opposite St. Margaret's Church on the east side of the High Street, going from London Bridge. As the jovially disposed Pilgrim would scarce pass an inn without turning aside to refresh himself, so the pious-minded would not let a church go by without offering up a prayer to St. Thomas, the memory of whom must fill his mind more and more as the shrine grew nearer and nearer, yet we can scarcely believe that either class were so bibulous or so devout as to halt at every inn or place of prayer. They would remember however St. Thomas's Hospital in High Street from which the present St. Thomas's Hospital is directly derived, and if the institution is now known by the name of the Apostle it seems originally to have been dedicated to the English Archbishop. Near at hand was St. Thomas's Church which would also seem to have a like origin. They had already passed St. Saviour's and right opposite the inn door we have noted St. Margaret's Church otherwise St. Margaret-on-the-Hill. It was not used after the time of Henry VIII, save as a court. You cannot turn over many pages of the *State Trials* before you come to the name. The Town Hall is now built on the site so that identification is easy.

I will just mention one other church, and that is St. George the Martyr, which is a little way along the line of the street. During the time of the Pilgrimage and long after, the houses did not extend beyond this. Hard by was St. George's Bar, where certain customs were levied. Here the Pilgrims turned to the left at what is now Dover Street, and might consider themselves already fairly in the country. Round about was marsh land, along which a causeway had of old time been built to carry the road, and though there would be patches of cultivation here and there, much must have been waste common and swamp. The change from Southwark was great. There was the crowded street, full of fantastically dressed figures, the street itself lined with noble and imposing buildings, here was the quiet and silence of the country, yet not on the road itself where there was much coming and going. All Chaucer's Pilgrims rode, but many did the journey on foot, either from need or from a penitential vow. Those with money could very easily hire a horse; no doubt many of them did so. There was a fixed tariff, which was twelve pence from Southwark to Rochester, another twelve pence from Rochester to Canterbury, and if you went on to Dover afterwards you must produce another sixpence, but then a penny went as far in Chaucer's time as one shilling and threepence does now, so that the charge though still moderate was not altogether trifling.

Along the road then we go till we come to the second milestone from London, where we call a halt at St. Thomas Waterings or St. Thomas à Watering. It was in the Old Kent Road at the corner where Albany Road now stands. Like many other things of which we speak we would find no trace of it to-day, but it was a well-known landmark in its time, and deserves some notice. The city had jurisdiction over Southwark and about here was the limit. There was a well or pool dedicated to St. Thomas where it was the custom for Pilgrims to stop to water their horses, and no doubt to visit the inn hard by and so take their last draught for the time of that famous London ale which Chaucer thought worthy of his praise. It had a more gruesome reputation as a place of execution for the county of Surrey, just as Tyburn was for Middlesex. If it had not quite so old and famous a history, yet many remarkable people came to a violent end there, among them the author of the *Martin Mar-Prelate Tracts*. References to the place in our old literature are common. They are of that savage satirical humorous style in which it was once the habit to treat such dismal things. There was an execution here as late as 1834, after long years of disuse. The place was chosen as the best way out of a legal difficulty. The story is told in the life of Lord Campbell who, as Attorney-General, had engineered the whole business. Many of our Pilgrims must have seen poor wretches dangling from the gibbet at that spot, but all along the road the gallows would be far from an infrequent sight, not that the rulers were merely cruel but the country was full of wild characters and society could not afford to house them or try to reform them. It did not profess to be very indignant, nay the sentiment on the subject of crime was curiously tolerant, and if the malefactor had wit enough to "pray his clergy," or agility enough to bolt into a place of sanctuary, he got off very easily, only if society fairly caught him, it made an end of him in summary fashion. But to return to our Pilgrims; here we have them fairly started with London some way behind, their journey more than well begun, yet it is necessary to pause awhile to say something of the remarkable man whose writings so preserved the memory of the Pilgrimage that he seems as much identified with it as St. Thomas himself.

CHAPTER VII

CHAUCER

What We know of Him—Facts of His Life—Varied Occupations and Fortunes—Adventures at Home and Abroad—Death and Burial—Curious Incidents in His Career—Portraits of Him, Literary and Otherwise—Fondness for Books and for Nature—Comments on Women—Ironical Humour—Broad Touches—Character of Harry Bailly—"The Tavern Sentiment"—An Objective Poet—*The Canterbury Tales*—Idea of the Work—The Supplementary *Tale of Beryn*—Places mentioned in the *Tales*—Theory about Harbledown—The French of the Prioress—Chaucer, Spenser, and Tennyson.

THE Canterbury Pilgrimage owes its beginning to St. Thomas, that it is still a vivid memory is due to Chaucer. It is necessary here to say some words about that great writer. Yet what remains to be said?

Erudite scholars, eminent critics, have discussed him again and again, not always to the increase of our knowledge and understanding. At least they have delved out every procurable detail, and viewed his genius from every possible standpoint. I here cite a few incidents, and make a few observations such as seem fitting to this link in my narrative. Even the baldest facts must be given with reserve. The word "chaucer" means shoemaker; it was not an uncommon name in London in the fourteenth century, so when we come across it we cannot always be certain that it is our poet. The scraps of authentic record are most tantalising. A piece of waste paper turns up; it is a memorandum of expenses in the household of a prince where Chaucer was a page; it notes the price of a pair of shoes or a cloak bought for him. Hard indeed from entries like these to reconstruct a life!

In the Middle Ages biographers confined their attention to kings and saints; no one thought of telling the life of a man of letters; when scribes took to such matters they did so uncritically, so produced what was of little value. Chaucer spent much of his life in the service of kings and nobles. His name appears in the State Papers, otherwise we would have known really nothing about him. Here are the main points.

He was born before 1340 in Upper Thames Street, in the city of London. His birthplace is probably covered to-day by Cannon Street Railway Station. His father was John Chaucer, citizen and vintner of London, a man of position and descended from people of position. Possibly he studied at Oxford or Cambridge, or even both. It is more than likely that he served wine to his father's customers. In 1357 we find him page in the household of Elizabeth de Burgh, wife of Prince Lionel, third son of Edward III. In 1359 he fought for his King in the French war, and fell into the enemy's hands. He was treated well enough. A prisoner of position was a valuable asset, so to starve or slay him were sheer stupidity. Next year he was ransomed, the King contributing £16 to whatever sum was required. A pound sterling, you must remember, *then* equalled £13 6s. 8d. *now*.

On his return to England he was made Yeoman of the King's chamber, as is mellifluously and royally written, *delectus valettus noster*, but fine words butter no parsnips and his duties were of the most ordinary character; the *valettus* had to make beds, bear torches, set the tables, go messages, and do such things as the King or his chamberlain should order. In return for this, he had his meals in the King's presence, though very much you surmise at the other end of the table. Like the modern maid-of-all-work he had his beer money, and stated provision of robes and shoes or their cash equivalent.

You gather he quitted himself well, for in about a year he rose to be an esquire of less degree. As such he had sevenpence halfpenny a day, and there was ample provision for dress. His duties now were to tell stories of kings and knights, to pipe or harp for the entertainment of the court, and to see after strangers and guests. Already he had a wife, Philippa, a lady of the Queen's chamber. Both he and she were in high favour with John of Gaunt, who granted them pensions and helped Chaucer to various preferments.

Of Philippa herself we know nothing certain. It is supposed that the married life of the pair was not happy or harmonious. Chaucer certainly had other loves; if Philippa had it would explain certain bitter touches in the poet's writings, but we have no evidence that she was anything but a model of propriety. It is surmised the couple had at least three children: Thomas, who became a person of importance; Elizabeth, who entered the Abbey of Barking; Lewis, for whom Chaucer wrote his treatise on the *Astrolabe*, a quaint gift for a child of ten! Thus we make certain of Lewis, but not of the other two.

Chaucer rose in the royal service, he fought in the foreign wars, he was abroad on state business in France, Italy, and Flanders, also it is probable that in 1373 he came face to face with Petrarch at Arqua. He had various pensions and emoluments, the chief was the appointment of comptroller of the customs of the Port of London, and in 1385 he was allowed to perform his office by deputy. It seems that he at once took the opportunity to go the Canterbury Pilgrimage —certainly for pleasure, possibly from piety. Next year, that is 1386, he sat as knight of the shire for Kent. It was customary to give grants in kind to favourites. In 1374 he had a pitcher of wine daily, a gift peculiarly grateful, even though he afterwards found it more convenient to commute it for a pension, but perhaps the commutation was the work of a government office. In 1398, that is two years before the end, he was granted a tun of wine, but much happened between these two grants. Perhaps like Florizel, Prince of Bohemia, "from his edifying neglect of public duties," but more certainly because John of Gaunt was out of favour, he lost all or nearly all his appointments and there came on him a time of depression. His wife died, also he was in straits for money, and it was not till his patron was again in power that the sun shone once more. He was gifted with various minor offices as well as several pensions, but even in the time of Henry IV, who succeeded Richard II in 1399, we must suppose him in want. At least he indited his *Compleynt to his Purs* for the King and was suitably rewarded. In the last days of 1399 he took a long lease of a tenement in Westminster, but before another year had gone, on 25 October, 1400, he died and was buried in St. Benet's Chapel, Westminster Abbey.

In after years many poets were laid beside him. The place, as all the world knows, is in the north transept and is Poet's Corner. In 1556 a tombstone of grey marble was put there in his honour. As the spot was known at that distance of time it was probably marked by some previous monument. It is from this tombstone that we get the date of his death. As late as 1868 Dean Stanley procured the erection of a stained-glass window with portraits and views of the Canterbury Pilgrimage over his grave.

One or two additional isolated facts may be given. On 1 May, 1380, Cecilia de Chaumpaigne executes a release from all liability, *de meo raptu*, and of everything else *a principio mundi* to the present time. The quaint legal expression "from the beginning of the world" must have tickled Chaucer's fancy. As for the tort itself, the bald translation would make it an ugly business, but we cannot be certain whether it meant mere abduction or downright ravishment. It has been urged that no consideration is expressed in the document, and therefore the wrong was not serious. It is possible there was a substantial *quid pro quo*, though there might have been reasons for not naming it in the deed, which as a deed was valid without stated consideration. Ten years later, on 6 September, 1390, Chaucer was robbed twice in one day by the same gang of highwaymen who must have dodged and watched him, knowing that he carried money. The values were considerable when we remember the then importance of the coins. Ten pounds were taken from him at Westminster, and nine pounds three shillings and eightpence at Hatcham by the Foul Oak. (Hatcham was a manor in Camberwell, Surrey, near Deptford.) It was royal money, but was forgiven him by his indulgent sovereign. The robbers were hunted down, and some at least were punished, *sus. per col.* is the brief and emphatic epitaph against the name of one of them in the public record. The third isolated fact takes us down nearly ten years to 1399. Chaucer enjoyed two pensions, one from the then King, Henry IV, and one from his predecessor, Richard II. With curious carelessness he lost the parchment grants of both and had to petition for and obtain fresh ones.

Chaucer had to keep the surely voluminous accounts of the Port of London in his department. He was the author of many works, from first to last he filled many pages of manuscript. He must have often signed his name, yet no authentic signature remains. We have no single scrap we can identify as of his handwriting.

Fortunately we have portraits. The chief is that which Thomas Hoccleve drew or more probably caused to be drawn on the margin of his *Regement of Princes*. Hoccleve lived between 1370 and 1450; he knew Chaucer well and held him in loving honour. The portrait dates from eleven or twelve years after

PORTRAIT OF CHAUCER

PAINTED BY ORDER OF HIS PUPIL THOMAS HOCCLEVE, IN A COPY OF THE LATTER'S "REGEMENT OF PRINCES."

the master's death; it is painted in colours. It presents a small thin man with white hair, and forked beard also white, the features are regular, the nose long and straight, the expression somewhat sad, a little ironical it may be, but firm and composed, as of one who knew everything that life could tell him, and had set his gaze steadily and composedly towards the end of all mortal things. There is not a suspicion of the mirth and gaiety and enjoyment in the pleasures of this world which must have lain there very evident in earlier years. He is dressed in a garment which reaches below his knee, a hood partly covers his head. The colour is black, as also are his stockings. He wears pointed shoes, one hand holds a string of beads. We have a fair total of portraits, some on horseback. None is so good as the one described, yet all have a general resemblance. The little figure does not tell us all that a portrait might, but we could not expect a Rembrandt or a Vandyke or a Raeburn at hand to put the very soul of the man present in his face before us. We are to be thankful for what we have.

In the *Prologue* to *The Rime of Sir Thopas* there is a word picture. The redoubtable Harry Bailly calls on the Pilgrim poet to come forward. He asks—

> What man art thou?
> Thou lokest as thou woldest fynde an hare
> For ever upon the ground I se the stare.

Then he tells the others to give him space, for—

> He in the wast is schape as well as I;
> This were a popet in an arm to embrace
> For any womman, smal, and fair of face.
> He semeth elvisch by his countenance,
> For unto no wight doth he daliaunce.

Is this Chaucer's picture of himself or even his picture as it would appear to Harry Bailly? Not altogether.

> Oure host to jape began.

Harry in fact did little else; he was a habitual and reputed wit, his jokes current in every tavern in

Southwark, and when he compares Chaucer's slender frame to his own ample proportions, he is obviously making fun after his kind. There is truth in the suggestion of our poet forgetting his rough companions, and staring on the ground as he mused on other things. Harry was clever enough to note, and perhaps to wince, under the ironical amusement of the other's glance as it dwelt on his rotund bulk and rubicund countenance, and so he calls him " elvisch," a word commentators expound as absent in demeanour, or rather as they say in Scots, " uncanny," something that the ordinary mind did not altogether fathom.

We have one strange recent note as to Chaucer's personal appearance. Robert Browning was buried in Westminster Abbey on the last day of 1889; his grave was dug in Poet's Corner, at which digging it was the duty or the pleasure of the Coroner of Westminster to attend; he took the chance to examine Chaucer's skeleton, and reports it that of a man about five feet six inches in height, which agrees very well with the portrait, and with Harry Bailly's description read backwards as it was evidently intended to be read.

I turn to the works.

The Chaucer canon is even yet not absolutely fixed, perhaps it never will be finally, but we know that he wrote the *Dethe of Blaunche the Duchesse*, *Troilus and Cressida*, *The Hous of Fame*, *The Legende of Good Women*, *The Parlement of Foules*, and more important than all, the *Canterbury Tales*. Unless you are a professed student in such things you may very well neglect the rest. The works confirm the impression of the life. He shows great knowledge of the world, and of all sorts and conditions of men. He has experience in the ups and downs of fortune, he has not always walked circumspectly or discreetly, but you learn a good deal more. He is a man of great knowledge and enormous reading. He knew classical Latin literature, especially Virgil and Ovid, for in his time no one studied Greek. He had a wide range of reading in medieval Latin which contained all the knowledge of the day; he knew everything that was worth reading in French and Italian. He was profoundly influenced by the great Italian masters, Dante, Boccaccio, and Petrarch, but the red blood of life ran headily in his veins; he was no mere scholar. He was passionately fond of books. After his day's work at the Customs House he would go home to read till he was dazed, but when the spring-time came and the green was fresh in the gardens that were everywhere around in the London of his day and the birds were singing as they sang then in the London streets, and when the daffodils began to peer, "for then comes in the sweet o' the year," he shut the quaint black letter tomes:—

Farewel my boke, and my devocioun!

Not only did he read the book of letters and the book of nature, he read his fellowmen clearly and truly if he did not go down to the very roots of their being, as Shakespeare does. He noted the dress, the habit of mind, the habit of body, the little foibles of women, the small prides, the broad faults, the nobility in humanity, the nobility in all ranks; and what he saw he could place before his readers. A graphic touch, a happy phrase, and the very man or woman rises before your eyes. Thus from out the darkness of the Middle Ages, his nine and twenty pilgrims come forth clearly portrayed; you would know them no better if they rode by you, along the Southwark High Street, and you looked at the apparitions with the eyes of your body, and felt after them with all the powers of your mind.

I will not quote even the most graphic lines in the *Prologue*, for that is a well-worn theme. His humour is rich and abundant, yet with a constant touch of irony, the irony of the artist, the irony of the great masters. You catch it in a phrase like "The Moral Gower". It is almost with a sneer at the doctrine of the Church that in the *Prologue* to the *Legend of Good Women*, he tells us in some striking lines that there is no doubt joy in Heaven and pain in Hell, but none has been there and returned to recount his experience. He will even mock at himself. The *Monk's Tale* in the Canterbury series tells of the tragic ruin of the great ones of the earth, but the Knight cuts the story short. "It is a great disease (grief)" to hear of such things—the Host is much plainer:—

> Sir monk, no more of this so God you blesse,
> Your tale anoyeth al this companye,
> Suich talkings is not worth a boterflye,
> For ther-in is ther no desport ne game.

Thus he abruptly ends a piece of which he himself felt the futility.

In a well-known passage in the *Prologue* he makes an apology for the stories he is about to tell, he must, he says, report exactly what was said, and he must not be blamed for it. The very apology, which is clearly ironical, since Chaucer himself was the story-teller, shows that the age had its own standards which in parts of the *Miller's Tale* and the *Reeve's Tale* (to name but these) Chaucer set himself deliberately to transgress. The stories, however gross, are exceeding humorous and mirthful. It is told of Robert Burns that as he composed *Tam o' Shanter* tears of joy and merriment ran down his cheeks. Chaucer must have felt like that when he thus wrote. His is not the coarseness of Rabelais, who talks filth for the mere love of the thing, nor the occasional grotesque coarseness of Dante, where the moral purpose even if you think it misplaced is apparent. It is the joy of the people in comic, indecent story. Harry Bailly, a real representative of the commons, is always making suggestive or improper japes, though so quaint and mirth-provoking that disgust were a mere pretence. When all this is frankly admitted there is much to be said in extenuation, if extenuation be required. The perpetual joke through the medieval centuries was the infidelity of married women, so that Chaucer who was in hearty sympathy with popular feeling should make this a stock theme is by no means surprising. Also he jested at the abuses in the Church, though he was no Reformer before the Reformation. There is almost certainly a personal note in the unconcealed bitterness of the observations on the female character, yet he has pictured noble and chaste women and pure-minded priests in the most affecting manner. In both he was true to life, for the Middle Ages with all their coarseness were peculiarly rich in saintly characters albeit its ideals were not those of the ancient or modern world. And then he utters the very truth: his characters in fact would have talked so grossly though not as wittily as he makes them; even their coarseness is healthy and natural.

"The tavern sentiment" is strong in Chaucer as it is with many great writers, Shakespeare and Scott and Dickens; but this only means that he found in the tavern things entertaining and attractive both for the body and the mind; it was a little globe where he studied in miniature the aspects of the great world. You might safely venture a step farther and say of Chaucer that like the cook of the *Prologue*—

> Wel cowde he knowe a draughte of Londone ale,

and like the frankeleyn—

> Wel lovede he by the morwe a sop in wyn.

You may believe also that the daily pitcher and the tun of wine came to the hands and the palate of no ungrateful recipient, yet you cannot believe him an inordinate wine-bibber, quite the contrary, otherwise he could not have been the man he was and done the things he did.

Bon-vivant, scholar, courtier, and diplomatist, he had enough work on his hands. There are traces in his life of a certain carelessness and hurry, as if now and again he had too much to do, and this is borne out by his works. Much he left unfinished, he breaks off abruptly as if tired, and he never completes the design. The *Canterbury Tales* is but a fragment, though a colossal one. He is an objective poet, his strength and his limitations lie together as is usually the case. His marvellous pictures of the Pilgrims are by one of themselves, a man of genius but yet of like passions, of the same world, of the same habit of thought. His keen wit plays about the abuses of the Church and the comic facts of life, but he accepts the doctrines of his faith without question just as he accepts the forms of government. To him the times are not out of joint. The sorrowing and suffering of contemporary humanity do not move him beyond measure. He is no reformer in Church or State. He is as much on the side of kings and nobles as Shakespeare. I point those things out not in a carping spirit. Chaucer like other great writers justifies his own existence and his own methods of work. It were mere folly to demand of him inconsistent qualities.

I turn to the *Canterbury Tales* which, as already noted, have kept the fame of the Pilgrimage alive, yet the odd thing is that they tell us very little about the Pilgrimage itself. The idea as a vehicle for story-telling is excellent. The Pilgrims start from the "Tabard" Inn in Southwark. The host, Harry Bailly, says he will go with them, and that each shall tell two tales going and two coming back. There are *Prologues* between which serve as links connecting the narratives. Therein mine host is always at his best, and not seldom at his grossest, but then as there were in all thirty-two Pilgrims, and there are only twenty-four tales, that is not one apiece for the outward journey. Chaucer does not even take his Pilgrims into Canterbury. He does not say it is even in sight, though as they have passed Harbledown they must be within a mile. Various reasons suggest themselves why he thus stopped short. I think he did so, advisedly, warned by his artistic instinct. To him and the men of his time there was something awful and impressive about the shrine of St. Thomas; he could not treat it in a jesting way, and he must have felt that it would be incongruous suddenly to adopt a profoundly devotional tone; it would have suited ill with the bulk of his work, it would have suited ill with the temper of mind in which he wrote the series. Still one feels the loss. A visit to the Shrine inspired by Chaucer's genius had been a precious literary treasure.

We have indeed an account, but not his account, by a contemporary, whose *Tale of St. Beryn* continues the series. It tells how the Pilgrims arrived in Canterbury, put up at the famous " Chequers of the Hope, which every man doth know ". They visit the shrine, go about their own amusements, and prepare to return. The story is not without merits; quite in keeping is the comical speculation of the most ignorant among the Pilgrims at the meaning of the painted windows. The prologue also includes an attempted intrigue between the monk and Kit the hostess of the " Chequers ". It is an imitation of Chaucer's manner, but it is a very pale copy of the great original. The imitation recalls Chaucer in an irritating way; you feel at every line the lack of the master's hand. Nor are there curious and intimate details which the author might perhaps have supplied had he thought it worth while, describing the shrine, the church, and the town. These might have made up in some way for the great blank, but we have them not, and I do not find that this prologue supplements or adds greatly to our knowledge.

To return to Chaucer's work. You doubt if such a heterogeneous assembly would in fact have voyaged together. Had a stronger common religious sentiment animated them, had they been marshalled and led by an enthusiastic priest instead of by the ribald host, the idea had seemed more feasible, but a band of pious enthusiasts would not have suited Chaucer's purpose. Yet secular as they professedly are, it is strange that the purpose of the journey so seldom occurs to them. Some stop to drink, but no one ever turns aside to pray at one of the numerous chapels on the route. The narrative is so wanting in exactness of detail that it is permissible to believe the journey done in one day. Dean Stanley, in his *Memorials of Canterbury*, assumes that this is meant, though he is too well informed not to know the thing impossible in fact. It is nearly sixty miles, the roads were bad and some of the party were bad riders; all no doubt had horses, yet they are all supposed to keep together, perhaps for fear of robbers, although there is no hint of any danger.

This must have been the best known and the most trodden road in the kingdom, for it was the great route through populous Kent and chief highway to the Continent. Whether this would make it better or worse, whether it would attract or drive away robbers, need not be discussed. The narrative does not mention stopping-places, but this is because it assumes the ordinary incidents of travel. In fact it took three days to reach Canterbury. If you walk it to-day it will just take you about that time. The first night you put up at Dartford, the second at Rochester, the third at Ospringe or at Faversham of which Ospringe is practically a suburb. Then roughly speaking what you lose by walking instead of riding, you gain by improvement on the road. In the *Tales* seven or eight points, if you include the starting-place, namely "The Tabard" at Southwark, are mentioned. The seven are "the Waterynge of Seint Thomas," Deptford, Greenwich, Rochester, Sittingbourne, Boughton-under-Blean, and a place "yclept Bob-up-and-down". This I think is clearly Harbledown, anciently called Harbeldon. It lies on a switchback hill and admirably suits the description. It is besides a place of considerable interest. This was supposed to be the locality meant by Chaucer till Mr. J. M. Cooper of Faversham, an ingenious local antiquary, discovered "Up-and-down-Field" in the parish of Thannington in or near Canterbury, which he would have to be the place our poet indicated. It may be pointed out that every field in a farm has its name, also such a name, you would fancy, not infrequent. Moreover there seems to be no evidence that the place was more than a field name. In fact it is mere wild conjecture, though it has shaken the faith of eminent Chaucerean scholars like Mr. Skeat and Mr. Pollard in Harbledown.

As the road by Harbledown was clearly the direct London road, little more than a hundred years after Chaucer's death, the evidence against the theory seems conclusive, but there is unfortunately a tendency among scholars to upset a well-established explanation simply to show their own wit. Even the learned Skeat is guilty of a like prank. No lines are more famous in the *Prologue* than those that tell how the Prioress spoke French "ful faire and fetysly":—

After the scole of Stratforde atte Bowe,
For Frensch of Parys was to hire unknowe.

The innuendo is obvious. The modern journalist says Mr. Skeat loftily is never weary of this jest, and he goes on to show in an elaborately learned note that the French of the Benedictines in Stratford atte Bow was most excellent Anglo-Norman French, which no doubt it was, and is exactly what Chaucer says. Mr. Skeat has perhaps (unbeknown to himself) some Caledonian blood in his veins, or surgical operations might be extended to others than men of the north—but I wander from Harbledown. Although those eight places are mentioned they are only so and nothing more; there is no local touch save in the case of Harbledown itself; in fact if you started the Pilgrims from Southwark, turned their faces right round, and made their destination the shrine of St. Alban at Verulamium, you could turn the *Canterbury Tales* into the *St. Alban's Tales* with changes of some half a dozen or so words. Yet one is content that this famous collection of stories which gives us the full measure of medieval life should be connected with Canterbury, however slightly, for that was the great place of Pilgrimage in England.

I will conclude those notes on Chaucer with this mention of him by two poets unlike to him and each other in many respects, yet like him in their command of English words and choice facility of phrase:—

> Dan Chaucer, well of English undefiled,
> On Fame's eternal beadroll worthy to be filed.

Thus Spenser, and Tennyson's verse is fitting complement:—

> Dan Chaucer, the first warbler, whose sweet breath
> Preluded those melodious bursts that fill
> The spacious times of Great Elizabeth
> With sounds that echo still.

CHAPTER VIII

THE MAIN ROUTE (*continued*). ON THE WAY TO DARTFORD

The Main Route—Aspect of the Country—The Fields—The Crops—The Cottages—The Castles—The Old Towns—The Churches—Deptford—The Bridge—The Ravensbourne—Greenwich—Memories of St. Alphege—Blackheath and Blackheath Hill—The Manor of Placentia—Shooter's Hill—Its Evil Reputation—Dartford—Its Connection with the Pilgrimage—Its Religious Houses—Dartford Bridge—The Story of Wat Tyler.

WE left our Pilgrims at St. Thomas à Waterings. Thence we take up their journey. In going to Canterbury they would do as we do to-day, they would follow generally the Roman road from London. In the universal confusion that followed the fall of the Roman power, the roads like everything else were neglected. They were covered with debris; also in after years, as towns grew up, parts went out of use. That the road is still the main route is because in going from London to Canterbury everybody would take the shortest way, unless some sufficient reason intervened.

As to the general aspect of the country through which the Pilgrims passed, it must be remembered that the population of all England was less, during the whole of the Middle Ages, than the present population of London. Also Surrey and Kent to-day are densely populated counties; they are the two counties of our Pilgrimage. We leave Surrey at Deptford long before we are out of to-day's greater London. Kent has this peculiarity; its valleys are densely populated, its hill districts are comparatively sparse, but the track keeps to the valley. London now stretches out along the main road to a great distance; you do not in any way get rid of it till you reach Dartford, and from Dartford to Canterbury towns and townlets are frequent. Then though this was one of the chief roads in England we would meet comparatively few people ; the houses would be scanty ; the towns of minute size ; thus Deptford and Greenwich, which we now approach, were mere fishing villages. Forests were frequent, their mast fed great herds of swine, their wood was burned in the open earth on " dogs," for as yet coal was not fuel. The houses were small, and tiled or thatched. No doubt tiling was more common in the towns than the country. In the side streets of our ancient cathedral cities there still exist dwellings the very pattern of those your fancy gives to the Middle Ages.

The fields of corn must have looked the same, though not so carefully cultivated; plainly this is true of other crops, as oats, barley, rye, and so forth. Remember that turnips and potatoes were unknown. Kent was even then famous for its apple orchards and cherry gardens, but hops, now the most characteristic product of the county, as well as the equally characteristic oast-houses to dry them, were absent from the landscape, for hops were not cultivated in England till 1524. The fields were even then separated by hedges, the commons of which we have now so often but the names were of large extent; most of the land was of comparatively little value, thus it was allowed to lie waste ; so it was better adapted for hunting and hawking, sports of which the Pilgrims must have seen diverting examples as they went their way.

There were no family mansions as we now know them, scarce anything between the cottage and the castle. Yet Kent was better off in this way than the rest of the kingdom, for its wealth and fertility were proverbial from early times. The more prosperous farmers had their moated grange. The great possessions of the Church were tilled by tenants, many of them thriving. The peace and prosperity were only relative, wealthy folk only found themselves secure in the walls of a city or castle. We have still many remains of castles. Each had a moat, crossed by a drawbridge. There were thick walls and small rooms, though sometimes a hall of considerable splendour. The medieval city was like a castle on a large scale; it had high, strong walls of masonry, round it was a ditch or moat, there were various gates with drawbridges to cross the moat. The streets were narrow, the houses had projecting fronts, underneath were the shops, each with its own picturesque name as in the case of inns. Some of the English towns, as Chester, Canterbury, Sandwich, Rye, Winchelsea, retain more or less complete portions of their walls and gates. On the Continent, the examples are more numerous and complete. A very good instance is the Haute Ville of Boulogne-sur-Mer.

One feature of the Middle Ages is still much as it was; that is the churches, however restored they cannot differ much externally. Many of the forms in which the exuberant piety of the time found expression have disappeared. Monasteries, roadside chapels, shrines, hermitages, are gone, though an occasional fragment survives to preserve their memory. Call it superstition if you will, the religious sentiment was at its very height in those days. The Church was everything, the Pope was greater than the King in theory, and sometimes in practice. It dominated and directed every department in human life; there were no Nonconformists and scarcely any heretics. The genuinely devout Pilgrim took large advantage of the opportunities of devotion presented to him, and we shall often turn aside with him.

The two first places we come to are Deptford and Greenwich. They are both mentioned in the *Prologue* to the *Reeve's Tale*, where the Host says:—

> Lo, Depeford! and it is half-way pryme.
> Lo, Grenewich, ther many a shrewe is inne.

Neither to-day nor then are they on the direct road, because you turn up Blackheath Hill, leaving both places on your left. "Half-way pryme" is said to mean about half-past seven o'clock in the morning, for "prime" meant from six to nine a.m., though it was often used for the end of the period, that is to say, nine. Deptford is only three miles from London Bridge, and Greenwich is about half a mile farther on, so Harry Bailly had some reason to speak of their slowness.

Chaucer's Pilgrims were not merely like other Pilgrims, but like the folk of the time, in that they were early astir and early to bed. They made the most they could of natural light, for artificial was dear and bad. The remark it will be observed does not imply that they entered the places at all. The speaker may have only referred to them as seen from the height of Blackheath Hill, most in fact leaving the two towns alone. Yet there were several reasons why some would visit both Deptford and Greenwich. The Ravensbourne Brook runs into the Thames at Deptford Creek. It is here we now enter the county of Kent, though in the Middle Ages this was not the fixed boundary, since Kent pushed some way to the westward. You crossed the Ravensbourne by a wooden bridge at Deptford, and in times of flood it might be more convenient to make a slight roundabout and get over dry-shod, instead of crossing higher up. In Deptford, also, there was this attraction to the pious, that at the east end of the bridge was a hermitage, right in the tide of traffic. It was dedicated to St. Catherine, and here masses were said from the time of Henry III to that of Henry VIII. Indeed, that latter monarch in 1531, on the very eve of the Reformation, gave £3 6s. 8d. for the repair of the chapel. The hermit had something more to do than sing psalms.

It was his duty to look after the bridge so that it might be kept in good repair. The spot was memorable for a battle in 1497, the outcome of a Cornish and Kentish rising against Henry VII.

A legend, sure theme of many a Canterbury tale, clung to the little Ravensbourne. The river rises to the south, twelve miles off in Keston Common. Here Julius Cæsar and his legions encamped during their invasion of Britain. They were in great straits for water. The sagacious leader noted the constant presence of a raven at a particular spot, and hard by he discovered a clear pool whence a brook trickled its moderate course to the Thames. The source is still known as Cæsar's Well, a fair, secluded spot so near huge, modern London. Hence the brook was called by the name it still bears.

Of the later renown of Deptford it is permissible to say a word. Here when the days of the Pilgrimage were drawing to a close, Henry VIII, " Father of the British Navy," founded docks and shipbuilding yards of repute for centuries and only closed in our own time.

It was here, on board the " Golden Hind," Drake feasted good Queen Bess and was knighted by her. It was here too that from the Guild or Brotherhood of the Holy Trinity of Deptford Strond arose the corporation of the Trinity House, still active and important. Deptford has also its memories of Evelyn, and Pepys, and Peter the Great, and in the Parish Registry of the Church of St. Nicholas there is this brief record of the sad end of a famous wit, " 1 June, 1593, Christopher Marlow slain by Francis Archer ". Marlow, the " Dead Shepherd" of *As You Like It*, was born in Canterbury. Deptford had an earlier name—Meretown, that is the town in the marsh. No doubt in still earlier days the ground between the base of Blackheath Hill and the Thames was difficult to get over, yet many of the Pilgrims would go on to Greenwich and implore the help of St. Alphege to whom the parish church is dedicated, for there were facts in his history that would appeal with peculiar force to them.

St. Alphege, like St. Thomas, had been Archbishop of Canterbury. Like him his remains rest in the Cathedral there. Like him he had died a Martyr to the faith and here at Greenwich was the theatre of his death. He lived between 954 and 1012; he was Bishop of Winchester and when King Olaf of Norway invaded our island he confirmed him in or converted him to Christianity, also obtained from him a promise that he would never invade England again. This promise he faithfully kept to the chagrin of his followers, who were therefore supposed to entertain bitter feelings against Alphege. He was made Archbishop of Canterbury in 1006. Five years later the Danes took that city, they carried off Alphege a captive and kept him for seven months until he should raise a huge sum as ransom. The good man recognised that procuring the amount must cause infinite suffering to a distressed community. He would do nothing. On 19 April, 1012, the Danes in their encampment at Greenwich prepared a huge feast. Inflamed with meat and drink they made one final effort to extort a promise from their captive, and when it failed they pelted him with the bones of the slaughtered oxen until Thrum, a convert of his own making, slew him in mercy. And yet the savages were already half Christians. Repenting when too late they reverently bore the body to London where it was laid in old St. Paul's. Eleven years afterwards Cnut conveyed the remains to Canterbury, where they were interred with all possible honour. Lanfranc, the first of the Norman Archbishops, was inclined to dispute the title of his predecessor to the high position of Saint, but he allowed himself to be convinced by Anselm.

Harry Bailly's wit, you note, condemns the ladies of

Greenwich as shrews. But we have only his word for it. Greenwich was a fishing village and in such the women do a great deal of the work; perhaps still more of the talk. Our host may have meant no more; if he did we know that according to his own account he had a terrible vixen for spouse. He never lost a chance of giving the other sex a sly hit, neither did Chaucer his portrayer, nor the monkish chroniclers, nor indeed the folk of the time in general.

Such of the Pilgrims as went to Deptford and on to Greenwich would swing round to the right, ascend the hill, and join the others who had taken a more direct way. This led straight up Blackheath Hill and over Blackheath, hugging closely the wall of Greenwich Park. The park was part of the Manor of Pleasaunce or Placentia. It was enclosed by Humphrey, Duke of Gloucester, the " good Duke Humphrey " of English history, in 1433, and within it he built the fortress known as Duke Humphrey's Tower. After all changes it is still a pleasant spot, so you cannot wonder it found favour in the eyes of royalty. Henry VIII was born at Greenwich; here he married Catherine of Aragon, here Mary and Elizabeth were born, and here on May Day, 1536, poor Anne Boleyn dropped that fatal handkerchief that seemed a sure proof of guilt to Henry's jealous mind, leading to her arrest and death when the month was little more than half run. There are royal memories of a more cheerful nature connected with Greenwich, till Queen Mary II procured the conversion of the Palace into the famous Greenwich Hospital we know so well, but the prospect from the hill had attractions for everybody. The eyes of the most devout would stray to the ships sailing up and down the stream. Quaint enough things those ships were with their high stems and sterns, their low middles, their two masts of which the larger one in the centre carried a great sail with the crow's-nest above, and the flag covered with heraldic designs rising over it all.

The ground over which they were passing had its own memories. Macaulay, speaking of the time of Elizabeth, calls it "Wild Blackheath," but an earlier age would not have thought it so. Some famous rebels congregated there. In 1381, Wat Tyler, Jack Straw and their followers were here encamped, and in 1450 Jack Cade followed their example. Here also, the year after, some of his followers in their shirts and on their bended knees craved pardon from the King for resisting his authority, a pardon which was by no means invariably granted. The heath had seen many noble pageants. Thus on 23 November, 1415, the Mayor and Aldermen of London, accompanied by 400 citizens all gaily attired in scarlet with red and white hoods, met Henry V returning from Agincourt, and here on 3 January, 1540, Henry VIII received Anne of Cleves whom he had already met at Rochester and dissembling his disappointment behaved as gallantly as he could under the circumstances.

Proceeding over Blackheath the Pilgrims went along what is now known as the Old Dover Road, and climbing Shooter's Hill descended to Welling. In later days the neighbourhood had an evil reputation for its bands of highwaymen, who naturally frequented open wild places in the neighbourhood of London. Hasted, the historian of Kent, says that Welling meant "Well End," because you had come over Shooter's Hill without being robbed. The etymology is not convincing; suppose in fact you had been robbed, what were you to call it? or suppose you were going the other way with Shooter's Hill and Blackheath still before you, which obviously must have been the case with 50 per cent of the travellers? Even on the outward journey you had Bexley Heath after Welling, and the highwaymen of Bexley Heath and neighbourhood in the eighteenth century were so notorious, it was said if you went after dark from Shooter's Hill to Dartford you were sure of being robbed at Shoulder of Mutton Pond. But we talk of a much earlier time, long before the era of the highwaymen, when the place does not seem to have been specially notorious. Crayford was memorable long before the Pilgrims' time for one of the last stands made by the old Britons against the Teutonic invaders. They were hopelessly defeated: thus the Saxons possessed the land till in their turn they went down before the Normans.

Dartford was an important point in the annals of the Pilgrimage. We count it to-day seventeen miles from Charing Cross; it was then considered a very fair distance, and glad enough the wayfarers must have been to conclude here their first day's journey. The people in the outskirts of London do all they can to attract the attention of the London excursionist. They supply his wants for their own profit. Dartford did this for the Pilgrims to such an extent that the end of the whole business was a heavy blow to the prosperity of the town. It was noted for its inns just as Southwark was. We have the names of ancient taverns; samples are the "King's Inn," the "King's Head," the "Black Boy," the "Hole (Old) Bull," the "Butcher's Arms," the "Dolphin". I cannot say that any of these can in fact show a medieval pedigree, but the names are ancient and fish-like enough. The "Bull," in particular, is still a fine example of an old Kentish inn. There was a good trade done in Pilgrims' signs by the Guild of All Saints in Overy Street and the Guild of the Virgin in Spital Street; no doubt they were the two ordinary varieties, the small vial to carry the sacred blood or the effigy of the Martyr's head with its brief Latin inscription.

A wider, more generous provision however was made for the Pilgrim than is anywhere now made for the stranger. If he was poor and needy there were several religious houses where was dispensed the profuse and indiscriminate charity of medieval times, the kindly charity that gave according to the needs and not according to the merits of the vagrant. There was also ample provision for his spiritual wants. As far back as the time of Doomsday Book there were three churches or chapels at Dartford; the number of religious foundations was much increased in after years. The parish church dedicated to the Holy Trinity had the north chancel sacred to St. Thomas of Canterbury; here was a chapel and an altar to him, dating from the reign of Henry III. Lofty arches were cut through the old church walls so that the altar could be seen by the passing Pilgrim. After the Reformation those arches were blocked up and the chapel became a vestry-room. When the arches were cut the church was enlarged so that it stuck right out into the road. No pious medieval builder would alter his plan or turn aside because he interfered with the highway; let the highway take care of itself would be his thought if not his expression. In this case the highway did, for it diverged round the obstruction. Also a cross was erected whereat the Pilgrim could pray even if he lacked time to enter the church. The town-folk cherished their altar and remembered it in their wills. Benefactions were often left to the light of St. Thomas.

The name of the town reminds us that there is a river here to be crossed. There was a regular ferry over the Darent from or before the time of Edward II. It was the property of the Manor, and very profitable it must have been. In 1235 a hermit, constructing a cell, set himself down on the spot. His duty was to help travellers. It was also his duty and probably his pleasure to collect alms wherewith, aided by the fruit from his little garden, he did well enough. In

THE MAIN ROUTE

Henry IV's time a bridge succeeded to the ferry; it was narrow and steep, but lasted till about 1750. The line of hermits was still kept up, only the priest in possession had the added duty of keeping the bridge in repair. The chapel attached was dedicated to St. Mary and St. Katherine; it drew its support chiefly from the passing Pilgrim.

In 1349 Edward III founded the Priory of Dartford. It was the time of the Great Pestilence, which may have inspired or at any rate quickened his zeal. It was for sisters of the order of preachers, had lands in London and elsewhere, numbered among its inmates members of the royal house, and was in its own day a very important institution. Hard by the bridge stood Trinity Hospital, dating from the time of Henry VI, 1452 in fact. It was built partly over the stream, into which piles were thrust to support it. We should now consider such a building eminently undesirable, but probably the object was to get a sufficient supply of water without trouble, an object which explains many minute details of our old towns. Its purpose was to house five poor persons, on whom were enjoined the practice of works of mercy and piety. To assist the wayfarers would be to fulfil both objects. When the Pilgrims got safe over the river they had to climb the steep ascent then called St. Edmunde's Weye, because it led to a chapel dedicated to the sainted King and Martyr. You remember that he ruled over East Anglia and that the Danes, tying him to a tree, shot at him with arrows till he perished. As our travellers rose up to Dartford Brent, they would pass the gallows beside the gravel pit. It was at this spot that heretics were burned in the reign of Queen Mary, yet even she did nothing to revive the altar of St. Thomas in the church. I have not yet exhausted all the religious institutions of Dartford. The Knights Templars had a house here, whose memory is still preserved in Temple Hill and Temple Farm; also there was a market cross dating from Henry VI's time. From the steps friars of various orders preached to the people as they went to and fro as their traffic called them; at this cross the people knelt and performed their devotions before they began buying and selling.

I must not forget to note that the great peasant rising of the fourteenth century took its first beginning at Dartford. It was the expression of a general discontent. A somewhat slight incident began the thing, just as a spark on a dry haystack raises a mighty conflagration. The well-known story is that the poll-tax granted by the parliament of Richard II was intensely unpopular not merely in itself but from the manner in which it was exacted. One of the collectors behaved so brutally to the daughter of a certain tyle-worker at Dartford known in history as Wat Tyler, that the enraged parent rushing at him with his lathering hammer smote him so strongly on the head that his brains fell out, and he fell dead. Great commotion ensued, men left their work and flocked to the spot, and the rising begun under Wat Tyler who was elected the leader. With him was Jack Straw and John Ball, the turbulent priest. Wat Tyler, whilst in talk with Richard II in Smithfield on 14 June in this same year, 1381, was supposed or assumed to be threatening His Majesty, therefore he was struck down by Sir William Walworth, the Lord Mayor. Tyler's death led to the dispersing of the rebels and the end of the rising. Walworth himself, as it happens, had some connection with Dartford, for his father was born there; having prospered in London he had given sixteen acres of land to Dartford Priory. There were various Wat Tylers, however, connected with the rising, so it is not at all certain that Wat Tyler the leader was Wat Tyler of Dartford, though the incident of the hammer that gave occasion to the rising is no doubt true. Wat's house or its successor is pointed out on the north side of the High Street. A hammer was found near the spot in 1834 and was enthusiastically adopted by local antiquarians as the very instrument of the blow. Alas! though of some antiquity, it was not earlier than Tudor times.

CHAPTER IX

THE MAIN ROUTE (*continued*). THE TWIN PATHS TO ROCHESTER

The Problem of the Ways—How Chaucer went—Stone Castle and Stone Church—The Watermen of Gravesend and their Charges—Remiss Churchwardens—Denton, Chalk, and Milton—Gad's Hill and its Robbers—A Legal Argument—The Road by Watling Street—Singlewell—Swanscombe and its Legend—Danes' Holes—Religious Houses at Strood—"Frindsbury Clubs"—Children with Tails—Rochester Bridge and its Chapels—St. William of Perth—His Shrine in the Cathedral—A Pious Innkeeper—Old Time Inns—The Good Works of Bishop Gundulf.

AT Dartford Brent we encounter what is perhaps the most difficult question that presents itself as to the route. The highway swings round to the left towards Gravesend, wherefrom it proceeds to Rochester and Strood, now a suburb of Rochester, in a fairly direct line. The Roman road, instead of making this curve, goes straight on with an occasional break till it joins the other at the "Coach and Horses" in Strood. The difficulties are more apparent than real. I have been in the district fairly often; sometimes I have gone one way, sometimes the other, which is, I think, exactly what the Pilgrims did. The Pilgrimage lasted for centuries, and during that time custom or convenience would make the tide flow more strongly for a period in one direction than another. We have sufficient authority to show that one or other was used, according to the whim or need of the individual pilgrim. Dr. Furnivall, whose authority is very high, thinks that Chaucer personally went by Watling Street as most direct. It is extremely probable that Chaucer did, in his own person, go the

Pilgrimage, but it is not absolutely certain. Assuming that he did, there is nothing in the *Canterbury Tales* themselves that settles this particular point. Even if he did, Chaucer was only an individual, though such is sometimes the power of a great work that he bulks more largely before our fancy than those thousands of anonymous shadows that flitted over the path through the centuries between the Martyrdom and the Reformation. We will speak of both ways.

Let us begin with the ordinary road through Gravesend. The first point of interest is Stone. The Bishop of Rochester of old time had a manor house here where he was wont to rest on his way to London; he proceeded in a leisurely, dignified fashion as was the manner of your old-time bishop. There was a castle here also, of which a stone tower still remains which the wayfarers would gaze on and pass by. The place then had and still possesses a most beautiful little church full of exquisite detail. It is hard to say why this village should have a strikingly beautiful church and the next, apparently just as important, or unimportant, one plain in comparison. It is the unexpectedness of genius; you cannot discover how the specially gifted artist came to plan this work and how a succession of workers in later years fulfilled and developed his conception. You believe that the ages which produced the few who could devise and execute such things likewise produced the many who could admire them. The Pilgrims lingered to gaze at a structure like Stone church with a passionate rapture, with thrills of emotion impossible for us to-day.

At Gravesend we have distinct traces of the Pilgrimage. Accounts remain of sums disbursed by the wayfarers, also there are or were certain dwellings called St. Thomas's Houses where tradition averred they stopped for rest and refreshment. There was also a regular ferry between Gravesend and London.

It was called the Long Ferry and belonged to the Crown. Starting from Billingsgate, it concluded at the Hythe or Landing Causeway in Gravesend. Many preferred to begin their journey by water; thus they came this way; also folk from the north of the Thames, not wishing to go round by London, crossed from where is now Tilbury.

Watermen had a bad reputation of old time for overcharge, perhaps having no skill in letters they could not thus defend themselves, whilst even in speech their talk was pointed and pithy rather than specious and logical. In 1293 the Jury at the Assizes at Canterbury presented the watermen of Gravesend, Milton, and London for that they took outrageous fares from their unfortunate passengers, nay it was gravely averred that they charged a penny for the journey between London and Gravesend, whereas it was well known that from the time whereof the memory of man runneth not to the contrary, the proper toll was a halfpenny! What answer could there be to so patent a fact? The watermen confessed their malpractices; they were soundly rated and ordered to content themselves with the lesser fare, yet were they incorrigible, for in 1313 they were presented again for the same offence. Alas! through the centuries things got worse instead of better, so that by the time of Henry VIII they were exacting twopence with barefaced audacity!

During that same king's reign there was a curious ecclesiastical scandal at Gravesend. In 1522 the Bishop of Rochester made a visitation. The churchwardens neither rang the bells nor assembled to meet him as they were bound to do, whereupon he took the extreme measure of prohibiting divine service. This was the last Roman Catholic Bishop of Rochester, no other indeed than Fisher, a man of learning and culture, for he was the intimate friend of Sir Thomas More and Erasmus, a man also of firm and resolute will. The Pope made him a Cardinal for his steadfast adherence. You remember Henry VIII's bitter phrase that the Pope might send him the hat, but Fisher would not have the head to wear it? That head as we have seen was presently spiked beside the head of More on the Southwark entrance of old London Bridge.

The Parish Church of Gravesend is dedicated to St. George, but that was after the days of the Pilgrimage. St. Mary's, the old church, was inconveniently situated as it was at a distance from the central life of the place; so in 1544 it was disused, whilst the Chapel of St. George was turned into the parish church. The Gravesend of those days was what we should now consider a village, indeed it was not incorporated until the beginning of Elizabeth's reign. On the adjacent Windmill Hill a beacon was placed in 1377. It served as a landmark, though its primary object was to warn of the approach of danger. I note this beacon because as the Pilgrims passed along they would come upon such objects with tolerable frequency. Our travellers speculated little as to the names of places they visited, however one notes that Gravesend, according to some, means the end of the hollow place; according to others, end of the grove.

Close to Gravesend is Milton. Here there was a Chantry. It was founded *temp*. Edward II, a little before 1322, by Aymer de Valence, Earl of Pembroke, and dedicated to St. Mary and the apostles St. Peter and St. Paul. The services were performed by one master, one priest, and two chaplains. These served the Parish Church at Milton till the Reformation. The after history of the building was diverse; it was in succession a private house, a tavern called the "New Tavern," finally a hospital, so that time in the long run restored it to something like the old uses.

To Milton succeeds Denton and Chalk. The church at Chalk was St. Mary on the Top of the Hill. At Denton there is St. Giles' Denton. These were small places. In 1778 Hasted notes that there were only two houses in the parish of Denton, which state of things seems to have been as old at least as 1650. The existence of the churches and the fact of the separate parishes indicate a larger population in medieval times. It can never have been dense. Perhaps the lonely ways were a little dangerous, at least the next place we come to was so decidedly, that is the notorious Gad's Hill.

Just as Shooter's Hill, according to Philpot (1776), was so called "from the thieving practised on it," so this locality reveals its nature by its title. "Gad" in Cotgrave's *Dictionary* means "to rove, to range," so we still have the phrase "gadding about". As a noun it signifies a club or wedge. It was then a lonely spot thick-set with woods on each side, and in early times notorious for its robbers. Those of our band who had money in their purses or anything of value about them approached it at nightfall with sinking hearts. In Shakespeare's day the Shrine of St. Thomas had been done away with, yet not so long before but that traditions of the Pilgrims to it still lingered. In the first part of *Henry IV*, Act i. Scene 2, the Prince and Falstaff determine to turn highwaymen, and Poins tells them of the suitable time and place, "to-morrow morning by four o'clock early at Gad's Hill. There are Pilgrims going to Canterbury with rich offerings and traders riding to London with fat purses." In Act ii. Scene 1, at the Inn yard, Rochester, the chamberlain says to Gadshill, "it holds current that I told you yester-night, there's a Franklin in the wild of Kent has brought three hundred marks with him in gold. I heard him tell it to one of his company last night at supper . . . they are up already and call for eggs and butter, they will away presently," to which Gadshill answers, "Sirrah, if they meet not with St. Nicholas' clerks I'll give thee this neck," with more to the like effect. The next scene is on the road by Gad's Hill. You remember that as the travellers are descending the height, they are set on by Falstaff and his crew and robbed, whilst the fat knight is presently eased of his booty by the Prince.

This of itself establishes the ancient and evil reputation of the place, but we have another, in some ways more curious and interesting though less known, reference in Leonard's reports. In the nineteenth of Elizabeth, Manwood, J., in trying a case, favoured the Court, as judges sometimes will, with reminiscences of like matters. He told how when he was servant, by which he meant no doubt pupil, to Sir James Hales, one of the justices of the Common Pleas, an action was brought under the statute of Winchester, 13 Ed. I, which made the locality liable for a robbery, against the folk of Gravesend for an affair at Gad's Hill. The defendants instructed Serjeant Harris to defend for them, and he brazenly pleaded " that time out of mind felons had used to rob at Gad's Hill". He urged so numerous were the robberies that the neighbourhood would be ruined if they had to make up the loss in every case! To this it was properly answered that usage, however long, could found no right to rob; so his ingenious plea went for nought. Obviously it was the duty of the well-disposed inhabitants to pursue the robbers with hue and cry so as to preserve peace and order on the King's highway, an they did not, they must take the consequences of their neglect.

Leaving this band of Pilgrims to enter Strood after their ill or good fortune on Gad's Hill, we turn to accompany the progress of those who followed from Dartford Brent the straight road of Watling Street. After about three miles the medieval way deserted

Watling Street for a short space making a detour to the right. The only apparent reason is that it thus took in Betsham or Bedesham as Hasted calls it, a very obscure place, now and always; it lies half a mile north of Southfleet, and if it was the true cause of the divergence, it shows on what trifling accidents the existence of the old way depended. It soon joins up again, and we follow on to Singlewell. Hasted spells it Shinglewell. The modern name would seem to infer that there was only one well there. If you restore the "h" the true intent becomes fairly obvious. There was an important well here with a roof of shingle; it served the Pilgrims both for halt and landmark; so widely known was it, that though in the parish of Ifield that parish itself was sometimes described as Ifield juxta Shinglewell. Here the village well is the modern form of the ancient fountain. You go on another mile, and there on the right of the road just beyond the turning on the left leading to Chalk is St. Thomas's Well. It still bears the old name; there still lingers the tradition of the Pilgrims who refreshed themselves at its waters, doing homage as they drank to the memory of the Saint.

Two places a little to the north of the route deserve a passing word. One is the hamlet of Springhead, rich in Roman remains, the other is Swanscombe between Northfleet and Southfleet, that is between the two lines of route we are considering. "The whole shire of Kent oweth it ever lasting name," says Lambard. The legend of "the moving wood of Swanscombe" is that the men of Kent met there to resist the Conqueror. They protected themselves from the heat with green boughs stripped from the forest. Whether William thought that the very ground was rising against him (a repetition, you note, of the story in *Macbeth* and elsewhere) or through this device exaggerated the numbers, I need not inquire. He agreed that they should have their ancient rights, chief of these the still subsisting "custom of gavel-kind," whereby the land is partitioned equally among the sons; there was no forfeiture for felony and so forth. Whereupon the men of Kent accepted him as their sovereign Lord.

More attractive to the Pilgrims was the fact that here was the famous and frequented shrine of St. Hilderforth. It had special virtues for those suffering from madness and melancholia. Round here are those strange excavations in the earth called Danes' Holes, the most famous of which goes by the quaint name of Clappernapper's Hole. Our travellers would accept without critical investigation the explanation that in these pits the natives had taken refuge from the Danes and other invaders, an explanation which to-day is still at least feasible.

At Strood the two bands united, for it was the most convenient place for them to cross the Medway, and at Strood they found opportunities both for devotion and refreshment. On the direct route was a pond or well again called St. Thomas à Waterings, and on the top of Strood Hill there was a Lazar house dedicated to St. Bartholomew, from whence the rise was called Spital Hill. Strood formerly was only part of the parish of Frindsbury, which lies to the east of it. Bishop Gilbert de Glanville (elected 1185) made it a separate parish and turned its chapel of St. Nicholas into the parish church. The Lazar house referred to was about a mile to the west of Rochester, just as we shall find the Lazar house at Harbledown is a mile to the west of Canterbury. The fact is significant. Leprosy was a highly contagious disease, so its victims were set some distance apart from the mass of their fellows, but they were not set so far that they could not be succoured and relieved, likewise they were placed by the main road that they might receive the alms of the passing traveller, especially the passing pilgrim. This same de Glanville was a very active prelate; he built on the north side of the main street at Strood the hospital of St. Mary, usually called Newark; its object was to provide hospitality for travellers, especially Pilgrims, and to help the poor and the sick. Noble objects indeed! yet hard is it to please everybody! The priory of St. Andrew's at Rochester Cathedral thought he had robbed them to found Newark, and they were bitterly jealous of the new foundation. In 1291 the monks had gone in procession to Frindsbury to pray for rain. It pleased them on their return to pass through the orchard at St. Mary's Hospital; they wished, they said, to avoid the violence of the wind. The hospital folk were indignant at the trespass; they too had their feelings; a dispute arose and the result was something like a pitched battle, to the great scandal of all pious souls. "And thus, out of this tragical historie, arose the bywoord of Frendsbury Clubs, a terme not yet forgotten,"—thus Lambard in his *Perambulation of Kent*.

The list of Bishop Gilbert's works is not yet finished. He built a quay of stones at the Strood end of the Medway bridge. He set some houses on it and raised a chapel dedicated to St. Mary whereat passengers might tarry for prayer. It is recorded that on 24 October, 1357, Queen Isabella, on her way through Strood, entering this chapel, made a donation of six shillings and eightpence, which meant a good deal then as we know, in honour of the Eleven Thousand Virgins. Ere we proceed over the bridge, we must tell again the not very edifying legend preserved by Polydore Virgil, employed by the Pope to collect Peter's pence in England, and the writer of a history of our country published at Basil in 1546. Once upon a time it was the fate of St. Thomas to pass through Strood. Some of the malicious inhabitants docked the tail of his horse. Now we know the Saint had a somewhat secular fondness for that animal; excessively indignant, he solemnly cursed those who had taken part in the outrage. Their descendants, he decreed, should be born with tails. Hence the quaint legend that every infant of Strood enters the world thus provided. There is much curious learning on this tradition to be found in Lambard and other old writers, some of whom say the insult was offered to St. Augustine, but the better opinion is as stated here. At least I prefer to believe so.

The name Strood, you will observe, is simply a form of *Strata*, or the paved way. The way is of course Watling Street which crossed the Medway at this point, first by a ford, but afterwards by a stout wooden bridge built on piles. In the years of desolation it was destroyed or more or less ruined at any rate, but a century before the Conquest there was a wooden bridge there, and this lasted till the fourteenth century, when a stone bridge was put up which endured till the nineteenth. The old wooden bridge was a dangerous structure. Edward I was in the city on 18 and 19 February, 1300, on each of which days he made an oblation of seven shillings to the shrine of St. William to be presently mentioned. He had hired a horse from a certain Richard Lombard, one of the train that transported his baggage. Crossing the bridge it was blown right into the Medway and there drowned. Richard had twelve shillings from the King to make up for his loss. Of the same period is the legend of the minstrel or harper, who made his living doubtless by attending bands of Pilgrims to lighten by song the labours of the road. He also was blown from the bridge into the Medway, and piteously besought the Virgin in a strange mixture of French and English to come to his aid. Our Lady was merciful and miraculously supported him whilst the tidal current bore him along, harping the while a hymn in her honour. He reached the bank a league from the city, where he was received by a great crowd who had watched his progress with wonder and anxiety. He returned to Rochester *magna comitante caterva*, and in the church there gave thanks for his preservation. Such is the story, the record of which he has left us in a Norman-French poem of ninety-nine lines.

Not till 1856 did the old stone bridge give way to another. The medieval stone bridge, which like old London Bridge had houses on it, crossed the river somewhat higher up the Medway. You got into the present track by going some way southward along the bank. The present bridge, a quite recent affair, is built like its immediate predecessor, a little way along the left bank on the site of the earlier structures and continues the road straight across. At the Rochester end there was also a chapel or chantry, that of Alleseelen or Allsouls. It was founded in 1393 by John de Cobham and Sir Robert Knowles and was served by three Chaplains, so there was opportunity for further prayer before travellers entered the town.

Rochester even in those days was an old and famous city with walls and gates, a great tower and a great church enclosing various shrines. Our Pilgrims had already seen the castle from the other side of the river, but it would not occupy much of their attention, even though the great square tower had been, it was thought, rebuilt by Gundulf, one of the most famous bishops of the See, unless indeed they passed that way during one of the sieges to which it was subject, which siege would more or less delay their progress. The Cathedral Church then of St. Andrew was another matter. They would enter it from the High Street by St. William's Gate, and perform their devotions at the two shrines of St. Paulinus and St. William of Perth. Paulinus was the third Bishop of Rochester and elected to that

ROCHESTER FROM ACROSS THE MEDWAY

See as early as 633; he was an active missionary prelate canonised in 1087. His body was interred in a magnificent silver shrine at the east end of the Cathedral; hither crowds of Pilgrims repaired for many a long day, but during the struggle of the monks with Bishop de Glanville they were hard put to it for funds, so hard indeed that they melted down the silver shrine to provide supplies. Perhaps they thought the silver was only an accident of the shrine; perhaps it was, but there is a fashion in such things. The devotion of the Pilgrims unaccountably, as they thought, became less fervent; they suffered both in honour and profit. How devoutly they wished for a new saint, and in the nick of time they had one in St. William of Perth!

William was in life a wealthy and pious baker in the northern city. Every tenth loaf he baked he gave to the poor; yet he prospered exceedingly. He determined to make a Pilgrimage to the Holy Land and let his business take care of itself; he set forth and in due time came to Rochester. The monks received and entertained him at the priory with all honour; he enriched them with valuable gifts and they sped him on his way with expressions of esteem and admiration, but he had got no farther than Delce Lane, when his servant, coveting his wealth, robbed and murdered him. What became of the servant no one cared to inquire, but the monks were on the spot forthwith. They reverently bore the body back and interred it in the cathedral with every honour. This was in 1201, and some fifty years afterwards Bishop Lawrence, making a special journey to Rome, succeeded in getting William canonised and " promoted by the Pope from a poore baker to a blessed Martyr". I have said that there was a fashion in Pilgrimages; the fashion ran strongly in favour of the new Saint; devotees flocked to the shrine in vast numbers. You can still see the stone steps in the Cathedral worn by their knees. The shower of offerings was so plentiful that with only two years' oblations the whole choir of the church was rebuilt. A chapel was erected on the site of the murder. There was a cross to his memory in Rochester, and it was from him that the St. William's Gate, already spoken of, derived its name.

This did not exhaust the attraction of the city and its great church. Among the treasures of the cathedral was a magnificent mitre of St. Thomas presented by Bishop Hamo of Hythe. Then as the band pursued its route through Eastgate they passed by St. Catherine's Hospital, otherwise "the Spital of St. Katherine of Rochester in the suburb of Eastgate," which was founded in 1316 by Simon Potyn of the "Crown" Inn, where the poor among them would be hospitably entertained. Mine host no doubt thought that one good turn deserves another, and that as he and his fellows had made so much out of well-to-do travellers, he ought to do something for the poorer class among them.

As you would expect there are many memories of old inns both in Strood and Rochester. Some at least were there in medieval days and some at least are still extant. Beside the "Crown" already mentioned, we have the "Bull," the "King's Head," the "Angel," the "Sign of Crispian," the "Swan," the "Red Lion," the "Star," the "Fleur de Luce," the "Capon," the "Noah's Ark". With all those attractions it is scarce like that our Pilgrims would pay much attention to St. Bartholomew's Hospital in Chatham founded in 1078 for poor and leprous persons. The indefatigable Bishop Gundulf was the founder, the greatest architect of all his fellows. Even if his claim to be the builder of the Keep at Rochester Castle be rejected, he certainly did much work there. He rebuilt the Cathedral Church and he raised the White Tower, still so conspicuous an object in the

Tower of London as well as St. Leonard's Tower, West Malling. We ought also to remember that his house for lepers still remains and does good work as a hospital. Our Pilgrims at length turn their backs on Rochester, toil up steep Chatham Hill, and enter a new tract of country.

CHAPTER X

THE MAIN ROUTE (*continued*). ROCHESTER TO OSPRINGE

Rainham Down and its Memories—The Cross at Newington—More Miracles—Crime in Holy Places—Roman Echoes—The Four-Went-Way—Sittingbourne—The Varied Fortunes of Schamel Hermitage—A Princely Alms—A Bid for Patronage—Old Time Feasting—Some Ancient Inns—The Legend of Tong Castle—Bapchild and Radfield—The Strange Story of "Judd's Folly"—Halt at Ospringe.

FROM Chatham Hill our Pilgrims passed over the open tract of Rainham Down. Here on New Year's Eve, 1539, the Duke of Norfolk attended by a body of nobles and gentles, " all in coates of velvet with chaines of gold," met Anne of Cleves, to convey her on to Rochester, where Henry VIII discovered her next day watching the sport of bull baiting. There was little to attract them in Rainham itself or its church with its walls of flint and perpendicular tower of an ordinary Kentish pattern. This tower served as a beacon, one of a line from the coast to London. A few may have stridden over the large churchyard to inspect a carved chest, an exquisite piece of ancient woodwork whose conjectural date is 1330, preserved in the building.

At Newington, some three miles farther on, there was matter more fit for their notice, not so much in the church though spacious and beautiful, as in the village itself. Here was a memorial cross commemorating that St. Thomas had confirmed a flock of children. Your medieval bishop was often a mighty haughty person; he was wont to perform the ceremony from horseback, and as you infer in a slapdash and perfunctory manner, but St. Thomas held the rite too solemn for this. Dismounting he placed his hands on the heads of the children, himself standing the while in the way.

Some fourteen miracles are recorded of St. Thomas in this little village. It is estimated that the number was more numerous, but for one reason and another all are not chronicled.

One story tells of two blind men on horseback approaching Newington on the way to Canterbury. By mistake one of them hurt the ankle of the other. Thereupon they fall into talk of their common calamity. Robert of Essex, so one was called, is moved to invoke earnestly the aid of the master. He sees a stone on the road! he is cured! Disdaining his wife's guidance, hitherto indispensable, he rushes off gaily to Newington, leaving his late companions far behind. Again, Godebold of Boxley has two lame daughters. They come to Newington Cross to pray. St. Thomas appearing to one in a dream, promises recovery. Immediately she is well and sound to the joy of priests and people. The church bells are rung as she gladly proceeds on her Pilgrimage. Her younger sister remains at the cross weeping bitterly, "crying like Esau" beseeching another blessing. The Saint is touched, again he appears in a dream, again promises and again performs to the universal content. "Cures innumerable," says the chronicler, were wrought at this cross.

Newington had other memories of religious houses of a less edifying character. Before the Martyrdom a nunnery was here, which had the Manor of Newington from the King for its support. There was dire strife between the Lady Abbess and her Sisters in the faith. Finally they strangled her in bed, and pitched her body into a pit, hence called Nun-pit. The King resumed possession of the Manor and packed the truculent sisters off to the neighbouring Isle of Sheppey. Later Henry II, being moved thereto by Becket, put seven priests in their place. Besides the vacant premises with the possessions thereto pertaining, he ordained them an allowance of twenty-eight weights of cheese from his Manor at Middleton, yet there was something cursed about the spot. One of the priests was presently murdered, and in this four of the brethren were concerned. Hard by there is Nunfield farm which possesses some carved stone, possibly a fragment of the old erections. Tradition says a nun was bricked up alive in a niche in the cellar. In such form do echoes of old time tragedies linger on to our own days.

Even at that early date Newington was set fair with apple orchards and cherry gardens. By one of those strange revolutions that time brings about, the hop, once all-prevailing in Kent, but as we know later than the days of the Pilgrimage, is again giving way to those more ancient products. They say the Romans brought the cherry to Kent. Be this so or no, here are sure traces of the all-conquering people. The Roman urns, at Newington, in a later age occupied the learned pen of Dr. Meric Casaubon, Prebend of Canterbury, likewise the prevalence of the sweet chestnut all round is put down to the invader.

There are great remains of earthworks hard by Keycol Hill which our Pilgrims climb out of Newington, but these, Roman or no, they would disregard as pagan abominations. Keycol Hill, sometimes known as Chestnut Hill, is seized upon by the antiquaries for their very own. Hasted is amusingly confident. "Keycol-hill seems to be the same as *Caii Collis*, or Caius Julius Cæsar's hill. Key Street, *Caii Stratum*, or Caius's Street." Key Street is a little hamlet on the farther or east side of the hill. It has the inevitable village inn with a huge gilt key for sign. It would be too great a shock for Dry-as-dust to assume that the hamlet was called after the tavern and not the other way round. Indeed the house is not a very old one, though doubtless there was always a tavern there, for here is the Four-Went-Way. The chief road from the Island of Sheppey crosses the Canterbury highway and goes on to Maidstone, again crossing before it reaches that town another Pilgrim track, and at Maidstone going off in various directions, both Canterbury and London being among them. The obscure inn at Key Street has no history worth tracing, but one must not forget that it and its kind were frequent along the route, though as we noticed they left fewer traces in stone or paper than the religious foundations of one sort or another which were just as frequent. The village ale-house was frequented by the more joyous type of Pilgrim, the type whereof Chaucer gives us, in the Miller, so memorable an instance.

As we pause at the Four-Went-Way, it is well to remember there were many religious houses a few miles distant on each side of the route to which some of the Pilgrims would make excursions. The way to Maidstone descends Detling Hill. On the southern slope of the same range was Boxley Abbey, famous for its image of St. Rumbold and its Rood of Grace. Boxley, as we shall find, is on another Pilgrim route, but that would not prevent an occasional visit from the main road. Had any made this visit they had already turned off by one of the roads to the right, which led by green and shady ways to the Abbey and its village. Again, at the Four Ways the road to the left would take them to Sheppey, and at Minster in Sheppey there was the ancient and pious foundation of the sainted Sexburga, widow of Ercombert, King of Kent, which in one form or other lasted down to the Reformation. As they crossed the Swale into Sheppey they would remember that here St. Augustine baptised ten thousand pagans on the Christmas Day after the conversion of Ethelbert in 597.

Passing the turning they approached Sittingbourne, more an overgrown village than a town. You recall it as one of the six places on the route mentioned in the *Canterbury Tales*, not without reason, for it owes its rise, if not its being, to the Pilgrimage. True it existed before. We gather from the name that here the tribe of Soedingan settled, and here were two watercourses or lanes, one still uncovered in quite recent times. The place was long, a mere adjunct to Milton, which lies a little to the north, and is now described as "next Sittingbourne". But then it is on the main route; so thirty years after the Martyrdom it emerges from obscurity. It was a convenient stopping-place, and presently furnished itself with every kind of accommodation for the traveller. Even in Chaucer's time it held only some ninety houses with four hundred and fifty dwellers therein. It is straggling to-day, and it was so then. Let us follow our Pilgrims through it.

They are scarce past Key Street when they come to Dental Chapel, whereof a villa called Dental House preserves the memory. The chapel was founded by the family of Savage of Bobbing Court. Bobbing is a parish you pass through on the way to Sheppey. Notorious Titus Oates held the living for some years. To the Pilgrims he had seemed a more inexplicable monster than he does to us, but his fame or ill-fame lay ahead in the obscurity of the future. The chapel at Dental was used for passing prayer by Pilgrims; it was only open in summer, when such travellers most thronged the road.

A little way beyond was Schamel Hermitage; it stood some way up the slope on the south side of the road at Water Lane Head; here was a chapel dedicated to St. Thomas and connected therewith various houses for the use of Pilgrims. The foundation dated from the time of King John, when a priest named Samuel was in possession; he said a daily mass, as well as looked after the travellers in some sort, in return for which he would seek their alms. It was a humble and not very prosperous institution. In Henry III's time the hermit was called Sylvester. The place was looked upon with dislike by Symon de Shoreditch, the then vicar of Sittingbourne, who on Sylvester's death carried off the altar and chapel bell to his own church. His successor, Boniface, continued this violent policy; he carted away the very material of the houses, so when the Queen as patron appointed Walter de Hermeston for new incumbent, he found nothing to do since his cure was non-existent; however in 1288 (16 Ed. I) an inquiry was ordered, the result being that the place was refounded solidly and firmly. It was in favour with royalty. In June, 1358, Queen Isabella passing that way as she went to Canterbury tarried at the chapel, and donated Richard de Lenedon the priest with twenty shillings. Two years later King John of France returning from captivity found time for a visit. Glad to be homeward bound, he was in a particularly liberal and pious frame of mind. His gift was twenty nobles, equal to one hundred and twenty pounds of our money, a very princely wayside alms indeed! The chapel ended like its kind in the last years of Henry VIII. Its bell went at five shillings, and the whole premises were let at six and eightpence a year.

It is not difficult to understand why the vicars of Sittingbourne had a special grudge at this chapel. It tapped in a most irritating way the stream of alms-giving which otherwise had fertilised their own immediate territory. Schamel was at their very gates and a perpetual sore to them. History has not recorded what the vicar said when he heard of King John's princely benefaction, and perhaps that is well, especially as there is no note of any gift even by the liberal French monarch to the parish church.

Canon Scott Robertson has investigated the history of old-time Sittingbourne with curious and scholarly care; he tells us it was divided into three parts,

Schamel to the west, the church with the houses round it, and Swanstree to the east. The church did not allow the crowd to pass by without some provision; there was a statue of the Virgin at the south-east corner of Chilton chancel under a niche with a fair canopy. To this Pilgrims and other travellers would do at least a passing obeisance. You infer that the Pilgrims did in fact neglect this church which had nothing specially connected with their saint, and that the statue was a desperate bid for some little notice.

At the end of East Street, Sittingbourne, the ground rises into what is now called Snips Hill. The earlier name was Swanstree. Hard by on what are now the grounds of Murston Rectory, was the chapel of the Holy Cross, or hospital of St. Leonard's at Swanstree. The hospital was for lepers and others, and it is only fair to Symon of Shoreditch to record that to it at least he was a kind and generous friend; you will note it was about a mile from the church and centre of the place, the regulation distance of the leper hospital. The Swanstree brethren as they were called were dispersed by Henry VIII. The reiteration of the common fate becomes monotonous, but it has this excuse, it impresses on the mind the magnitude of the change in the whole life of England.

We know well enough by this time the Pilgrimage was much more than an ascetic succession of alms and devotion. However virtuous the wayfarer, he had his cakes and ale, and ginger was "hot i' the mouth". On the Swale marshes, a mile to the north of Sittingbourne, lies the just-mentioned town of Milton. The reputation of its oyster beds dates from Roman times, and was well maintained during the whole of the Middle Ages. They then belonged to the Abbot of Faversham, to whom they had been gifted, possibly in a fit of devout abstraction, by King John. Thus it might seem almost an act of piety to consume them. The day was far dis-

THE MAIN ROUTE

tant when such delicacies were packed straight off to London. They were enjoyed on or near the spot. So the oyster must have been a common article of diet in the Sittingbourne taverns, of which there was an inordinate number. First there was the "Lion," which in name and site is an inn 500 years old. It had royal patrons at times. Here Henry V, returning home after Agincourt, was feasted by Squire Northwood at a cost of nine shillings and ninepence, which went at least as far as nine guineas would to-day, or our traveller might seek the "White Hart," near the church, whereof the structure, some 400 years old, still remains strong and firm though now put to less festive uses. There are accounts extant of dealing with "the wife of the Lion," or "the wife of the George," for so mine hostess was quaintly termed. Also we have the names of places like the "King's Head," the "Seven Stars," the "Cherry Tree," the "Falcon," the "Angel," the "Adam and Eve," the "Plough," the "Bull," and so forth. The merriment of those antique hostelries is strange and ghostly, "Dead and gone, like old world wine," and we sigh as we pass on.

Some of those who feasted with Henry most like viewed the procession seven years later that carried his body in solemn state on its way to Westminster for burial. There was no halt here as at Canterbury, Ospringe, Rochester, and Dartford, but the mere fact of the progress would be a sight never to be forgotten by folk far and near. It was in 1416, during his reign, that the Emperor Sigismund had passed through with a retinue of 1000 men, the most splendid visit, it is alleged, ever paid to England by a foreign sovereign. These last two processions were obviously common to the whole route.

Another mile, and the Pilgrims reached Bapchild. They had passed over ground sufficiently high to give them a view of the Abbey and Church at Minster in

Sheppey as well as the ancient craft on the waters of the Swale. They would note Tong Castle, which raised its height between them and the water; no doubt they received with unquestioning credence the ancient legend of how Hengist obtained from Vortigern as much land as an ox-hide would enclose. You foresee that the ox-hide was cut into strips, and so easily made to surround the considerable space on which the strong tower afterwards rose. The chaplain, if unusually learned, might quote from Virgil the parallel case of Carthage. Tong, or Thong, he would remark was the same thing, so the very name was evidence for the story. He was not likely to know that the legend was world-wide.

At Bapchild there was an oratory supposed to date from 694, when an old-time King of Kent had held a great Council for Church purposes. Some vestiges of the walls are reported by Hasted in 1798 as still visible, though not to be discovered to-day. Bapchild is one of those curious names which excite your curiosity. According to this same Hasted it is compounded of two words meaning "moist" and "bleak". After Bapchild comes Radfield, and then Green Street, which to-day make practically one long straggling hamlet, though then there was no doubt space between them. At Radfield there was another opportunity for prayer and almsgiving at the free chapel founded there in 1190 by the prior of the order of St. John of Jerusalem. The priest must sing daily mass for the soul of King Henry II and perform various other pious functions unnecessary to mention. Henry died the year before the foundation. In spite of his penance and repentance, the guilt of the Martyrdom still attached to his name. This may have moved the prior to provide special intercession for him. In the time of Edward VI the chapel was reported to have fallen down, the owner being unknown. Perhaps that merely meant it was out of repair, for the result of Mr. Littledale's inquiries is that it was only cleared away a century ago. It stood at the forty-second milestone from London, and some three miles farther on there was another oratory called Stone Chapel on the north of the road. "Some broken walls of flint" are all that remain.

It was difficult utterly to destroy every vestige of those ancient foundations. They were built to last, as their pious founders thought, for ever; we see they did in fact endure for a very long time indeed. When they were secularised the building was used for some humble, rural purpose, or it was left alone, for it did not pay the toil necessary to its destruction. The present century is like to be more cruel than all its predecessors. The route is one of the most populous in England; new houses are built, new methods are introduced, and the last crumbling wall is swept away because it breaks the dull uniformity of the modern plan. True our own time has shown a revived interest in medieval and other ancient remains, but it has not gone so far as to preserve the slight vestiges of a shrine like Stone Chapel.

Our wayfarers are now on the summit of Beacon Hill, where once stood the Ospringe beacon. Presently they will reach Ospringe itself. First they must climb another hill known in later days by the odd name of "Judd's Folly". The explanation is curious, and has at least its beginning at the time of which we speak. The prior and convent of Rochester held land hereabout. At the Reformation, when these were ended, the land passed to the Dean and Chapter of Rochester as in some sort their successors. In the time of the Commonwealth, the Dean and Chapter were suppressed and the land sold to one Daniel Judd, who was a great purchaser of property of this description; he did very well out of his bargains, and in 1652 "built the present elegant seat after a design of Inigo Jones," and comfortably established himself under the firm persuasion that the new order was to last his time at any rate. As we know he was mistaken. Back came Charles II, past his very gates. How ruefully must Daniel have contemplated the royal progress! The Dean and Chapter started anew into life and Judd needs must quit! "Judde House commonly called the Folly House," says Hasted (1782), the reason of which name is abundantly obvious. It seemed to a later owner not quite suitable for him at any rate, so he called it Syndale House. The term still lingers on as the name of the hill.

Ospringe was an important point in the Pilgrimage. Situated within ten miles of Canterbury, it was with most of the wayfarers their last halting-place. Thence you began the final stage of the way. Thus it was at Ospringe that the body of Henry V lay in state under a hearse which then meant a funeral monument, just as it had done at Canterbury and was again to do at Rochester. There are various points of interest here as well as at Faversham which is hard by, to the northeast, though about a mile off the main road; so we shall follow the example of our Pilgrims and tarry here a little.

CHAPTER XI

THE MAIN ROUTE (*concluded*). THE LAST STAGE TO CANTERBURY

The Maison Dieu at Ospringe—Its Various Fortunes—Religious Houses at Faversham—St. Crispin—St. Crispianus and St. Erasmus—The Poor Nuns of Davington—The Forest of the Blean—Boughton Hill—The First View of Canterbury—The Hospital of St. Nicholas at Harbledown—Its Long History—Erasmus and Dean Colet—Treasures of the Hospital—The Black Prince's Well—" Blue Dick "—His Outrageous Proceedings—On the Threshold.

OSPRINGE, a big parish five miles in length and two miles in breadth, is on the north side of the London Road which crosses the parish eastward. The chief object for Pilgrims was the *Maison Dieu*. There were two divisions stretching on the two sides of the stream which gives the place its name. Here was a royal manor whose Lord, Henry III, has the credit for the foundation of this house; about 1235 it was fully staffed, had master, brothers, secular clerks, and so forth. These were as usual to pray for the Royal Founder, his predecessor and successors. They were to care for Pilgrims, wayfarers generally, and lepers. The separate part across the stream was for the lepers, it is thought: so again you note here is a leper house a mile from Faversham. Medieval England had even worse plagues than leprosy, to wit the Black Death which a century later wrought havoc there in Edward IV's time, or perhaps it was that the lepers had carried their gruesome disease across the water; at any rate the master and one of the brethren perished, whereupon the others fled, panic stricken. The Crown, resuming possession of the vacant site, held it for some half century, when Bishop Fisher of Rochester prevailed on Henry VIII to hand over the property to St. John's College, Cambridge, which still has it and still presents to the living.

If the *Maison Dieu* held out insufficient attraction to the Pilgrim there must have been numerous small hostelries clammering for his custom, or he might go a little afield. Half a mile to the south lay the church with its hamlet, and as we have noted a mile to the north was Faversham, always from early times a place of importance. Antiquaries to-day dig about it for Anglo-Saxon remains, since here was an early Saxon as well as a Roman cemetery, but our Pilgrims cared not for such heathen matters. The salt pit at Ospringe, whence salt was procured from sea-water, seemed to them worth all such vain antiquities; also at Faversham there were legends and sights well worth notice, for here was a wealthy and powerful abbey of the order of Cluny whose pleasure it was to entertain the very great and whose duty it was to house the very small. They performed their part so well that though a royal chamber was reserved for the King in the *Maison Dieu* where His Highness might repose himself as he passed that way, yet he usually preferred the hospitality of the Abbey. Then in the church at Faversham the north aisle was dedicated to Thomas of Canterbury also on the wall there was portrayed his Martyrdom. In this chapel there hung St. Edmund of Bury's light, to which as late as 1529 a certain Robert Fale of Faversham left " One cowe ".

Here too was an altar to St. Crispin and St. Crispianus. Old legends averred they had in Faversham, toward the close of the third century, plied their trade as shoemakers. They had fled to escape persecution from the Roman emperors. The very house in Preston Street where they had worked was pointed out. It was long an object of interest to brethren of the gentle craft, yet oddly enough neither of these, nor even St. Thomas himself, was the favourite saint at Faversham. From some whim of fashion St. Erasmus was first by a long way. Do not suppose for a moment that this was the cynical scholar of the Renaissance, the friend of More and the new learning, the man who was not much in favour with either side. Our Saint was Bishop of Antioch and was terribly tortured by the Emperor Diocletian, to little effect, however. He was soundly beaten with clubs, yet no bruise appeared on his fair skin; molten lead, pitch and brimstone were poured over him, only to his refreshment, and he was loaded with heavy iron fetters, which melted from him like wax; he escaped from his prison without breaking the seal on the door, and so was given up as hopeless. The learned are gravelled to explain why he was in such favour at Faversham, perhaps it was through such surprising legends, perhaps it was the belief that prayers said to him on Sunday availed during the whole week, but whatever be the cause the fact is certain. Innumerable citizens at Faversham remembered him in their last wills.

We have not yet exhausted the interest of this town: half a mile across the Creek there was the Nunnery of Davington, founded by Henry II in 1156. The ladies were Benedictines of the order of Cluny. They were ill-endowed with this world's goods, were known indeed as the poor nuns of Davington, and possibly were too much occupied in solving the ancient problem of making both ends meet to give much attention to the passing pilgrim, but the house which was dedicated to St. Mary Magdalen lived its own obscure life through the centuries and only fell with the others.

Now our Pilgrims are on the main road again pressing forward in the last stage of the Canterbury journey, yet are they scarce started, at least only gone a half mile from the *Maison Dieu*, when there is another wayside oratory especially for their behoof. When the Pilgrimage stopped there was no further use therefor. Deserted, it stood like its fellows, a pathetic memorial of times that will not return to England.

Little more than two miles farther on they entered the parish of Boughton-under-Blean. Boughton means the town in the beech-wood, reminding us that our path is about to take us through the forest of the Blean. The big, handsome, finely situated church dedicated to St. Peter and St. Paul had not for our friends any special attraction, but near the west end of Boughton Street, which is some distance from the church, there was another of those roadside shrines dedicated to the Holy Trinity. The fabric held out in some sort till the eighteenth century, which truly prosaic and irreverent age used the last fragments to mend the parish roads. A poorhouse (that modern leper hospital) was built on the site. Again at the hamlet of South Street a hospital for lepers was founded in the eighth of King Richard II by Thomas-at-Hurst. According to Doomsday Book, there was a fishery here, value tenpence, and salt pans estimated at sixteen pence.

South Street is not on the main London Road. At Brenley Corner you turn to your right for it. The side road is known as Key Street, and Hasted, confident as before, puts it down of course to Caius Julius Cæsar. This way passes by the church, and through the hamlet at South Street, which local information affirms the oldest part of the parish, perhaps the only part before the Reformation where there was anything like a village. There certainly is a local tradition mentioned by Hasted that the London Road turned off here and approached Canterbury towards the south. In 1868 Mr. J. M. Cooper wrote a long letter to the

Athenæum on the subject, and succeeded in raising considerable doubt upon the matter. There were various reasons why one might wish to avoid the steep ascent of Boughton Hill. On the other hand the way was longer and less direct, but not much longer and not much less direct. We shall presently find Erasmus returning from the Pilgrimage with thoughts of the old and the new crowding his mind, for the end was almost in sight; passing along the main road we traverse to-day without any hint that there was any other. I have already touched on this question, and here will only say that ground was of little value, and tracks ill-defined and not fixed quantities, so that some may have gone straight on and others turned to the right, which theory seems to me to solve all difficulties. Boughton must have been of importance as a religious centre, since the neighbouring parish of Herne Hill was originally a Chapelry to it, and like enough almost the only religious house in the surrounding wilderness, for the King's ancient Forest of the Blean stretched and in some sort still stretches from Boughton to the very outskirts of Canterbury. It was a neglected tract from the earliest times. Doomsday notes it "1000 acres of unproductive wood, not yielding acorns". Our kings, scarce knowing what else to do with it, granted time and again huge chunks to Christ Church, Canterbury. Also King Stephen gave other parts to Faversham. Altogether it was computed to contain 6250 acres, extending from the sea on one side to Chartham on the other. Our kings hunted wild boars in its thickets. It was a favourite haunt of outlaws; the few inhabitants, charcoal burners and other woodmen, were half savages. A century ago it was still of ill-repute, through smugglers who gave part the name of Dunkirk as of a free port. The church left this corner of its possessions for centuries severely alone. It was an extra-parochial district, and indeed not till 1840 did it receive spiritual attention. You would fancy that steep Boughton Hill set close with trees must have been a lurking-place for robbers, but I cannot find that it had any traditional reputation like Shooter's Hill or Gad's Hill. Perhaps that shows the road may really have gone some other direction, but perhaps the forest was too desolate even for robbers!

As the Pilgrims crested the hill from the hollow where Dunkirk lies, they saw at length the object of their thoughts and dreams. There, framed at the end of a long stretch of road, rose before them the great tower of Canterbury Cathedral crowned with its figure of a cherub, whence its name of the Angel Steeple. However careless, however gross was the mind of many, therein still burned a flame of mystic piety ready to burst forth on fit occasion. Devout awe and thankfulness filled their souls; throwing themselves from their horses they fell on the ground in an ecstasy of adoration. There were hymns and prayers, half-choked with tears. Then again as they proceeded, the hill shut off their view, and so they came at length to Harbledown.

Here the woodland lies thick around, and so the country retains some vestige of its ancient look. Also this is true of the village itself, for here yet exists that ancient medieval foundation, the hospital dedicated to St. Nicholas which Archbishop Lanfranc founded in 1084, less than twenty years after the Conquest, for those stricken with leprosy, and though leprosy is long gone from our midst, the house is still there drawing its ancient revenues, doing worship in its ancient church, fulfilling its ancient and beneficent task of giving help to the poor and needy. It lies on the slope of the hill.

Harbledown is well described in three famous lines

HARBLEDOWN HOSPITAL OF ST. NICHOLAS, NEAR CANTERBURY

of Chaucer, at the beginning of the *Prologue* to the *Manciple's Tale*:—

> Wite ye nat wher ther stant a litel toun
> Which that y-clept is Bob-up-and-doun,
> Under the Blee, in Canterbury weye?

The name means the pasture down; it is elsewhere described as being situated in the Blean wood. It was a sort of oasis in the wilderness, noted for its salubrity. Leper hospitals were placed in choice spots, just as in our own time in the outskirts of London you shall find asylums for the insane planted on the finest of the Surrey Hills. Hard by the hospital there is a famous well known in early days for its medicinal properties. The house was near three centuries old when the well got the name by which it is known to-day, that of the Black Prince's Well, from its shadowy connection with the famous warrior. Dean Stanley suggests that it was on account of the well that Lanfranc raised his leper hospital on this particular spot, but you recognise other reasons. It was on the high road, and so a fit subject for the alms of those who passed by its gates. Lanfranc could not foresee that within a century one of his successors was to undergo martyrdom, and that a result of that martyrdom would be to increase enormously the number of pious travellers. You would like to recover details of the daily life of the hospital in its early days. We have one or two notes that enable us to some extent to do this.

The house was directly under the Archbishops of Canterbury, who from time to time issued statutes for its governance. We have those of Archbishop Winchelsey, of date 1298, which was four years after his consecration. A simple and uniform dress was provided for the brothers and the sisters as the inmates were called, without which they must not be seen outside the gates. They were not to be garrulous, contentious, or quarrelsome. Those who were given to such vices were solemnly admonished, and if the warning was of no avail, expelled. They were not to wander without licence, especially they were not to haunt Canterbury overmuch or to stay there overnight. You gather that they had a natural human desire to vary the tedium of the hospital by visits to the nearest city. It was only the merely poor or the slightly affected who would be allowed out at all. Outside you believe them the most persistent of beggars.

After the Reformation, Archbishop Parker issued, in 1560, another set of rules. These followed the lines of the old ordinances. If they were disobeyed, the erring brother or sister was to be stuck in the stocks, and fed on bread and water. The legality of this punishment has been questioned, but there is reason to believe that it was never, in fact, inflicted. Offences against morality were purged by the oath of six brothers or sisters. If the inmate on whom suspicion rested was not able to get the requisite number to speak for him or her, the doom of expulsion was pronounced. It is interesting to note this survival of the old English method of trial by compurgation. A priest attended to the spiritual wants of the hospital: he had eight pounds a year, which was deducted from the allowance of the inmates. There are regulations of later Archbishops. Whitgift in 1591, Abbott in 1618, and Sancroft in 1686, quite modern rules in fact!

Besides the priest the hospital had and still has a master and a prior; the master was non-resident, the prior was one of the brethren chosen by themselves. The number of inmates has varied from time to time, but before the Reformation all were indwellers. They lived in the ancient conventual manner. They had a common dining-hall and dormitories for sleeping. As one brother was made prior, so one sister was prioress. They had an annual feast on the name day of their patron saint, St. Nicholas. Repairs were provided for by a "reparation noble," value six shillings and eightpence, which each inmate had to contribute. The buildings of the hospital you now see do not date from those early times; in fact the almshouses and the *frater* or common hall are only of the seventeenth century, but the church or chapel of Lanfranc still remains. It is large, with a nave and two aisles, for the hospital was once a parish of itself, or at least extra-parochial. It is known as the Church of St. Nicholas of Harbledown.

A window is still shown called the Lepers' Squint; the picturesque legend is that the lepers of the hospital, shut off by the terrible malady from the society of their fellows, gazed through this window that they might receive, as it were, some crumbs from the Holy Table. This story you will safely reject; the window is eight feet from the ground for one thing. The parish of Harbledown always had its own church, that of St. Michael, on the other side of the road. It was "restored" in 1829, wellnigh beyond recognition. The peculiar attraction of the church at the hospital is that with its old timbered benches, its old font and pews, in its very bareness and desolation, it gives you a rare and distinct impression of immemorial antiquity. Outside there is a yew tree said to be one thousand years old—it certainly looks it! Henry II has such an ill name in all matters of the faith that it is well to remember he was here a generous benefactor. In 1173, in the nineteenth year of his reign, he endowed it with an annual allowance of twenty marks from his Canterbury rents. The sum is paid to this day by the King's Chamberlain. It was to ease those afflicted with "poverty, old age, and bodily infirmities," and thus forced to take refuge in this retreat. Although built for lepers, it was by no means for them alone. Yet one curious gift was specially theirs. Between 1114 and 1122 Ralph d'Escures, otherwise Rudulfus de Turbine, who had been Bishop of Rochester, was Archbishop. His rule was singularly uneventful; at least it is recorded that he gave a penny a day charged on his Manor of Lyminge to provide milk for the lepers in this house.

With it all, the hospital was never at any time richly endowed. The inmates had a keen eye for the passing stranger. A brother stood ever at the gate. He had a small alms-box stuck on the end of a pole which he thrust, you might say, in the faces of the Pilgrims, the while earnestly beseeching an alms, but no Pilgrim was like to pass this house, for it contained a most precious relic—no less than a part of the shoe of St. Thomas! It was bound in brass, and set with a jewel; this the devotee kissed on his knees. He needs must give something for the good of the house, to use an expression which suggests rather irreverent and incongruous ideas. It was in favour of the hospital that the wayfarer must go at a slow pace up the steep hill and so could scarce pass without notice.

I turn to the famous visit paid to this hospital in 1512 by a great writer of the time—two great thinkers indeed—for here were Erasmus and Dean Colet, both friends of the new learning, both inclined to look with impatience on things which an earlier generation had received with unquestioning reverence. The account, though often given, must here again find place. The narrative is by Erasmus. It is from his *Peregrinatio Religionis Ergo*. He tells how he and his friend Gratian, to wit Dean Colet, were returning from their Pilgrimage to Canterbury, where we shall again meet them. A little after leaving t e city they found themselves in a hollow and narrow road with steep banks. On the left hand was the hospital of a few old men, who whenever they see a horseman coming run out to greet him, sprinkle him with holy water, and offer him the shoe of St. Thomas to kiss. The passer-by does what is expected both as to kissing the shoe and giving alms. Our travellers were going *from* Canterbury and so down the hill, but so steep is the way that the descent would almost be as slow as the ascent. Colet was on the left hand side, so got the full benefit of the shower of holy water, to the quiet amusement of his friend, who notes that he put up with it, though not inclined to be at all grateful, but the shoe was too much. What did the old man want him to do with it? he shortly demanded. The poor brother was a little put out at the unexpected question. It was the shoe of St. Thomas, he said. Colet turned to his companion in a temper not lessened, you believe, by Erasmus's open enjoyment of the scene. "What, do these brutes imagine that we must kiss every good man's shoe? Why, by the same rule they might offer his spittle to be kissed or what else?" He rode on in high disdain leaving the brother wondering what strange new species of priest this was, for you may be quite sure that no breath of the new learning had yet come to disturb the life of this old-world hospital set in the Blean Wood. Amused as was Erasmus he was also considerate; he stopped to console the old man with a donation before he spurred on his horse to follow his irascible companion. They go down the hill to the village, up the next steep ascent which immediately follows. As they crest it Erasmus, you fancy, looked back at the old brother still staring after them in dumb, stupid wonder. Then the place vanishes and it seems to us to slip back into its old obscurity. You still are shown the almsbox and the jewel, though the fragment of shoe is vanished, and that may help you to realise a scene itself, to us now dim and far distant, though then something novel and portentous.

The hospital had other wonders to show such Pilgrims as entered its ancient walls. There was a collection of mazer bowls, and one at least of great antiquity. The rim is silvered gilt, at the bottom is a medallion of Guy of Warwick—of all people in the world! There is a Norman-French inscription stating that the valiant champion killed the Dragon. Where he did so is doubtful; it may have been at Harbledown, but the existence of the mazer bowl is scarce sufficient evidence. Not for us here is the story of this redoubtable medieval warrior, but I may mention the legend to which the inscription refers. On his travels he found a dragon and a lion fighting in a forest near the sea; he determined to engage the conqueror, who turned out to be the dragon. Guy lustily belaboured his scales, but to no purpose, until the monster unconsciously uncovered a soft place under his wing. The champion was alert to seize his chance; he thrust in his sword two feet, the dragon gave a dreadful yell, and expired.

There is not much here native to the soil of Harbledown, and it is hard indeed to say how this particular mazer bowl got there. You wish Dean Colet had not been so hasty during that memorable visit of his in 1512. You are sure his remarks on the Bowl had not been less racy than those on the Shoe.

There was one more noteworthy thing at Harbledown, that was the Black Prince's Well, which lies on the slope of the hill to the west. In the early months of 1376 the Prince lay in the Palace at Westminster sick unto death. Some memory of the days when he followed this road seems to have come to him, for he sent for water from the well in the hope that it might relieve his malady. It was in vain; he died on Trinity Sunday, the 8th of June, in that year. It is merely a tradition, though I think a likely one. The Prince was, at any rate, no stranger to Harbledown, for it lay directly in the road to London. It was pure water and famous water; it may be that the mere fact that he stopped there to drink gave the font its name. Tradition is hard to kill in that ancient hollow of the Blean Wood.

I have yet one other memory of Harbledown, though it be by way of anti-climax. In Puritan times the incumbent was Richard Culmer. Had some one told the Pilgrims of his advent in a future age they would have cursed him with every word of execration, for he was no less than " Blue Dick," a bigoted Puritan who, procuring to himself a ladder and a pike, smote the gorgeous window of the transept of the Martyrdom, and thus, to use his own graphic phrase, " rattled down proud Becket's glassie bones ". Our Pilgrims crest the hill, eastward from Harbledown. They have the great bulk of the cathedral fair in their view, rising over the roofs of the walled and gated medieval town; they are on the last morsel of the journey, and as they turn round St. Dunstan's Church there is the West Gate right in front of them; yet on the very threshold we must arrest our steps to say something of the Holy City, the goal of their Pilgrimage, which they are about to enter!

CHAPTER XII

THE STORY OF CANTERBURY

The Place before the People—The Roman City—Its Remains To-day—Early Christians and their Churches—Coming of the Northmen—The Pagan Tribes—Red Ruin—Queen Bertha—Mythical Canterbury—The Ancient Legend of Pope Gregory—The Coming of Augustine—Conversion of Kent—St. Augustine's Abbey and the Priory of Christ Church—Their Rivalries—Archbishop Cuthbert's Device—Victory of Christ Church—Limits of Saxon Canterbury—Some Famous Archbishops—Old Town Life in Canterbury.

THE story of Canterbury goes a very long way back indeed, over two thousand years, with a possible break of a century. About the very early inhabitants we know little. Geology tells us something, for the place is rich in the debris of past ages, broken fragments that incite rather than satisfy our curiosity. Once the sea rolled over the site which in time became a shallow tidal estuary, a swamp from which rose the heights behind the dense aboriginal forest. There were folk in the swamp who lived in rude huts suspended over the water. At various depths under the soil you find primitive weapons and utensils of this early people, but above ground is there anything left to mark pre-Roman Canterbury?

Within the old wall to the east of the city there is the huge earthern mound, called the Dane-John. It now stands alone, but there were formerly two other mounds of like kidney, though smaller, to the south of it, where is now in fact the Railway Station. They were removed to make way for it. Some would have those mounds early British forts; other antiquarians put them down to Saxon or even Norman times.

When Cæsar landed in 55 B.C., the place must have

THE STORY OF CANTERBURY

been one of some importance, though we do not know that the great Roman ever passed through. Its British name was Dur-Gwern, which is said to mean the marshy river. From this the Roman name was obviously formed. It was Durovernum, which is, so to speak, classical Latin for Canterbury, the medieval term being Cantuaria. Cæsar pays Kent the compliment of being the most civilized part of Britain, which from Cæsar's point of view was not saying much, though Shakespeare thought it worth while, many centuries afterwards, to paraphrase the laudation. The Romans occupied Britain through something like four centuries, and in no part were they more in evidence than in Kent. The conquered people had no separate life apart from the Roman Empire, and Canterbury was to all intents and purposes a Roman city. It became from the first, what it is in these later days of railway travelling, a station on the way to the Continent. The great Roman road called Watling Street passed through on its progress to London and beyond, for the man of Roman times, our Pilgrims and ourselves, all in turn have trodden the same mighty thoroughfare.

The Romans had three great fortresses on the Kentish coast, or what was then coast. These were Reculver (*Regulbium*), Richborough (*Rutupium* or *Rutupiæ*), and Lymne (*Portus Limanus*). The ways from those uniting at Durovernum to cross the Stour thence moved on to London. There is much controversy as to the size of Roman Canterbury. No doubt it was a walled city, but much smaller than the present town; thus the whole Cathedral precincts lay outside. Margaret Street and Sun Street, and part of the High Street were within it, but the rest must be guess-work. The boundaries shifted from time to time. The *Pax Romana* was as strong as the *Pax Britannica*. In this corner of Britain there was no rumour of war in the memory of generations, so the city would spread beyond the fortifications, and these in time would be neglected.

This Roman Durovernum has not altogether passed away. The Roman bricks were so strong and durable that the medieval masons used them wherever they could. There is a great deal of this old material incorporated with what of medieval Canterbury has survived. Also the foundations of the Roman city are still there, seven or eight feet below the streets of to-day. When labourers are excavating for drainage works and so forth, they come across pieces of tesselated pavement, all manner of fragments of pottery, horse-shoes, dice, bracelets, knife-handles, brooches, pins, bronze statuettes, and above all coins of every sort in very considerable profusion.

In Roman times, too, Christianity was introduced; indeed it is just possible that one of the most famous churches in Canterbury, that is St. Martin's, and the ruin or rather the site of another near it, that is St. Pancras', may date from those ancient days. As St. Martin was not one of the very early saints of the Church, since he flourished 316-400, this would imply a reconsecration, which again is possible. The temptation is strong to link on our present forms of faith in some such material way to those distant days, but there is no sure evidence to found on.

In the early years of the fifth century of our era the Romans departed to defend their own imperial city from those persistent attacks of the northern barbarians which led to the ruin of the Empire. The Britons were left unable to defend themselves. Jutes, Saxons, Danes, Norsemen, rushed in on a defenceless land. Kent was from an early period one of the main objects of the invasion, and Canterbury fell among the first cities. For a century there is muddle and confusion and darkness. You do not regret the darkness, for there must have been endless suffering and unspeakable horrors. Durovernum was taken, plundered, and left desolate. One or two significant facts point to this. No less than five burial grounds of the Roman period have been unearthed at Canterbury, not one single pagan Saxon was there or in the near vicinity.

The Teutonic invaders were of course pagans, and they stamped out Christianity so effectually that such of the Britons as were left, forgetting their religion, conformed to the heathen gods of the Norse mythology. The very name Durovernum was forgotten. There is no connection between it and "Canterbury," whereas "Dover" and "London" still retain without much change their ancient titles, evidencing an unbroken life all through.

However in 565 we have Ethelbert as King of the Kentish men with Canterbury as his capital city, and Canterbury is a shortened form of Cantwarabryg, that is the Town of the men of Kent. He had married Bertha, daughter of the Christian King of the Franks. It was stipulated she was to enjoy her own faith; hence she brought with her as chaplain the Bishop Lindhard. Ethelbert's palace was where the Cathedral now stands. The east part of the Cathedral precincts is bounded by a large portion of the city wall still remaining strong and entire. Here there is a postern gate from which you may gain what is to-day called Lady Wootton's Green. Close to the left of this is the site of the Queeningate. The name still remains, and that is something, for it perpetuates one of the oldest memories of Canterbury. Through this gate Queen Bertha was wont to pass on her way to Christian service at the little church of St. Martin's, where Bishop Lindhard officiated to the Queen and the few faithful, mainly, if not entirely, her own personal attendants. Some think that through this gate Ethelbert and his suite also passed on high days a little way south-west to St. Pancras', then a heathen temple where he worshipped his gods—strange rude idol figures.

Ethelbert was a born commander; he was *Bretwalda*, or ruler of Britain, and he was lord of the smaller Kings south of the Humber. He had a long reign of sixty years, and there is ample evidence that he was broad-minded, wise, and moderate. Bertha must have thought the gain would be enormous if she could convert her husband. She may have aided, but the determining cause came from without, from the eternal city itself.

Our Pilgrims at the gate or on the way, if they had heard in some form or other the narrative I have just given, would only now begin to prick up their ears. The doings of the days of darkness would have seemed to them merely evil and not worth attention. Moreover, the average human being has only a limited amount of mind to give to anything, and in medieval times this was directed entirely to the Church and its legends. Even if the Pilgrim did hear of very early Canterbury, it would not be the sober narrative we have summarised. Some scholar among the band may perchance have conned Geoffry of Monmouth or his like, so would announce with full belief that Canterbury was founded 900 B.C. by Lud-Hubris, a British king, with other quaint and remarkable details which I shall not here repeat. These legends be it remembered had their own value, they profoundly influenced English literature for one thing. They were universally credited; indeed Edward I on one occasion overawed an Archbishop by reminding him that he was descended from Brutus, grandson of Æneas! Something of the same imaginative touch made this same Edward hale from Scone the Stone of Destiny and fix it as the base of the Coronation chair in Westminster Abbey rather than go to Kingston-upon-Thames, where the authentic crowning seat of the old Saxon kings is in existence. But this is by the way.

The story of the introduction or rather re-introduction of Christianity into Kent has been often told. It is one of the most familiar incidents in English history, yet it is not to be neglected here and must be once again briefly set forth. When Gregory the Great was merely monk and not yet Pope, he was one day passing through the slave-market at Rome. His attention was attracted by three boys of fair complexion, white skin and flaxen hair, which showed strongly against the swarthy hue of their fellow-captives. Inquiring of the keepers of the market who they were, he was told they came from pagan Britain. They were the nation of the Angles or English. "They are well-called Angles, for they have the faces of angels; and what is the name of their province?" "Deira," was the answer. "May they be plucked from the ire of God and called to Christ's mercy," said the monk, playing on the word Deira, which is the same as two Latin words, *De ira*, meaning from the wrath. "And who is their King?" was the next question. "Ella," said the slave warden. "Allelujah," said the priest, continuing his word-twisting, "the praise of God shall be sung in their land."

There and then he determined he would do what he could for the conversion of Britain, but it was not till he sat in St. Peter's chair that he had the power to put his ideas into execution. Then he sent Augustine, prior of the Monastery of St. Andrew on the Caelian Hill at Rome, the monastery from which Gregory himself had come, with forty monks to Britain.

Our country was still thought, as in Roman days, on the very confines of the world, so that it was with shrinking hearts that the missionaries set out; yet set out they did, and in 597 landed at Ebb's Fleet, which is three and a half miles south-west of modern Ramsgate.

Here there is a break in the chalk cliffs that marks it as a suitable landing-place. Communications passed between them and Ethelbert. He was already half persuaded; he would see them in the open air where their dreaded magic would have less power; so the memorable interview took place near the spot of their landing in the Isle of Thanet. Ethelbert listened to their Latin hymns, gazed on their silver cross and on their painted and gilded figure of the Christ. He agreed to receive the missionaries into his royal city, where they were to make such converts as they could, and so in procession they marched into Canterbury. Here he gave them the plot of ground still known as the borough of Staplegate, which long retained peculiar privileges and exemptions, not yet, it is averred, altogether vanished. It is a little way to the north-west of the Cathedral, near where the church of St. Alphege now stands.

Very soon Ethelbert came completely over to the new faith. On 2 June in that same year he was baptised, most probably in the church of St. Martin. His whole tribe followed his example; witness the 10,000 christened in the waters of the Swale on the Christmas Day following. There was a speedy end to idol worship. The pagan figure that stood in what was afterwards the church of St. Pancras was smitten by St. Augustine with his own hands, then the place was consecrated as a house of Christian worship, to the discomfiture of Satan, whose grotesque efforts in opposition are set forth in quaint detail by the monkish chroniclers. Ethelbert was a generous benefactor to the Church, he gave Augustine his royal palace, he himself retiring to Reculver. On the site of the palace the priory of Christ Church was founded, and the first church there was the beginning of the Cathedral. This was within the walls of the city, but he gave him, just outside and near St. Pancras', a piece of ground on which was built the Abbey of St. Peter and St. Paul, with which afterwards the name of Augustine was joined. This last name effaced the others, so that for the greater part of its existence it has been known as St. Augustine's Abbey.

Here the Christian clergy were to be educated, and it was also to be a place of burial for Saints and Kings. Hence it was outside the town, because the Saxons followed the Romans in the habit of extra-mural interment. Long ere this Augustine had been consecrated as first Archbishop of Canterbury, and when he died he was interred in St. Augustine's: here Ethelbert and Bertha were also buried and many of the later Kings and Archbishops and Saints. This burial had a curious consequence to be noted presently, but a word will conclude the history of this great Abbey. It lasted down to the Reformation, rich and splendid indeed but not specially connected with the main thread of our narrative. After it fell like the other great religious houses, it was soon used for all sorts of common, nay you might think base purposes—public-house, brewery, and tea-gardens and so forth, whilst just behind it swine were housed in the scanty ruins of St. Pancras'. Then some seventy years ago the ground was acquired for the purpose of a missionary college, which is still called St. Augustine's. There has been a good deal of more or less tasteful adaptation and rebuilding and a great deal of excavation and the site of St. Pancras' has also been acquired for the college, so that here, as indeed is the case elsewhere in Canterbury, there is a curious revival, in however dim and shadowy a manner, of old times, old customs, old institutions.

It was natural that there should be rivalry between St. Augustine's and Christ Church; to put it vulgarly they were both in the same line of business, they competed for favour, importance, popularity. You wonder the common founder did not foresee this, and take some steps to prevent it, but from one or two things we gather that Augustine, whatever his merits, was no student of human nature. He may have thought that as Christ Church was a cathedral church to which the Archbishop belonged, this would give that house the superiority, but as early as 610 a papal order was procured from Rome that the bishops were not to intrude in St. Augustine's.

A church or monastery was important according to its possession of relics, the earthly remains of Saints and holy men, or things immediately connected with their persons. Now it is noted St. Augustine's was a great burial-place. The archbishops themselves were taken there after death, and there too were the remains of the founders of British Christianity. This gave St. Augustine's such a decided preponderance that Christ Church was in despair. Archbishop Cuthbert, who died in 758, did something to restore the balance; he first procured from the Pope permission to be buried within his own cathedral. When he felt his end approaching he directed the monks of Christ Church to keep his death secret till he was safely interned in the precincts. Then with something as near a grin as the occasion permitted he vanished from the world! A device of this sort was dear to the medieval mind, and no doubt the monks chuckled as they carried out his behests. When the obsequies were duly performed they tolled the bell which announced that the Archbishop was gone. Immediately the monks of St. Augustine appeared on the scene to claim the body of Cuthbert as a new addition to their charnel treasure-house; they were told he was buried in the Cathedral and the Pope's mandate was flaunted in their faces! You imagine their discomfiture as they crept back to their own Abbey! After this most of the archbishops were buried in their own cathedral; there was always some sufficient reasons for the exceptions.

This might not have availed to turn the tide of popular favour and interest, were it not that the murder of Thomas in 1170 made Canterbury one of the world-famous centres of medieval Pilgrimage, and obviously the one famous spot in Canterbury was the Cathedral, the scene of the Martyrdom. It will be remembered that the Abbot of St. Augustine's hospitably entertained the knights just before the murder, in fact that event was fatal to the supremacy of his own house, for it raised the cathedral to such an eminence that this monastery outside the gates became quite subordinate. But we are passing beyond Saxon Canterbury; one or two words must be said ere we leave it.

Its extent is a matter of some controversy, but we know that the Saxon wall was wider than the Roman one, for it embraced the Cathedral and its close. The chief gate to the east was Burgate; there was a gate in the High Street, but it was some way east of the present West Gate. I will not discuss in detail the causes that made the Archbishop of Canterbury the highest ecclesiastic in England. Canterbury was in close connection with Rome and Rome was the centre of authority, whilst the Christianity of the north of England was largely due to St. Columba and his Celtic monks. When in 664 the Council of Whitby determined that the Roman practice of holding Easter should be followed, the decision was ultimately a victory for Canterbury. Again, at the decisive moment, London was not sufficiently Christian to be chosen, and so under Archbishop Theodore, who was consecrated in 668, all the English churches agreed to obey. Of the other archbishops before the conquest Dunstan (960-88) was probably the most famous; he it was who reconstituted the Abbey of St. Augustine which only bore that name from his time. Stigand was the last Saxon archbishop; he was not really a bishop, for his predecessor, Robert the Norman, had been outlawed by the English, but was not dead. Also he acknowledged a rival Pope, so though he submitted to the conqueror this did not save him, for he was deposed in 1070.

Kent did not keep its supremacy, but sunk to a subordinate position to Essex and this told on Canterbury. Also that city was taken and destroyed by the Danes. It is difficult to estimate the population, which must have fluctuated, but does not seem to have been more than about 5,000; yet it had fourteen parish churches within the walls, and immediately outside were others, making the number up to twenty-two! Such was the exuberant piety of those early times! In the Middle Ages the Church was all in all, and there was always great activity in church building which absorbed much of the intellectual activity of the period. Our energies are too much distracted to do more in this direction than feebly copy, but this singleness of purpose had its own defects. Any accession of wealth or energy or ability had but one result, to increase the number and splendour of the churches. No one asked were there not too many already for the population? Was there nothing else waiting to be done? Such questions had been deemed suggestions of Satan. Hence the multiplication of shrines and chapels on the route and in old Canterbury.

Many of the archbishops after the Conquest were famous men—Lanfranc, who succeeded when Stigand was deposed, and Anselm who followed him, not the least. Lanfranc divided the property of Christ Church into two parts, one for the Archbishop and the other for the monastery. He also made the Archbishop of York submit to Canterbury by the pious fraud of producing certain forged documents. I will only mention two others. Stephen Langton, who had much to do with

Magna Charta, but is best known for our present purpose as presiding over the translation of St. Thomas's remains in 1220; and Simon of Sudbury, who was enthroned on Palm Sunday, 1376, a great builder and in many ways a benefactor to the town. Before the Reformation it was the custom for the Mayor and Aldermen to visit in state his tomb in the cathedral, that they might offer up prayers for the repose of his soul. The West Gate, as we now know it, was his work, and he rebuilt the wall between that gate and the North Gate, though of that piece there is scarcely any sign to-day above ground.

The mention of the Mayor and Aldermen reminds us that Canterbury had all this time a civic life of its own distinct from the life of its monks and priests. It carried on its crafts and trades by guilds and mysteries, so that no stranger was allowed to enter and practice without going through the strict training of the time. These guilds hindered free trade but they promoted social life, and they must have aided their poorer members. Like everything medieval, they had their religious side, for each guild had its chosen church, moreover the brethren were bound together by common religious ceremonies. As regards the Rulers, there was first a Portreeve, then two Bailiffs, as presiding deities. Under Henry VI a mayor was made chief officer, and under Edward IV Canterbury was created a county in itself and had its own sheriff. Warham was the last archbishop but one of the old faith. To him succeeded Cranmer, under whom there was the destruction of the Shrine and the end of the Pilgrimage, for it was not revived under Cardinal Pole, though under him England was nominally for a few years again joined to Rome.

As we know where the wall stood we can delimit exactly the extent of the medieval city, and as a good slice of the walls still remain we have some idea of how it looked from the outside. There were seven gates besides Queeningate already noted, the oldest was Worthgate, supposed to date from Roman times. It was a single arch in a massive wall, but it and its fellows save West Gate have all vanished.

CHAPTER XIII

THE CATHEDRAL

As We know It—The Saxon Church—Fire and Invasion—Building and Rebuilding—" The Glorious Choir of Conrad "—William of Sens and William the Englishman—Notable Things about the Cathedral—Becket's Crown—The Crypt—The Black Prince's Chantry—His Life and Death—His Burial and Tomb—The Angel Steeple—Christ Church Gate—The Priory of Christ Church.

I TURN now to speak of the Cathedral, the scene alike of St. Thomas's murder, his burial and enshrinement. I give but a few notes, so that we may approach it in the company of our Pilgrims with the advantage of fuller knowledge.

Canterbury Cathedral is a building of many styles and dates and changes. It did not show to all generations as it shows to you to-day. It was not till less than half a century before the end of the Pilgrimage that the Cathedral took the external shape we know, for about 1495 the central tower, the Bell Harry, or Angel Steeple, as it is variously called, was raised to its present height from above the level of the rest of the building. It is this additional piece of tower that gives the Cathedral its impressive dominating aspect. Before the days of Thomas, on the same site, there was a cathedral of much the same shape, though not quite the same size. However, to turn to history.

First is a piece of legend. Here in the days of early British Christianity King Lucius built a British or Roman church, and albeit the Saxons desecrated it to use as a temple for their pagan gods, it was restored to its right purpose when King Ethelbert in 597 gifted it to Augustine.

Now no doubt in Augustine's time there was a house of prayer on the spot, but it must have been built or much adapted by that saint. In church matters it is usually held that imitation of the old is the greatest wisdom, also it was natural that models should be drawn from Rome so that this missionary church among the heathen English should be on the plan of the old Basilica of St. Peter's. The altar stood in the apse at the west end; behind that was the episcopal throne. There was another apse at the east end where later the chief altar was placed. Also it possessed a crypt. The catacombs at Rome, where the early Christians found a hiding as well as a burial place, and where they celebrated worship in the days of the pagan city, had a strong hold on the imagination of the early Church. The crypts of so many cathedrals were a pious effort after imitation.

Then we are told that Archbishop Odo (942-59) raised the walls and made a new roof. It was slow work, for execution lagged far behind conception. For three years the place stood roofless. The monkish chroniclers assert that no rain fell during that period, an amusing sample of monkish legend, because I presume they meant that the rain fell hard by yet not on the church. Half a century later the Danes attacked the place and did much damage; then followed the Conquest, and the year after the Cathedral was burned down. This at least gave a clear field, of which the energetic Lanfranc, who got the See in 1070, was not slow to take advantage. He set to work to rebuild on a more magnificent scale from the very foundation. He also rebuilt the monastery, for it must be understood that Augustine did not merely found a church but a colony of monks to take charge of it, and thus constituted the priory of Christ Church.

These re-erections were on the same site and the building took seven years. Anselm followed Lanfranc, and under him the east end of his predecessor's church was again levelled and rebuilt by Prior Ernulph. Ernulph's work was continued by his successor Conrad, who made such a splendid business of the choir that it was called "the glorious Choir of Conrad," a name of which the memory still remains, though from its dedication by Archbishop William in 1130 it had an existence of less than half a century.

It was in this church that St. Thomas was murdered in 1170, and some of Lanfranc's work which was then there still exists, especially in the Transept of the Martyrdom, where original features were retained in honour of the Martyr. In 1174 "the glorious choir" was destroyed by fire. That was a very constant and terrible danger. People had more furnishings in their great churches, they lived more in them, and obviously their mechanical appliances for fighting a conflagration were puerile as compared with ours. You are not surprised to hear repeated stories of burnings and wide spread havoc, yet on each occasion the populace seemed struck with terror and surprise. Perhaps they assumed a supernatural protection for the church, so were amazed and confounded that the fire blazed fiercely in spite of everything. This story has often been told of their wild conduct after the fire of 1174. They tore their hair and beat their breasts and cursed and blasphemed God and His saints, nay even St. Thomas himself whom they had come to regard as their peculiar friend and patron.

In due time preparations were made for starting work afresh, and William of Sens was chosen to rebuild the Cathedral in more than its pristine splendour. He was disabled by accident in 1178, but his work was continued by William, a native Englishman, who in 1184 finished the choir in the east part of the church. Then between 1378 and 1410 the nave, which had remained substantially the same as Lanfranc built it, was taken down and with the Transept rebuilt by Prior Chillenden. Finally Prior Goldstone II, in the last years of the fifteenth century, raised the central tower to its present position above the level of the rest of the building, and so the outside became, on the eve of the Reformation, what it has remained ever since, for, with one exception, only minor details have been altered. This exception is the north-west tower of the nave. It seemed to the authorities of the last century that its unsymmetrical shape spoilt the proportions of the Cathedral, so, though it dated from Anselm's time, it was pulled down in 1834 and a new tower, after the pattern of the one in the south-west corner, was erected in its place.

Some striking peculiarities of the Cathedral are the result of this long architectural history, here briefly summarised. It is of great length, as much as 514 feet in all, whilst the height of the central tower is 235 feet and of the west tower 130. Then the choir is raised high above the nave, whilst the Trinity chapel is higher still. Also the east ends of the choir are curiously contracted, which contraction makes the church seem much longer than in fact it is. The height to which the eastern parts are raised above the level of the nave gives, as Dean Stanley puts it, the idea of church piled above church. The reason is this: The fire of 1174 was partial, it had not destroyed the chapels of St. Anselm and St. Andrew, which stand respectively to the south-east and the north-east. Again, it was proposed to make the new Trinity Chapel of the same size and in exactly the same position as the old, for it was here St. Thomas said his first mass after being made Archbishop. The device to preserve those two chapels and the erection of the new Trinity chapel caused this narrowing and this impression of length, a result probably not altogether intended or foreseen. A further chapel of a circular shape was added at the extreme end. It is usually known as Becket's Crown, though the name has evoked comment. It has at least the sanction of long usage. The supposed origin was that here was kept that part of Becket's skull which had been cut away by Richard le Bret with such violence that he had broken his sword.

It was the policy of the monks to show discretion in the arrangement of their treasures. It would not do to heap everything together, and thus, even in the case of the one saint, Thomas, various parts of the Cathedral had to be visited before the whole of the relics of him could be seen. It was to this new Trinity Chapel that his remains were translated from the crypt on Tuesday, 7 July, 1220, the red-letter day that was known as the Feast of the Translation of the Relics, and chiefly, no doubt, owing to the fact of a more congenial season it was the great popular festival of the Becket cycle or year, exceeding even 29 December, the anniversary of his death.

It has not yet been explained why the eastern portion of the Cathedral is so raised. This is on account of the unusual loftiness of the crypt which is beneath it. This was obviously not so liable to be attacked by fire and generally not so subject to alteration as any other part of the church; it is therefore the oldest part. The west portion is usually called Prior Ernulf's crypt as it was built by him in the time of Archbishop Anselm, but this was before the new Trinity Chapel, which is the work of William the Englishman. The crypt below it with its higher vaulting and the massive piers which he found necessary for the greater pressure from the new chapel above are also his work. The crypt was dedicated to the Virgin as Our Lady Undercroft. Her altar stood between the two divisions of the crypt already mentioned; just behind it, to the east, was the original tomb of St. Thomas ; here the chief relics of him rested for the half century between 1120 and 1170, when they were translated to the chapel above.

There were various chapels in the crypt, but the most interesting was the Black Prince's Chantry which he founded at the time of his marriage in 1363. For the required permission to do this he gave Christ Church his manor of Vauxhall, now a grimy London district, but through all changes the property of the Cathedral. By a strange fate that chantry is to-day the place of worship for the descendants of the French Huguenots. This use, though venerable, is of course long after the events with which we deal; it dates only from Elizabeth's time. Perhaps it was not very logical to house this little non-episcopal sect in a corner of the Metropolitan Cathedral. A high churchman of to-day indulges in a covert sneer at the "Walloon Meeting House," but most Englishmen are glad, nay proud of the fact, both as a reproof to the extreme ecclesiastical spirit and because of the sympathy shown an industrious persecuted community whose descendants have since done well in England and for England. Here is one of the most striking illustrations of that genius for assimilation of the best blood of other folks which has made England great and prosperous.

This is not a guide to the Cathedral or even an account of it, except in so far as it is connected with St. Thomas and illustrates the history of the Pilgrimage; for this reason it will neither be necessary nor desirable to give anything like an account of the vast number of tombs and monuments which it contained even before the Reformation. By this time the reader understands very well that its great interest for medieval Christianity was that it held St. Thomas's shrine. Of other shrines I will not here speak, but one grave must receive at least passing mention. As all the world knows, the Black Prince is buried in Canterbury Cathedral. His monument has always been an object of attraction. He is as ever a national hero to all generations of Englishmen. Henry VIII, who scattered the ashes of St. Thomas, had thought it infamous sacrilege to disturb the dust of his great ancestor. Even "Blue Dick" the Puritan fanatic here stayed his hand. It was reported that Cromwell set a special guard to preserve the grave from injury. Time itself has dealt gently for wellnigh six centuries with that impressive monument, has mellowed and made venerable, not ruined or broken.

The Prince dates from 1330; he was born at Woodstock, the eldest son of King Edward III and Philippa of Hainault. He studied at Queen's College, Oxford, and did much in 1346 to win the battle of Crecy. Ten years afterwards he fought at Poitiers, where he took the French King John prisoner, and on 19 April, 1357, passing through Canterbury they made their offerings at the shrine of St. Thomas and proceeded the next day to London. In 1363 he married his cousin Joan, the "Fair Maid of Kent". He made his will on 23 April, 1376, and died on 8 June that same year, to the universal and loudly expressed grief of the whole nation. Such is a bald record of his life's story.

In his will he had given elaborate directions for his burial. It was to be in the Cathedral church at Canterbury, where lay the body of the true martyr, "My Lord Saint Thomas" (*Monseignour Seint Thomas* in the Norman-French of the original), in the middle of the chapel of Our Lady Undercroft, right before the altar. This direction was not observed in order to do him greater honour. For seventeen weeks the body lay in state at Westminster and then was carried to Canterbury by the way over London Bridge, exactly the way that our Pilgrims have followed. It was laid down between the high altar and the choir whilst the solemn funeral service, illustrated with every elaboration of rite, was celebrated. Thence it was moved to the tomb, not in the Undercroft but close to the shrine of St. Thomas in the Trinity Chapel. There he still rests, there you see the fine effigy, in complete armour, the head supported by the helmet, whilst above are his arms and shield blazoned with the armorial bearings of France and England. Around his tomb is a long Norman-French inscription telling what has been from the beginning, the most expressive of common-places, that death is the inevitable end of all earthly glory. There is much in Canterbury Cathedral to give point to all sorts of curious contrasts and moral maxims. The Prince desired to be laid there because it was the burial-place of St. Thomas, so if anyone of the period had wished to describe the exact situation of his tomb he had said it lay to the south of the shrine. To-day if you wish to indicate where that shrine once stood, you would say it was to the north of the Black Prince's tomb. History has changed its judgment of St. Thomas more than once, his place scarce finally settled even now, but the lustre of the name of the Black Prince has ever shone with rare and radiant splendour.

These things require some notice. On the Angel or Bell Harry Tower there was a noted gilt figure of an angel, the Archangel Gabriel in fact, stuck on a pinnacle, though that has long since disappeared. The name of the Bell Harry Tower was from a bell presented by King Henry VIII, so that the more beautiful and poetical is also the older name. The present bell in the Tower is of date 1603; it is rung for Curfew and as passing bell when King or Archbishop dies. The Cathedral and priory buildings which were *imperium in imperio* were surrounded by a strong wall of their own as they still are. The chief gate is still Prior Goldstone's, otherwise Christ Church Gate, that beautiful example of the perpendicular style which you see as you pass up Mercery Lane. It dates from 1517. The precincts were widely different from what they are to-day. South of the Cathedral stretched a considerable Cemetery in two parts, the outer for laymen, the inner reserved for the brethren. A wall which stretched southwards from St. Anselm's Chapel held them apart. On a mound in the cemetery close to this wall there stood a campanile used for tolling the passing bell. The beautiful Norman arch which gave entrance is still in existence though its site has been moved. Here was a place called "The Oaks," no doubt from the trees there, whilst "The Elms" is perhaps the original name of a spot hard by strangely called the Homers. This is corrupted French for elms (*Ormeaux*) or a man's name of the thirteenth century or something else!

Attached to the Cathedral was the Priory of Christ Church. So important was the Priory that you might say the Cathedral was attached to it; at any rate here was a huge monastic institution of which the numerous buildings stretched to the north of the Cathedral, a somewhat unusual, but here the only available, position because just outside to the south runs Burgate Street, which of old was the chief way through the town, thus cutting off any free space on that side. Professor Willis is the great authority for the architectural history of the Cathedral and of the Priory of Christ Church, and to his learned page the reader must be referred if he should wish to go thoroughly into the subject, but I may run over one or two of the buildings to give some idea of the size and importance. Chief was the Archbishop's hall or palace which stood to the north-east. One must remember that notwithstanding all the attractions of Lambeth, the Archbishop had here his official residence during the whole period of which we treat. The hall was noted for its quaint and splendid banquets of which we have many curious accounts. Then the prior was a very important person, and he as well as the other great officials had their own places in the blocks of buildings. Still the great majority lived a common life, they slept in one or other of the huge dormitories, they took their meals together in the *frater*, they drew their supplies from the buttery and they studied or walked in the great cloister, they consulted together in the chapter house, and if they were ill or off duty as it were, they retired to the infirmary, itself a huge institution to the north-west with a cloister, hall, and chapel of its own.

To the north of all this was the Green Court, which had a gate giving on the outside world though you passed first by the Almonry, whence the benefactions of the priory were distributed. Again to the north of the Green Court were the stables, stable-yards, and other buildings which served the more material wants of the monks. Great part of those buildings still exist in a more or less perfect condition, so that it is possible under skilled guidance and with careful attention to reconstruct the vanished life of the priory. They have suffered much from the changes and neglect of 400 years since the Reformation, when the monks were scattered on the dissolution. The Dean and Chapter practically partitioned out the buildings to suit themselves, also part was made into a school, the famous King's School of Canterbury. The Archbishops from the Reformation to the Commonwealth kept up their residence in some sort, but on the Restoration were dispensed from doing so, and it is only within the last few years that the Archbishop of Canterbury has recovered an official residence beside his own Cathedral. As the clergy of post-Reformation times were married and each lived with his own family, whilst the common life was at an end, you at once see how great changes and rebuilding must happen ere the old could be made to serve the purpose of the new. A great deal could not serve that purpose at all and was either destroyed or left in picturesque ruin, but all this is a modern story. During our period there was this huge Priory in full working order attached to the Cathedral.

CHAPTER XIV

THE PILGRIMS AT THE SHRINE

Outside the West Gate—The Entrance—Aspects of Old Canterbury—Pilgrims' Hostels—" The Chequers of the Hope "—Mercery Lane and Its Wares—Entrance to the Cathedral—Its then Aspect—A Masterpiece of the Middle Ages—The Pilgrims' Round—Old World Treasures—The Shrine of St. Thomas—Its Glories—Tribute of the Pilgrims—The Blood of St. Thomas—His Well—Pilgrim Stories—*The Tale of Beryn*—The Visit of Erasmus—Other Holy Places in the City—The Supremacy of St. Thomas.

WE rejoin our Pilgrims outside the West Gate, yet not immediately do we enter the city. Just where the London Road turns to the right, into what is now St. Dunstan's Street, there stands the church of that name, well worth our visit. It is very old, plainly has pieces of Saxon work, and so is earlier than the time of St. Thomas. Dunstan had been Archbishop of Canterbury, a saint himself and one of our Saint's predecessors. The very name suggests to us something ludicrous. The monkish chronicler that imagined the comical adventure of his hero with the powers of darkness, armed with a weapon no more powerful than a tongs, did the memory of his hero serious wrong. We are apt to forget how great a figure Dunstan made in the religious history of England, yet the child-like faith of the medieval world was not repelled by a touch of the ridiculous; nothing here marred the devotion of the Pilgrim. The church had another attraction more directly connected with St. Thomas. It was here that Henry II on 12 July, 1174, began the final stage of his penitential pilgrimage, to be completed by the scourging in the crypt to the wonder of all Christendom. In the last days of the

Pilgrimage there was another relic placed here, the interest of which time has not altogether destroyed. As we passed over London Bridge we noted that to the south gateway the head of Sir Thomas More had been fixed after his execution in 1535. It remained there for fourteen days, then his daughter Margaret Roper procured its removal, and had it placed in the Roper vault of this church. She had married one of this old family whose house was just over the way. There is a memory of it still remaining in the ancient gateway of date 1500.

No sooner were our Pilgrims finished with St. Dunstan's than a small chapel in a field on the other side of the way, that is across what is now St. Dunstan's Street, craved their attention. It was dedicated to St. Thomas and stood at the foot of the hill called after it St. Thomas's Hill. It was founded in 1187 by that crusading Primate, Archbishop Baldwin, when his scheme for a much more magnificent institution at Hackington near by had fallen through, on account of opposition from the monks of Christ Church.

What with delays on the road from perils or prayers, it might turn out that the city gates were locked and barred ere the Pilgrim got to them. At sunset down went the portcullis over the gateway and up went the drawbridge over the moat or ditch. It was a complicated business to let our band into the town after dark through the main gates. This difficulty was discounted by ingenious caterers for their own profit. A number of houses for entertainment of belated travellers existed outside the walls. The "Star Inn" is specially mentioned. After supper, in the moonlight, or after sunrise in the early morning, the Pilgrims gazed curiously at the walls and spires of the town they were about to enter. The West Gate is one of the most important specimens of medieval architecture in England. The Pilgrims before 1380 saw a portal of quite other aspect. It was an ancient Norman structure whereon was stuck the Church or Chapel of the Holy Cross. In 1380 Archbishop Sudbury pulled down this gateway and erected the much larger one we see to-day. He also rebuilt the Church of the Holy Cross on the south of the gate, where, hopelessly restored, it still stands. As for the gateway, with its strong towers, its battlements and its chamber over the arch, it must have looked then just as it does now. A walled city usually means narrow space, also one building is put to various ends, thus this West Gate was used as a Guildhall in early days, and almost down to our own time as a prison. One of the marked surprises of old Canterbury must have been to come from all the cramped quarters and narrow ways to the huge spaces and noble breadth of the Cathedral.

It is now broad daylight, the gates are open and we with a hundred others press forward. The number would vary with the season of the year. It might be an ordinary day, and even then the tale would be greater in summer than in winter, or it might be the anniversary of the Martyrdom on 29 December, which would draw a mighty crowd, but the great event of the year was the Feast of the Translation of the Relics, on 7 July. Then also the annual Canterbury Fair, called Becket's Fair, took place. This did not end with the Pilgrimage, so it must have supplied a popular want. Greatest of all, your pilgrimage might hap, by chance or design, on Jubilee time, which was every fifty years from 1270 to 1520. Then the crowd from all parts of Christendom was enormous. In 1420 there were 100,000 folk crammed into the city. Along the street our band proceeds to the accompaniment of drum and pipe and bagpipe. It is a narrow street, lined with small houses made of wood and thatched, the wood ornamented and carved into grotesque shapes, and the upper stories overhung, so that you could walk under a colonnade instead of on a pavement. The street is far from clean, to put it mildly; the folk you meet have bright, various coloured dresses from which you easily tell what is each man's rank and business, also, by appropriate signs over the various shops, you have just as little difficulty in classifying the houses.

You find the city a network of narrow lanes and passages. Ever and again you would come upon some branch of the Stour, crossed by a narrow bridge. In the sideways many of the houses were mere huts, covered with thatch; on the other hand, the town was full of large and imposing buildings. Beside the Cathedral there was a dozen or so lesser, but still imposing, churches. They were much in evidence, some right in the middle of the street; two stuck on the top of the gates, and others with their cemeteries by no means exactly "toed" the street line. Then there was the mass of the city wall, the huge square Castle, St. Ethelbert's Tower, the Dane-John and its then existing fellows, to impress the stranger.

Had our band entered yester eve, they had put up at one of the numerous Pilgrims' hostels with which the town was fairly crammed. One was right in their way; this was Eastbridge or Kingsbridge Hospital which still stands to the south of the street, just where it crosses the river. Though of earlier date it came to be called the Hospital of St. Thomas the Martyr. Here Pilgrims to the shrine were housed, they had the night's lodging and fourpence for the day's food. Here on the wall is a mural painting of the murder of St. Thomas, in fit keeping with the sights of the morrow.

The entertainment of Pilgrims in Canterbury was a huge business, whether of charity or profit. The town authorities did their duty. In later times, at any rate, they set up a post in King Street before the Court Hall, with information as to lodging and victual for the use of strangers for the current year; also they enjoined innkeepers not to press unduly their services on Pilgrims. Since wayfarers were of such various ranks some classification was inevitable. The very greatest, as crowned heads and their kin, were put up at St. Augustine's Abbey. The apartment over the gateway was a choice and favourite spot. It had scarce seemed so to a royal person of to-day, but your medieval monarch did not take kindly to seclusion; probably the view of the street outside was the attraction. There were various places within the precincts of the Cathedral for the pious traveller. To the east of the Infirmary Chapel was the Homers or Meister Homers. Here the prior entertained his specially favoured guests. Again, where there is now the Deanery, Prior Goldstone II (1495-1517) had raised the New Lodging, which was also for better-class folk. On the other hand, at the south-west side of the Green Court were Chillenden's Chambers, where they housed a rather lower set, who probably did very well, since they were under the charge of the cellarer. There was the North Hall, which was at the north-west of the Green Court, for a quite inferior class; the famous Norman staircase, one of the choice bits that remain of the old Priory, gave access to this. Moreover it seems that near the North Gate, but outside the bounds, there was a Strangers' Hall for such poor Pilgrims as it was not thought proper to admit inside.

Turning away from the precincts altogether, I note that all or nearly all the numerous hospitals and religious houses at Canterbury took upon them the entertainment of Pilgrims. I will not weary the reader with a bare enumeration of names, but one famous house of the secular kind requires particular mention. This was the "Chequers of the Hope," at the south-west corner of Mercery Lane, just where it joins the main thoroughfare of the town. It extended a good way

Christ-Church Gate BCB

down the lane on one side, and westward along the High Street on the other, and as the Pilgrims would go straight from the West Gate and turn down Mercery Lane to get to the Cathedral, they could not fail to notice it, which was one reason, no doubt, why it became the most famous of all. Here Chaucer's Pilgrims are supposed to be lodged. At least they are taken there in the supplementary and contemporary *Tale of Beryn*, which shows the fame of the place. The name, it is said, means the sign of a board for play upon a cask, though according to others the " hope " is really a hoop. This inn was built, or at any rate repaired, by Prior Chillenden; it was mainly of oak and chestnut. Its form was after the fashion of the " Tabard " at Southwark. You rode into an open court, round which were galleries from which various rooms opened. By means of outside stairs, you reached the central piece of the building, to wit, a huge hall resting on wooden pillars known as " the dormitory of the hundred beds ". The court of the inn had a partially flat roof, whereon you could walk. There was a very fine view of the adjacent Cathedral from it. Crowded as old Canterbury was, we know that there were gardens within it. This inn had its own spacious garden with herbs like selvage and hyssop and Canterbury bells. The " Chequers of the Hope" lingered on, though not as an inn, till recent times. It was burnt down in the closing years of the last century. But there still remain the cellars, which are of vast extent, and a certain amount of stonework,—interesting relics of an earlier world.

The great way to the Cathedral was then, as now, down Mercery Lane and through Christ Church Gate. As its name implies, it was a good trade thoroughfare and the houses were of a good trade class. You were able to walk safe from weather under the projecting first story and inspect the wares at your leisure. Obviously the dominant note would be Pilgrim knick-knacks, souvenirs of Canterbury which to-day in another form is still the staple article. Here was a great market for Pilgrim signs, the *ampulla* or leaden bottle, presently to be filled with the precious St. Thomas's blood or the *caput Thomae*, the head of St. Thomas, in one or other of many shapes and sizes, usually in the form of a medal. These signs were borne with some ostentation as a proof to all the world that the bearer had been at the shrine signified by the token. Here is a case in point. Giraldus Cambrensis, in the twelfth century, tells that he, returning from Canterbury through London, visited with his companions the Bishop of Winchester. That prelate notices the sign of St. Thomas round their necks and is led to observe, evidently they had just come from Canterbury. You infer that there must have been a great traffic in the city in such things, and so tradition says. Nay, a foundry for casting leaden signs is reported to have existed in the precincts of the Cathedral. Now, for the last century or more, the earth at Canterbury has been pretty well scrutinised and riddled. But few have turned up. Some were fished up from the Stour, and, indeed, the chief preservers of such things have been the rivers, especially the Thames. It may be that the Canterbury native thought less of them than the stranger, so there was no local demand, and the visitor safely conveyed away all that he bought.

Our Pilgrims emerge from the attractions of Mercery Lane, enter the precincts by Christ Church Gate, and move on towards the south-west door of the Cathedral. The way lay through the cemetery, where were buried those who had died during their visit to Canterbury. The cemetery for the monks of the priory was some way to the east, and separated from the other by a wall and a gate. The exterior of the great church was very much then as it is now. The dominant note everywhere was St. Thomas. Over the south porch the three murderers were pilloried, so to speak, since their three effigies were exposed to popular execration. Erasmus noted them during his visit, in the early years of the sixteenth century, and names them, oddly enough, as Tuscus, Fuscus and Berri; evidently he meant Tracy, Fitzurse and Breton. Before entering, they gaze at the figures in the niches, now vacant, or only lately filled up. Then, arranging themselves according to rank, they more or less devoutly, but at least with the outward aspect of gravity, entered the nave. Here a monk met them ready to shed holy water over their heads from a sprinkler.

The church was not so bare as it is to-day. It was full of variety, animation and movement. There was a bewildering choice of shrines, a profusion of images, gaily-coloured banners, multitudes of chapels, each with its own attractions. The great size and height of the church, the elevation of the choir above the nave, and of the Trinity Chapel above the choir, impressed all beholders. The windows also were filled with the most glorious painted glass, of which a few fragments yet remain,—precious relics of vanished glories. As the soft light streamed in and fell in coloured rays on the pavement, the effect, even on the ignorant, was great indeed. Not only did the medieval world know how to build a cathedral, but was skilled to trick it forth. And it was at its very best in the embellishment of Canterbury.

A monk showed each band round, though each did not follow the same order. Usually the Martyrdom was the first place visited. A Latin distich over the door said that this was the sacred and noted place where St. Thomas suffered martyrdom. The story of the tragedy was told again in the splendid glass of the window, given by Edward IV and his queen. The Martyrdom, you remember, was in the north-west transept. The place had been cleared and re-arranged; but part of the wall and part of the pavement is even to-day judged to be the same as it was in the time of St. Thomas. A rough wooden altar marked the exact spot where he had fallen. This was "the altar of the sword's point," and here some of the relics were shown by the attendant priest, who explained and described, and improved the occasion for the spiritual and temporal welfare of the church. The relics of St. Thomas were disposed at appropriate places, where they were like to produce the most effect. Thus, here in a tabernacular casket was kept the point of Le Bret's sword, which had broken as he struck at the head of St. Thomas. And here were also some of the brains enclosed in rock crystal. It is unfortunate that the accounts we have belong to the last years when the cult of St. Thomas was a dying superstition. We can only imagine as best we may the feelings of the devotees. Chaucer might perhaps have told us, if he had continued his tales and brought his Pilgrims to the shrine, but it must have been Chaucer in his most serious mood; I think it was his delicate artistic perception of fitness, his own sense of propriety, that made him hold his hand when he reached the precincts of the holy city. The prologue to *The Tale of Beryn* is amusing and useful, but the hand is not Chaucer's, and there is no touch of a high note throughout.

The Pilgrims would go next to the crypt, to which some steps on the right gave convenient access. Dark and gloomy, it may have seemed after the rich light of the church. However, a great multitude of lamps was suspended to the pillars. The peculiar attraction of the crypt was that here had been St. Thomas's first tomb until the translation of the remains to the Trinity Chapel just above. In accordance with the scheme, already stated, part of the relics was retained, to wit, the haircloth shirt and drawers he had worn at the time of his death. It is possible that here was also kept, set in silver, that part of the skull which had been struck off

RELIQUARY, DEPICTING THE MURDER AND ENTOMBMENT OF
ST. THOMAS OF CANTERBURY. LIMOGES. 1200 A.D.
IN THE BRITISH MUSEUM

THE PILGRIMS AT THE SHRINE

by the Le Bret sword. But what of Becket's Crown or Corona? Was not this part of the body shown there? Many explanations have been suggested. The relic may have been moved from the one place to the other; it may have disappeared for some time; it may have been stolen by the guardians themselves, and replicas, so to speak, from some other body here substituted. In fact the genuineness of any of the relics is extremely questionable. Only a fraction can possibly have been genuine, and even these were liable to be purloined by the very monks that watched them; for a pious fraud was not merely allowable but praiseworthy upon occasion.

Those things the common crowd were allowed to gaze on, but more distinguished visitors were admitted to see the treasures of the Chapel of Our Lady Undercroft, to whom the whole crypt was dedicated. The gold and precious stones here were enormous in amount and value. The Pilgrims would next ascend to the choir where a great mass of relics not connected with St. Thomas, and therefore of subsidiary interest, were kept. But the mere number was impressive, for there were more than four hundred items. The monk in charge handed them, or the chief of them, to the visitor to be kissed, naming the special one in every case. Among the more curious were some of the earth from which God made Adam, Aaron's Rod, part of the table of the Last Supper, part of the stone upon which Our Lord stood when He ascended into heaven, a part of the prison of St. Peter,—but one cannot follow the articles in detail, though the arm of St. George must not go without this brief mention. There were fifty-six separate reliquaries stuffed with every kind of relic. There were three heads and eleven arms of saints, and four of the fifty-six reliquaries contained pieces of the true cross. We are told that Plegmund (890-909) brought "the blessed Martyr Blaise" at a great price from Rome, and thus founded, so to speak, the collection of sacred curios which was not exceeded by any church in Christendom.

Only a fraction of the Pilgrims can have done the church thoroughly, venerated all the relics, worshipped at all the shrines. Even to inspect the ecclesiastical dress and furniture, of which the Cathedral possessed great store, would occupy much time.

The especially privileged were then taken to the sacristy in St. Andrew's Tower in the north aisle of the choir. Here was the rough wooden blackthorn stick which had served St. Thomas for episcopal staff, and the stained and frayed handkerchief and the rags which he had used. There was next a move to the apse at the extreme end of the great church known as Becket's Crown. Here was a golden image of the head of the Saint, and the altar possibly contained at one time, at any rate, that part of the skull which I mentioned in connection with the crypt.

Finally came the holiest of the holies, the shrine of the Saint in Trinity Chapel, behind the great altar. The Pilgrims, who approached it from the lower part of the church, ascended the steps on their knees; you trace the mark to-day in the hard stone. The shrine as we know is completely gone, but there is a long hollow in the pavement at the western end which shows exactly where it stood. The mark was made by generations of kneeling Pilgrims. It is still possible for us to understand with some exactness what the shrine was like, because shrines were constructed on one principle. The base was of marble or stone, not solid but with recesses or arches, into which the devotee might thrust some part of his body, so as to get the most advantage from the healing power of the relics. The virtue of the Saint was active throughout all the shrine. In this substructure was laid the *feretrum* (feretory) or chest containing the whole or part of the body. It was covered with gold plates, and over it was a gold-wire netting on which was fastened a great wealth of jewels. This shrine was surmounted with three finials of silver-gilt, the centre piece weighed eighty ounces and the others sixty each. All this was protected by a wooden cover, usually kept locked, but raised when the shrine was to be shown.

This was the supreme moment of the Pilgrimage. As the cover was raised, the silver bells attached to it tinkled musically and the diamonds blazed, the priest exhorted and the Pilgrims' minds were moved to the highest pitch of devotion. One of the monks stood by and pointed out with a white rod the most precious objects, telling the value and lauding the donor by name. This was in French, the language of the court and of culture. The most precious gift was the *regale* of France whereto the figure of an angel pointed. It had been given by Louis VII on his pilgrimage, and a wonderful story was told of the manner. The Archbishop who took him to the church noted the stone as it flashed in a ring on the King's finger. He begged it for the Saint, but the King showed some reluctance, for he thought it a talisman. But he offered a hundred thousand florins instead. The Archbishop agreed, and the incident might have been considered closed, when all of a sudden the stone of its own accord started from the ring and stuck fast in the shrine, as if fixed by a goldsmith! The King needs must leave the gem where it was, to the wonder of succeeding ages; finally to sparkle on Henry VIII's finger, and to be a trophy so precious that even the pious and orthodox Mary preferred not to restore it to the Church. However, the wooden cover was at length let down on this mass of splendour, and the Pilgrims turned away. Some, it may be, to say prayers at other altars and venerate other relics, but the most were content with having done their duty and fulfilled the object of their journey.

No other tomb was allowed to come near the shrine for a long period. It was the greatest honour possible to the Black Prince to place his body hard by. Afterwards there was laid the body of Henry IV and that of Archbishop Courtenay, the last for no very obvious reason now discernible. Before the Pilgrims left the Trinity Chapel and the neighbourhood of the shrine, they were urged to make their offerings, as already at the various points in their progress. I note that the sum of seven shillings, in coin of the period, was a fair and usual donation for a man in good position.

One thing remained. The Pilgrims must get their bottles filled with the blood of St. Thomas, now wondrously diluted, but still believed of efficacy. A stone on the south side of the Trinity Chapel, worn away as if with much use, is pointed out as the spot where the Pilgrims knelt to receive the filling of their bottles from the spring in the precincts, called St. Thomas's Well. Into this, the blood and the dust taken from the Martyrdom had been thrown. It miraculously ran blood and milk at various times, but it disappeared with the fall of the cult.

The prologue to *The Tale of Beryn*, and the account of the visit of Erasmus, give us some valuable hints. The lines in the *Tale* which tell how the "lewd sots" stared in amazement at the painted windows and made the grossest mistakes as to the subjects, is a genuine piece of observation. And there are many other touches showing that the author, to use an expressive vulgarism, "knew the ropes". What follows when they came out of the church is sufficiently probable, as it is certainly sufficiently amusing. One cannot say that the lower comic note is overdone or unnatural, but there is nothing else. One can only say that the account is useful as far as it goes.

THE PILGRIMS AT THE SHRINE 173

The visit of Erasmus and Colet is between the years 1511 and 1513, twenty-five years or so before the end, and in many ways the shadow of that end is over their narrative. They were impressed, as men of all ages have been, by the majesty of the Cathedral, which from afar off " strikes religious awe into the beholders ". Erasmus describes the sights of the church and gives some sly knocks *suo more* at the relics. The treasures were so great that Midas and Crœsus were beggars in comparison with the monks. Suppose this wealth were sold for the poor ? The suggestion was not well received! There is a description of the shrine in its magnificence. In the sacristy they are shown pieces of rag, of which the Prior offers a small fragment to Colet as a great favour. Colet shows his contempt very plainly ; but the Prior prefers not to notice it, offers a cup of wine to the strangers and courteously dismisses them. Erasmus was a friend of the Archbishop, the learned and moderate Warham. The Prior was Goldstone II, who had built what is now the deanery, the central tower and Christ Church Gate. Erasmus, Colet and the Archbishop were all adherents of the new learning ; we have no information as to the beliefs of Goldstone, but probably a man of his ability and culture was touched with the spirit of the time. Erasmus looked at everything critically and cautiously, not prepared to break with the old, yet not content entirely to accept it. One would have liked an earlier narrative from some devotee of superior mind who would have reproduced to us the spirit with which the true and earnest believers approached the shrine, but this perhaps we could not expect; at least, we have it not. The monkish expressions of devotion are mere stereotyped formulas, and the others mere ludicrous narrative or sceptical criticism. It were not difficult to carp at the views of Erasmus, to show that either he goes too far or not far enough. But the discussion would lead us far afield, and we refrain.

The churches and religious houses beginning with St. Augustine's Abbey, which came next after Christ Church, possessed relics of their own, noteworthy and precious, at least so the men of that time believed. The whole city, to the pious mind, offered opportunities for praise and prayer. There were crosses at the various markets, nay, in almost every street, and the continual chiming of the bells, from all the churches beginning with the Cathedral, was a perpetual reminder to devotion. But the dominant note was ever St. Thomas. He was commemorated on the city arms; hospitals went by his name; there were altars to him in the minor churches. His shrine was the very core of the town. At stated intervals the pageant of St. Thomas was performed. A car drawn by ten horses went through the chief streets. Thereon was an altar. A boy dressed in appropriate costume represented the Saint. Four other boys, armed as knights, struck him down; blood flowed plentifully; an angel spun round and waved its wings; a man concealed in the altar supplied the motive force and also the blood, by some —for the time—ingenious mechanism. He received the moderate remuneration of twopence. So popular was this strange show that, though it fell with the shrine, it was thought worth while to revive it in Mary's reign, though no attempt was made to restore anything else that had reference to St. Thomas the Martyr.

CHAPTER XV

SANDWICH AND THE SANDWICH ROAD

St. Thomas at Sandwich—Former Importance—Its Decline—The Journey There—"Heart's Delight"—Wingham Church—Chestnut Pillars—An Absurd Memorial—Traditions of Guilton—Ash-next-Sandwich—A Green Level—Richborough Castle through the Ages—Coins and Oysters—A Thunderstorm—The Maze of Sandwich Streets—Hospices and Hospitals—Some Quaint Points from Their Records—The Vanished Gates—A Golf Carnival—Houses by the Sea—The Bells of St. Clement's—Farewell to Sandwich.

THERE are places near Canterbury so connected with the history of St. Thomas and the Pilgrimage that it is proper to speak of them; one such place is Sandwich. From here St. Thomas sailed for France after his quarrel with Henry II, and here it was he landed in that fated December, 1170, and thence proceeded to Canterbury in that triumphant procession which suggested to more than one monkish writer the entry of Christ into Jerusalem before His crucifixion. Richard Lion Heart disembarked here on his return from Austria, and went on foot on a Canterbury Pilgrimage to give thanks for his liberation; the Black Prince came here with King John as captive—to mention but these. The reason was that which gives such a strange piquancy to the history of the place.

It was once a great port for the Continent, and the sea, which is now a good two miles off, rushed strong up the broad estuary of the Stour where there lay near a hundred ships with their some 1500 sailors, but all that is over and gone; the harbour became silted up. A great vessel, the property of Pope Paul IV, went down right in front of the haven and it was believed much aided the process. Between 1500 and 1600 the town was done for as seaport; it was left to decay. It was not thought worth while to pull down the old houses or change the old paths. Gates and walls are almost gone, else had it been a relic more precious than Winchelsea; yet this, which was once the greatest of the Cinque Ports, is still noteworthy.

Although the royal visitors mentioned and hundreds more obscure whose names are altogether forgotten made their Canterbury Pilgrimage from the Continent by Sandwich, yet neither in the town itself nor on the way to the North Gate whereby they entered the Holy City are there many relics of the cult of our Saint, though the extinction of the town as a Continental port almost coincided with the end of the Pilgrimage. Reasons suggest themselves; Sandwich, however important, was only one out of several havens, also the journey between it and Canterbury—some twelve miles—would always be performed in a day, thus you would not expect Pilgrim chapels and shrines, and houses of entertainment, in the path. Here are some notes of a visit paid to it from Canterbury with some hours' wandering through the town and its vicinity.

The way between Canterbury and Sandwich runs in an almost direct line; it is the Roman road from Richborough and has not, I think, varied much within historic memory. In leaving Canterbury you pass the cemetery gate and along the old wall of St. Augustine's Abbey, for you do not now emerge by the North Gate. Then leaving St. Martin's on your left you climb to the top of one of those low hills which ring Canterbury round. The road, like many in Kent, is switchback; it is not crowded with traffic, albeit the motor is not infrequent. There are pleasant hop-fields and green lands, a very wealth of old houses, some charming churches, and an occasional windmill. You turn to look at a horse nowadays even on these country roads.

Two splendid Kentish specimens caught my attention for a moment as I descended the hill to Littlebourne; they were drawing a farm-cart and were encased in a sort of network covering, to keep off the flies or the heat; they were decorated with gay rosettes, perhaps there was some rustic festival afoot. The ticket which as required by law bore the place of their domicile, announced it as "Heart's Delight," a charming destination for a bright May day, but their way, alas! was not mine.

After Littlebourne came Bramling and then Wingham, a peculiarly delightful village with many a quaint house, each of which filled you with a desire to become its tenant for the delightfully ridiculous legal period of 999 years. The inns and the church are in their own way equally attractive; perhaps the Pilgrims found them so, or they divided according to their taste; however, I gave the preference to the church where there are things worth the seeing.

The door stood open but no one entered save myself, so that as I moved softly about the ticking of the clock in the huge tower fell on the ear with startling distinctness. There were some very old stalls in the choir. I was not surprised to find they dated from the thirteenth century; they certainly looked it. I touched them with reverence. No doubt they were for the priests, but a Pilgrim must have sat on one many a time thinking of the near end of his journey. A familiar object like this brings us into more intimate touch with the past than the sculptured effigies of knights in marble. I admired the chestnut columns that held up the nave; they must have been old and yet looked firm and fresh and strong. The oddest thing in Wingham Church is a preposterous monument to the illustrious members of the Oxenden family, " whose ancestors have flourished in this county for several ages," which boast is justified, since there are records of them from the sixteenth down to the nineteenth century. The monument bears date 1632 and is a curious example of the art of the period. It is tricked off with comic cherubs, shamelessly undraped, also you have marble fruit and foliage in exuberant profusion. The corners are decorated with the heads of oxen with truncated horns, though this is due to mischief-makers who have struck off the points at unknown and probably different dates in past generations, a quaint popular protest against this monstrosity in marble.

The next place in the road is Guilton and to that succeeds Ash-next-Sandwich. I had read with interest J. R. Planche's *A Corner in Kent* which deals with Ash and the country round it; perhaps it had raised my expectations too high, and it may be I was unreasonably disappointed. In old pagan times Guilton, tradition avers, possessed an idol of solid gold three feet in height. At Guilton Mill there are the remains of a great Anglo-Saxon cemetery, which I did not visit. The village has its usual record of old inns. The "Ship" at the Canterbury end and the "Lion" at the other, to name but two. Places of entertainment with those names have been here from time immemorial. The church stands on a little height at the side of the main thoroughfare. It is big enough and even imposing though obviously restored. The steeple is peculiar, whence its commemoration in an ill-natured couplet of some antiquity.

> Ash church with its peaked steeple,
> A bad parson and worse people.

The present generation are entitled to hold the verse entirely irrelevant, as regards themselves. I found the church door fast locked, but in the porch there was prominently displayed a list of forbidden decrees leading off with the familiar sentence, "A man may not marry his grandmother".

Has any young man of Ash, bored to death with

the abomination of desolation in the winter months, greatly daring, revolved in his mind a breach of this canonical law as a relief from the monotony of existence? There is no record in authentic or even legendary history of any such! The spacious churchyard is thickly crowded with monuments. In that peaceful district they are left undisturbed slowly to decay. A countryman was loitering there, with what purpose I know not; he explained to me, in his slow Kentish drawl, that they were tacking on additions to the City of the Dead. He dwelt with some pleasure on the view from the height, a sleepy but pleasant landscape, an expression in earth of slow, regular, peaceful, monotonous lives. The chief thing moving was a windmill a little way off; the only windmill I had seen in motion for I don't know how long. He explained that such things were little used by the modern farmer or miller.

A little way farther on and I entered the green level plain which lines the coast. The country had quite a Dutch look and in the distance were the towers of Sandwich; ditches took the place of canals; there was a sprinkling of windmills. The Flemish refugees who fled from Alva's persecution in the Low Countries must have found themselves quite at home in Sandwich. They, in their turn, made their mark. The bulbous tower of St. Peter's Church, bits of house architecture, even some words peculiar to the district, all remind of the Netherlands.

Just before entering Sandwich a notice, at a road to the left, directed me to Richborough. After a mile's journey I came on this ancient and famous Roman fortress, so majestically mounted on a cliff, by what are now the scanty waters of the Stour. You remember that was the great Roman stronghold in Britain; it guarded one exit of the Wantsum, till that broad sea channel, which at the other end entered the estuary of the Thames at Reculver, became silted up. It was perhaps the place in Britain best known to the Roman world in the days of the later Cæsars; witness the testimony of Lucan and Juvenal and Claudian. The second of these has commemorated the flavour of the oysters taken from its shore. The soldiers of the garrison showed a keen Epicurean relish for those delicacies; witness the incredible amount of oyster shells excavated here or hereabouts, also it is averred as many as 140,000 coins have been delved up from among the ruins. Its Roman name was *Rutupiæ* or *Rutupium*. It is to the Saxons that it owes its present name of Richborough or the King's Town. The northern barbarians huddled therein and even built some sort of rude palace. Also when they became Christians they needs must have a church which probably stood on the mound now called "St. Augustine's Cross". Of church and palace there are no tangible remains, above ground at any rate, but the Roman work that was before them remains strong and solid after them. I had been there once before many years ago; the place then lay open, for I remember exploring some way the underground passage in the middle, but now I found it enclosed and protected with wire whilst a board declared the price of admission as threepence! There was no one to receive the money or open the gate; it was only when returning that I found I should have got the key at a cottage some distance off. I scarcely regretted for I saw all over the enclosure as I crept slowly round it. The cliff rises abruptly from the river, and the side towards the east, left open, was sufficiently guarded by nature; the other three were enclosed by a wall whereof huge fragments remain, flint and rubble and lines of red tiles all bound together by that Roman cement which time seemed to make stronger and harder. There was nothing in the enclosure save the mark of some excavations, a few sheep pasturing, some poultry, and one or two trees. The space, beautifully clean and bare, was evidently carefully tended.

It was a stormy day and I was fortunate in encountering only the tail end of a heavy downpour. There were frequent flashes on the horizon and the thunder, "that deep and dreadful organ pipe," sounded strangely appropriate amidst those grim and hoary ruins. Then the sun came out and lighted up the broad plain. I sat down on an outlying block of masonry, on the edge of the side that overlooks the Stour, protected by a jutting mass that projected over my head. It looked insecure, as if about to topple over and grind me to powder, but I reflected that which had remained so many centuries was not likely to crash down on this particular hour, nor did it! It was a Saturday afternoon but no visitors were expected, else some one had been at hand to throw open the gate. I circled round the whole enclosure but no human being was visible. A little foolish train of three carriages rattled past at frequent intervals by the river-side at the base of the cliff, and when it was gone there was nothing but the call of the wind in the tree-tops. Familiarity, according to a well-known saying, breeds contempt, but in the hours I passed at Richborough that afternoon, it always seemed to grow greater. It is not merely its long record, for that record we are like to misread; we trace it back to the beginning of the Christian era and thus gain an impression of commencement; it is rather a termination, one of the ultimate works of imperial Rome, the result of the centuries of Roman history; an outpost of her dominion, the last erected, the last to fall. It was already old and hoary when the Pilgrims, as they left Sandwich by the Canterbury Gate, on the way to the Holy City, saw it crowning the cliff on their right. Only a very few, if indeed any, turned aside for closer inspection; they would gaze on its huge bulk with somewhat of the same unreasoning awe with which the Saxon visitors at Rome contemplated the Coliseum. Their mind was full of the thoughts and feelings of their own day and in such Richborough had no place, but the Pilgrimage rose and flourished and passed away, and Richborough remains in all essentials but little changed. Already old in their time, it scarce seems older to-day, touched then and now with the true touch of Roman permanence.

As the day wore on I left Richborough and entering the Canterbury Gate, or rather passing over the site of it, I was soon wandering in the narrow streets of Sandwich. A curious and intricate jumble, they form for the stranger a sort of maze of town architecture difficult to unravel until experience gives the key. You are continually missing the point at which you aim, continually passing the same spot, yet the space enclosed by the ramparts is comparatively small, for a brisk walk of twenty minutes would I think take you completely round it. Do not regret the lost way; in every corner there is some little bit of old-world architecture delightful to your sight. It were worth coming to Sandwich merely to see a beautiful house like Manwood Court, where was once the Grammar School which is now housed in more spacious quarters outside the ramparts. Those ramparts have done much to preserve the antique aspect of the place. Of late years golf has given it a new prosperity, and there are many new houses, but these have been erected in the new suburbs, outside or away beyond the golf links, by the sea, and so do not mar the past.

The connection of Sandwich with the medieval church was very close, for Canute gave it to the priory of Christ Church, Canterbury, St. Thomas's own house. It contributed the respectable number of

RICHBOROUGH CASTLE.

40,000 herrings to feed the monks, also it supplied their clothing. In the Moat Sole there is the Hospital of St. Thomas founded by Thomas Ellis, a prosperous draper of the place, about 1392. At the Reformation and after, it escaped the royal fangs, and there and at one or two other foundations of a like nature, some poor and aged and honest brothers and sisters still have a secure haven for their declining years. I found this ancient foundation a very modern and far from imposing structure; the porch is ancient though encased in new masonry, but it is quite distinguishable. I thought it a very charming morsel of antiquity. I was more taken with St. Bartholomew's Hospital which stands outside the town on the right hand side of the Dover road. It dates from the twelfth century. It is a strange jumble of old and new buildings each inscribed with the name of the particular brother or sister, its tenant for the time being. It is mixed up with a farm, I persume its property; the whole is dignified by an ancient, spacious, and beautiful chapel. Content with my inspection of those two, I made no attempt to hunt out St. John's in the Corn Market.

The *Customal*, a sort of ancient history of the town first put in writing in 1301, though even then it was a digest or record of things already antique, contains many quaint details as to life in those old hospitals. Thus at St. Bartholomew's the brothers and sisters were wont after dinner o' Sundays to assemble in their common hall, where they had of the master a penny apiece, wherefrom each contributed a farthing towards a jug of ale, " which they drink together to promote brotherly affection," and then before they left they bent them in prayer " for the founders and benefactors of the Hospital and for all the faithful living and dead ". At St. John's each inmate had daily a mess of porridge, a farthing loaf, and a farthing beer money " if their income would admit of it ". If the dwellings went out of repair, they lost the beer money till all was trim and trig again. On Sundays they attended the churches with pewter dishes, beseeching money to buy meat for Sunday's dinner, and when herrings were plentiful, they were down at the harbour begging. All this and much else is set forth in quaint medieval Latin, translated for us by Boys in his *History of Sandwich*. Evidently they considered begging a good work, but it was not the only support of the Hospital. A vagrant hog found in the streets or poultry swimming in the Delf water were forthwith impounded for St. John's.

Thomas Ellis, besides the hospital in honour of St. Thomas, founded the chantry of Thomas the Martyr in St. Peter's Church. Unlike the hospital it did not survive the Reformation; its property went for forty-seven shillings in the second year of King Edward VI. As to the special provision for our friends, one of the chief, perhaps the original purpose of St. Bartholomew's, was to entertain Pilgrims and travellers. Assuredly no needy Canterbury Pilgrim could have been turned away from St. Thomas's Hospital. At St. John's house there was a number of single rooms called the Harbinge, for the special accommodation of travellers; likewise, a brother and sister of the community, having the official title of "Harbingers," looked specially after their comfort. In New Street there stands the old house with its spacious and delightful gardens called "the Friary," and here are some remains of the old-time establishment of the White Friars or Carmelites. Since hospitality was the duty of all those establishments, you cannot doubt of the entertainment of wayfarers. If those ancient religious of all denominations begged persistently and shamelessly, at least they spent their gettings without stint, and where they were most wanted.

Nearly all the Pilgrims from Sandwich to Canterbury coming by sea, presumably were provided for their passage; most of them, I fancy, were men of some means, and preferred the inns of the town to the plain fare of the hospitals. In the cattle market there is the Congregational Chapel dating from the reign of Queen Anne, quite a respectable antiquity for a building of the kind. Here it was said was an inn specially used by self-supporting Pilgrims. I know nothing as to the antiquity of the present inns. I noted the "Three Kings Yard," which seems to hint at a very old hostelry, at least the name has the right medieval smack. I went along the High Street and out at the Barbican, that quaint medieval passage or gate, always reproduced in pictures of Sandwich, and walked about a little in the Haven. It is not quite deserted, for, when the tide fills, one or two barges rise lazily from the mud and crawl past the bridge, and out into the marsh, after which they are tugged, or perhaps if the wind be favourable, sail towards the main. There are some fragments of the Town Wall hereabouts which you easily pick out. By the Fisher's Gate you return to the town by Quay Lane. This is the only ancient portal extant. In Boys' *History* are illustrations of the other gates then standing. Sandown Gate is a solid, square building, not altogether unlike the West Gate of Canterbury. Woodnesborough Gate, though the top of the arch is broken away, looks sufficiently picturesque and imposing, and Canterbury Gate is again somewhat like the West Gate of that city. The *History* quoted was published in 1792. The author would not have had the gates engraved unless they had been even then objects of interest. It is too late now to grieve for the folly that levelled them to the ground.

There is, still, a small fragment left of the Sandown Gate. As the name implies it leads to the downs and the sea. It ought to be called Golf Course Gate. On this Saturday afternoon all sorts of vehicles were streaming through it on their way to the Course, and I went there too. There was some important match on, so the place was crowded. The local constabulary were hard pressed to give order and regularity to the traffic. It was a full mile distant from the town over the downs, or perhaps one should say links. They strike you as most excellent for the purpose, for here the links of the north which gave birth to the game, and conditioned the rules thereof, are reproduced by nature in very close fashion. I went on an additional mile to the sea, where the houses of a new Sandwich are springing up, huge and "replete with every comfort," no doubt, yet monstrous, hideous, formless, as if the architects had taken for plan the distorted visions of a rich man's nightmare, such be the strange growths that the last few years have raised on this once lonely shore.

On Sunday morning I got me again to the Ramparts and sought a seat on the Mill Wall; it was under the shadow of St. Clement's, the chief church of the place. The exquisite Norman tower with its quaint arcades stood out perfectly outlined in the clear air, from it there pealed forth the sweet note of its melodious bells. Past it motors hooting loudly, as they dashed round the street corners, sped at a mad pace and in quick succession through the Sandown Gate on towards the links. Through the trees I saw the masts and sails of a barge slowly moving from the haven. The bells seemed the plaintive, pathetic note of old-world faith calling in vain to men intent on pelf or pleasure. Presently the bells of St. Peter's and St. Mary's echoed from the near distance in a confused, sweet jumble of sound. With such music in my ears, I loitered for some time in the Rope Walk, and then after a final glance at the old houses of Strand Street, set my face towards Woodnesborough, where they say was once a temple to the great god Woden. Thence round by Ash and towards Canterbury.

CHAPTER XVI

THE PATH OF THE KNIGHTS, STONE STREET, SALTWOOD CASTLE AND LYMNE

Picking up Stone Street—Its Character—Its Great Age—Changes on It—Lessons from a Chalk Pit—Villages on the Way—The West Wood—The Prospect of Kent—Saltwood and its Castle—Restorations, their Good and Evil—The Postern Gate—History of the Castle—Its Connection with the Martyrdom—Tradition of Archbishop Courtenay—The Primate Then and Now—The Eloquence of Z. Cousins—On to Lymne—The Great Fragments of Studfall Castle—The Scene from Below—The Church and the House on the Cliff—Their Debt to Studfall Castle—Antiquities and Antiquaries—John Leland, Dr. Stukeley and R. Smith—" The Nun of Kent ".

THE way by which the knights who murdered St. Thomas rode from Saltwood Castle to Canterbury is still a high road though it leads through a somewhat remote tract. It was already centuries old before their time, for it is the ancient Roman way called Stone Street which ran from the ancient Roman *Portus Limanus* to Canterbury. It holds so many points of interest that it well deserves some notice in this book. I here set down the account of a journey along the road and back again with notes of a visit to Lymne and Saltwood.

It is not altogether easy for a stranger to pick up the Canterbury end of this ancient way; you are usually told to take the old Dover road which runs south from the cattle market, and turn to the right past the Cricket Ground. I did so. I was further directed by an ancient country dame to take a turning to the left past a public-house, which I also did. The road became narrow and was vanishing rapidly into a by-lane; then I talked with a countryman doing some carting work; he tried to explain to me where the original Stone Street was. He pointed to a narrow track which, ascending a hill, disappeared in a wood. Your rustic is all very well for a simple statement, but he lacks facility of expression, and gets confused when it is a question of detail; possibly I misunderstood him, at any rate I floundered about unfrequented ways for a mile or two; they were delightful through thick woods and by ancient secluded cots, but they zigzagged far too much to support the dignity of a Roman way. In the end I floundered on to Stone Street; there was no mistaking its long straight line.

I fared better on the return journey and happened on what seems to be the true exit. Worthgate, you must note, was the oldest gate in Canterbury; it was a single arch which pierced the outer wall of the Castle, and if not itself Roman must have succeeded a Roman portal on the same site. It is unfortunately gone, but if you leave the city by the site of Wincheap Gate, you leave the spot where it was a little on the right hand. Proceed along Wincheap Street till you come to Hollow Lane on the left; it has no promise; there is a touch of the slum about it; never mind, the houses soon vanish. Plod your way upward for it is a steep narrow lane which twists about just a little. Keep right on; you border an open field and the road becomes straight as an arrow flight; it is shaded on both sides by noble trees, is a charming piece indeed. It is assuredly the ancient way though curiously desolate; why, it is hard to discover, for it goes straight into Canterbury. Some more frequented thoroughfares cross it at right angles, and then after two or three miles one of those cross-roads turn into it and you have the recognised way; you have gained it almost in a straight line from Worthgate.

I have had occasion several times to talk of the Roman Road. It was really a solid mass of layers of large and small stones, bound together with that hard Roman cement which holds to-day as firmly as it did then. The top of this mass was made smooth and on it were laid large flat stones, a sort of pavement in fact. You see at once why the Roman Road in some cases has lasted down to our own time, but it does not twist and bend as a modern road does ; it runs straight along up hill and down dale. The ancient engineer wanted to get between two points and was not concerned to serve the needs of savage villages, if any such existed. Then it is a narrow way sufficient, I suppose, for the passage of two chariots or of a solid but narrow body of men along its pavement. For what else was it wanted?

If you look on the map it appears still to run with perfect straightness, and in fact it does so for long tracts. Some authorities say that even where it diverges you can trace the old way by the side of the modern, pursuing its rigid course. I cannot say I noticed this. It does bend a little in going up-hill, has a peculiar twist of its own, owning as it were, though ever so little, the need of suiting itself to the steep. Those twists are, I think, original, others are the work of the weaker human peoples who used it after the imperial race had vanished from the scene. Thus it here and there broadens out so that the distance between the hedges on either side is about double what it is in the secluded part ; again it wobbles a little, you cannot now tell why.

Think of its enormous age! In its early centuries land can have been of little value ; now and again people would stray off it, over a hardly defined border, and the stray way hardened into the main path. Both at the Canterbury end and at the sea end, its irregularities are most pronounced ; it naturally gets a little confused among the suburbs of Canterbury, and at the other end, after you pass Westenhanger Station and come out on the main road which runs westward from Hythe, it takes a turn to the right to get to Lymne. A straight line, it has been noted, would carry you past

Shepway Cross where of old time the Lord Warden of the Cinque Ports was installed with all manner of ancient rites; here also the court of Shepway was once held in the open air. A little farther, at the foot of the cliff, there was once the open sea; perhaps *Portus Limanus* had a landing-place here, and the Roman soldier would step from his trireme and march straight off for Durovernum, as he called Canterbury.

You meet various object lessons which suggest causes for a deflection of the road. Thus a few miles from the sea end there is a very old and now disused chalk pit; it causes a considerable hollow in the hill, and were it not masked by a thick growth of wood would make a very conspicuous object in the landscape, as the chalk pit on the hill above Aylesford does for instance. Now this chalk pit is right in the middle of the way which bends very decidedly to the left to get round it. One readily believes that once the road went straight on and perhaps a section was destroyed when the pit was fashioned, at a time when no one was particularly interested in rigidly keeping to the main way. Stone Street is the boundary line of every parish through which it passes. Thus it was there before the country was divided into parishes. When that division was made, it was inevitable it should be selected as the limit of the local division.

The natural centre of the village is the church; round it the houses cluster, though we sometimes find them scattered for some reason we cannot now discover. Although you touch on some half dozen parishes, yet the church or the village is not built by the way. Lower Hardres is at the Canterbury end and Stanford at the other, but if you wish to visit Petham or Upper Hardres or Monks Horton for instance, you have to go to the right or the left.

I would not to-day call it very lonely; there are a good many scattered houses, not very old and not very modern, an occasional small hamlet also along it at intervals, and it is too charming a route to be neglected by the prying motorman or the cyclist, nay ! on Whit Sunday I met a huge motor bus with a party of excursionists pounding across Farthing Common and through the West Wood !

West Wood is a charming forest of trees at about the highest part of your passage. Much of it has been cut down, and you are warned off from the rest by a notice which from its archaic language does not lack entertainment; it makes mention of Mockbeggar Farm and Rhode Farm whence permits have to be obtained, the wherewith lacking you are threatened with dire treatment at the hands of keeper and woodreeve. It were worth while trespassing to encounter so archaic an official ! You journey along the sixteen miles or so very pleasantly; the ground is on the rise from the time you get clear of Canterbury till you top the range of low hills, and then you have a tolerably steep run down towards Lymne.

At the highest point a huge undulating plain bursts upon you all at once. It is bounded by the sea. In the vast sweep are clumps of trees, villages, churches, country seats, white roads serpenting in and out—a pleasant country landscape; in short " the prospect of Kent " is neither startling nor imposing, but it is very delightful for all that, and never fails to charm; such is the road along which the knights travelled on the morning of Tuesday, 29 December, 1170, and along which they returned in the darkness of the winter night after they had done their cruel work.

Saltwood Castle itself is not on Stone Street but two or three miles east of it, about a mile north of the town of Hythe. You leave Stone Street by the first turning to the left after passing Westenhanger Station. Whether the road is an ancient track or no I know not. It is pleasant with fair prospects. The country is made up of small hills ; on the tops and in the hollows are houses for the place becomes more and more populous. Then you pass Sandling Station and presently find yourself in the village of Saltwood, which has grown much of late years. Passing through, leave the church on the left and unexpectedly you pop upon the Castle. Centre of a natural amphitheatre, it nestles in the hollow of the hills. The Saltwood Brook runs through the grounds and the meadow stretches by its banks making what is called a " haugh " in the north. To the south the heights open to give you a glimpse of the sea. You are hard to please if you be not content with this for your place of abode ; others have thought so too, for in 1882 it was elaborately restored and no doubt possesses all the comforts of a modern residence. The restoration has been admirably done. As the outer wall is now complete I assume it patched up here and there, but it is so well that you do not distinguish the old from the new, not that the wall maintains its original height all round, but there is enough to enable you to gather exactly what it once was like. Those restorations are to the wanderer loss as well as gain ; he may or may not be glad that something is done to preserve an old building especially if it be done judiciously as here. Alas! the place is now shut for him. It were unreasonable to expect the inmates to open the gates at all hours to Tom, Dick and Harry ; do so, and life were scarce worth the living. If it be left ruin, you are allowed to wander over at your will, or a small tip smooths the way. True, Saltwood is shown during some months in the year, on Wednesday afternoons up to six o'clock, but I think it was not the month, and assuredly it was not Wednesday, and it was certainly after six o'clock.

I promenaded, no one objecting, the grounds, peered in at the gate, and circumnavigated the ancient pile, in short I saw as much as I cared to see, save that I missed the remains of the Hall. As for the room where the knights are said to have planned the murder in darkness, there could be no certainty of identification, even if the story be true. The knights, be it remembered, did not come of set purpose to murder Thomas; they may have contemplated his death under certain conditions, certainly not the deed of sacrilege in the transept. The spacious moat is now dry. It was of old fed from the Saltwood Brook which ran on my left. The principal gateway is sufficiently imposing; you see over it the arms of Archbishop Courtenay, who built the central portion at any rate. The thing I spied with most interest was a curious, little, furtive postern door in an angle of the wall on the west side, opening in the direction of the village. It was a quaint touch of human nature in the midst of a field of splendour. In old days many a youth of high or low degree crept through it at eventide, bent on some amorous intrigue with a village maiden; again, it let in secret messengers laden with dark affairs of state—at least you guess so, but the postern preserves its secrets! Sure it is the Knights did not come out this way, they assembled their followers in the spacious courtyard and came proudly marching through the main gateway and so across the winter hills to Stone Street and Canterbury. Yet the last look I gave to the castle was towards the quaint little postern.

Saltwood has an old history, nay some have put down its first beginning to the Romans! This may or may not be, there is no Roman work therein discoverable to-day. Some affirm that Oyse, King of Kent and son of Hengist, built or rebuilt it in 488. It was an early possession of the See of Canterbury. In St. Thomas's time it was held as we know by De Broc; the right to it being a subject of embittered controversy between Archbishop and Knight. After the martyrdom the Crown held it for some time, then King John in one of his pious fits gave it back to the See. It became a favourite residence of the Archbishops, though the castles and palaces of those great folk were so numerous that they could hardly give much attention to any one in particular. The great name here is that of Archbishop Courtenay, who was Primate from 1381 to 1396. Here he lived much, built much, worked much. Yet the most definite legend preserved is ridiculously trivial, albeit instructive. Some hay or straw had to be delivered at the Castle; the rustics brought it, not in carts " as ought to be done to an Archbishop, but slovenly in sacks on their horses' backs ". The uncourteous peasants were summoned to Saltwood, and were soundly rated by the Primate who assigned this penance: All were to march in procession, bare-legged, each with a sack of straw on his back, so open at the mouth that the straw might appear, to disgrace them for their disrespect. What a very important person your Archbishop once was, to be sure! To-day you may note an elderly clerical gentleman slip down to a railway station and take a ticket to Canterbury and thence walk or drive to the Cathedral without any state at all. Thus the Primate of all England now enters his cathedral city. Ah! but it was very different; long ago, an Archbishop was considered by himself and everybody else something very much out of the common, and looked at from that point of view the story is at least possible.

The Archbishops finally lost possession in some form of law for in 1536 Cranmer exchanged it with Henry VIII for other land. No doubt the Crown had the better of the bargain; however, it fell presently into private hands and so has continued. On 16 April, 1580, an earthquake shook down good part of the castle which lay more or less ruinous till restored as already set forth. Through all the years it has been a point of interest. In the *Gentleman's Magazine* for

December, 1802, a correspondent signing " Z. Cosens " unbosoms himself thus to the sympathetic Sylvanus Urban. " What veneration and awe thrilled through my veins to think I was about to ask admittance where monarchs had been sumptuously entertained and where some of our greatest prelates have lived in regal state."

When Z. Cousins enters the ruins of the great hall his note becomes even more enthusiastic. " And pleasing indeed must have been the view, whilst the venerable prelate was gracing the festive board, to have beheld the vast expanse of the encircling stream which, whilst it conveyed the idea of perfect security, added a charm to the surrounding landscape over whose plains and through whose enchanting glades the timid deer might be seen mantling her slender limbs in successive leaps from the eye of the intrusive traveller." After those eloquent words aught further were sheer anticlimax.

I have said that at the sea-end of Stone Street you turn a little to the right to find yourself presently in the ancient village of Lymne. It is ringed about with a collection of new dwellings which by contorted shape and strange name make a daring effort after the picturesque and charming. They miserably fail! you will not find them worth a second look. Lymne itself is composed of old but not strikingly old houses, though it contains two fine specimens both on the left hand of the principal street. The village is delightfully placed on the edge of the cliff. Here is a little church with a square impressive tower, and cheek by jowl with it stands the old house called Lymne Castle. Peering over the edge you see, half-way down the slope, huge formless masses of masonry scattered over a wide area. Other masses are concealed in the woodland or the hollows. From the mounds and hillocks everywhere you infer that there must be more fragments under the ground masked by the turf or by some depth of earth. At the base of the slope is the great plain known as the Level of Romney Marsh, and then still farther out is the sea, higher than the level of the marsh, wherefrom it is held off by huge embankments of sea-wall, some parts of which are very old indeed. The stone fragments proclaim themselves for Roman work. Here is a ruined stronghold of the imperial race now known as Studfall Castle or the fallen or ruined place.

The picture from the top was beautiful and striking, but it gave me no clear impression. I crept down by a steep road, crossed the Military Canal and so on to the marsh. I halted where the road branches off to Dymchurch : thence I fancied I was able to trace out the outline of the fortification. There are great gaps on three sides ; you gather those were walls ; the fourth was open to the sea or the port, there it was sufficiently defended ; naturally you are guided by the analogy of Richborough, though that last is much smaller whilst much more complete. From my standpoint I had the view in reverse order ; I was on the plain above which were the ancient remains of Studfall Castle and above that again the church and the houses of Lymne perched on the cliff. Down the winding road I came, were queer little dwellings of brick and wood, puny things beside the huge blocks that lay a little way off ; at one part of the road a large modern country house was in process of erection ; sheep were peaceably feeding amidst the blocks, the cuckoo was calling from every thicket its strange mocking call which had rang in my ears all the way along Stone Street, and ceased not amid the Roman ruins. The bells of Lymne Church were calling to morning service. The worship they celebrated was scarce older than the ruined Roman stronghold.

The church itself has a more intimate connection with those remains, for Lanfranc, they say, took therefrom the materials wherewith to build it. Perhaps

THE PATH OF THE KNIGHTS

those same materials supplied the original walls of Lymne Castle beside it. That castle was said first of all to be a Norman watch tower and then it was the house of the Archdeacon of Canterbury. Later it was a farm and now a rich man has swooped down thereon. It lies wellnigh hidden away amid a crowd of new buildings which contain all that can satiate the rich man's fancy. I had scarce seen it at all but the postern of the huge gate stood open, so I caught a glimpse of the old house behind. You assume it restored perfectly, the partitions and so forth run up by the farmer-folk judiciously removed, but as farm-house it retained its old look, not much altered and you roamed about it very much at your ease. I wish the rich man had gone elsewhere. Over the great gate was a very new coat of arms engraved in stone, a ship and the motto *Deus dabit vela*. I pleased myself with giving many various meanings to the simple Latin phrase. You must console yourself with the reflection that the original ancient house is there, however hidden away, and that all about it is very well looked after.

I crept up from the marsh level by a road if possible steeper than the other, finding a childish pleasure in touching some of the blocks as I passed, admiring a piece of tower here and there. Finally I emerged on the top near the Post Office and betook me to my original station, at the edge of the churchyard. Of course the ancient foreshore wherever you look is now dry land, but you can trace it eastward, it is said, as far as Hythe, though I confess I failed to do so. Not merely has the sea receded and then been banked out, but all sorts of other changes have taken place. The River Lymne or Lemanis, it is supposed, joined the sea about here, but it has wildly altered its course and now discharges at Rye, that is if it be indeed the Rother.

If you want to know all that can be known of Lymne and its antiquities you must consult the learned work of the late Charles Roach Smith, published in 1850, but since then the world has changed a good deal, and when the author talks of "its lone aspect at the present day, its isolation from highways and byeways," you remember that it is over sixty years ago; the place now strikes you as anything but isolated.

It was only at the close of the Pilgrimage that the critical spirit began to apply itself to antiquities. Hitherto men gazed at them in stupid wonder. John Leland, almost our first antiquary, was of the time of Henry VIII; this is how he speaks of it: "Ther remayneth at this day the ruines of a stronge fortresse of the Britons hangging on the hil, and cummyng down to the very fote. The cumpase of the fortresse semeth to be a X acres & belykelyhod yt had sum walle beside that streechid up to the very top of the hille. Wher now ys the paroch chirche & the archidiacons house of Cantorbury . . . About this castel yn tyme of mind were fownd antiquities of mony of the Romaynes."

Dr. Stukeley, that learned if not altogether judicious antiquary, has some interesting notes on the place in 1722; he is struck with the manner in which those "prodigious parcels" had been cracked and broken and tossed about "as if Time was in a merry humour and ruined it for sport; but I believe it was the effect of design and much labour"; yet the "impenetrable solidity of the mortar" had held much of it together. Its ruin is largely due to landslips. How can even Roman work stand out against the forces of nature?

I have wandered a little it may be from my allotted path to tell of the wonders of Studfall, but be it remembered that Stone Street was one of the ancient ways to Canterbury; along it also bands of Pilgrims progressed to the sacred city. I note in conclusion that a mile to the west of Lymne is the hamlet of Court-at-Street, where is the ruined chapel at which Elizabeth Barton, the "Nun of Kent," some time an inmate of the Priory of St. Sepulchre at Canterbury, made those strange revelations which foreshadowed the last struggle for the old order of things.

CHAPTER XVII

THE WINCHESTER ROAD

"The Pilgrims' Way"—The Old Road—The Course It Would Take—Dread of the Forest and the Swamp—Along the Hill Slope—Roman Influence—Heathen and Christian—The Rise of the Pilgrimage—Relative Importance of the Ways—Some Writers on the Subject—Far-fetched Theories.

I HAVE spoken of the various tracks by which the Pilgrims made for Canterbury. One chief road remains. At first it might seem the greatest of all because it is known emphatically as The Pilgrims' Way. It is still called so in the common talk of the various districts through which it passes. It is not complete, but huge fragments of it exist and you are usually able to trace the parts between. One thing has given it prominence; it is by far the most picturesque of all the routes, secluded and beautiful, it is now rarely trodden save by the local peasant or the vagrant wanderer. Of late, owing to the keener interest which an always more educated community takes in its past, it has entered into the World of Letters at any rate, but this cannot materially increase the number of those who use it. The ordinary theory of this road is as follows: A number of people came from the south-east of the Continent as Pilgrims; they crossed the Straits to Southampton, thence proceeded to Winchester. Here they were met by men from the west of England and parts of Wales and Ireland, the whole band then proceeded to Canterbury along this path, which became in time known as the Pilgrims' Way.

This is true enough, but it is only a small part of the truth. It has long been recognised that, ages be-

KIT'S COTY'S HOUSE

fore St. Thomas, this road was in existence as a great main way running between the west and east of England. It seems probable that in very early days the chief English road lay east to west and not north to south. The Thames made a natural division. The Continent, with which there was always some important communication, was for a good space roughly in line with the south coast. Remember that all the great invasions of England were south of the Thames. Another thing makes us think that the south of England was the most important part of the island. Those mysterious remains known as megalithic are there the most important. Accident has fixed one great mass not very far from Canterbury, another not very far from Winchester. The first is represented by Kits Coity House, with the subsidiary groups at Addington and Coldrum; the second by Old Sarum, Stonehenge and Avebury. Old Sarum, it is believed, is the antique British capital, and the mammoth masses of stone connected with it were developments or copies on a grander scale of those important though less mighty masses in Kent in the valley of the Medway. Sure enough a road ran between them, which road would be continued westward at any rate. No doubt there were minor roads, branching off here and again.

The late Mr. Grant Allen, basing on the well-known historic fact that the Phœnicians obtained metal from South-West Britain, urged that tin was borne along this way from the far West to the far East for shipment, so he called it "the tin road". Assuming this road, we ask what course would it take? Here I am only concerned with it after Winchester, but apart from St. Thomas why should it run between Winchester and Canterbury? Mr. Hilaire Belloc, who is an authority on the subject, has pointed out that there were various Kentish ports of almost equal importance for which some inland town was required as a common centre. This centre might have been in various places in the Canterbury district, but Canterbury had advantages, geographical or fortuitous, that gave it the pre-eminence; things of a like nature gave Winchester the chief place in another direction.

In feeling after the probable course we begin by large exclusions. Great part of the south-eastern district was covered by the Forest of Anderida, dark, dismal, sometimes impenetrable, full of wild beasts in fact, and of evil demons in fancy. The road would leave this alone; again the marshy ground of the valleys was to be avoided, as difficult if not impassable. Over a great part of this way there runs that great mass of hills called the Downs; their low heights of chalk are often very beautiful, though that in this connection does not count. How were it to march upon the top of those hills? Obviously "No," for there you would be exposed to wind and weather, you would have to go endlessly up and down, since the heights are not level. There would be constant difficulty about food and water, especially water; for if you had too much on the stagnant plain, you had not enough up there; besides, in early days every man's hand was against that of his fellow; there on the top you were a conspicuous object for all your foes, that is for the remainder of the human species in the part where you happened to be. The plain had dangers of the same kind. There the folk of the district dwelt, there you were always liable to sudden attack.

There remains the hill-side, where Nature had already provided something of a path. It is characteristic of the North Downs that they rise gradually from the flat plain up to a point, and thence get suddenly steeper. The junction of the two slopes was the very place for the road, and there it was. That this is also the choice way through the land is an accident. Trees came to line this road by chance or design,—yew trees it is usually

THE WINCHESTER ROAD

said, but in the parts I have myself trodden I have not found the yew predominant. To-day this line of trees touches the route with mystery and romance. I have often sat to watch the line drawn along the hill-side, something hinting at the life of man, but not the life of to-day, for it was away from the fields and any visible use.

The road naturally took the south slope of the hills. In our cold damp climate we treasure up our scanty supply of sunlight, both for heat and dryness. Here the little maximum was attained. I doubt if the importance of dryness is generally appreciated; it is incredible how little most of us know of anything like natural conditions, we are so used to our roads that some of us pass our whole lives without ever straying from them. To know what a cart-track can become in even a moderate rainfall is a new experience; it is impassable in the strictest sense of the term.

How long the ancient British polity lasted can only be matter of conjecture. At length the Romans came to inaugurate a system of road-making which put old conditions to defiance. Roman work not only strikes you with admiration but with awe and a certain touch of terror. There was a direct brutality about their methods, a serene and sovereign contempt of obstacles and dangers, a proud consciousness that they were building for all time. At this very day I suppose the most solid masonry existing in Britain is in the walls of Verulamium or Richborough and the firm structure of roads like Stone Street. This particular primitive track did not suit them as a whole; so it is supposed to have gone largely out of use; not altogether, indeed, for the Roman civilisation never resulted in the complete culture of the Island. The time came for the strangers to go, whereupon things swang back more or less into their primitive conditions. I say nothing of the centuries of anarchy, but when the

Saxon tribes had finally conquered Britain and submitted in their turn to Christianity, there came some sort of settled government in however rude a form. To the legendary King Arthur there succeeded the real King Alfred ; also the enthusiasm of Pilgrimage arose. It is well to remember, however, the Canterbury Pilgrimage was only one, though it came to be by far the greatest in England. Winchester itself, where was the shrine of St. Swithun, was an important centre two centuries before the period of St. Thomas. It was obvious that people from the west of England would use this old direct road to Canterbury, and that they would be here joined by those foreign Pilgrims who came by way of Southampton. Winchester, which was the old capital of England and always an important city, was marked out as the place where the tide first took volume and bulk.

Wherever the Pilgrims passed, they were prominent, sometimes revered, sometimes dreaded, always noteworthy. It was worth while for both priest and merchant to seek the patronage of the more wealthy, of whom there was a good number. Charity was then the first and most sacred of all duties, and to be charitable required a provision of houses and food; very few were found to cavil at those vagrant paupers and say to them, "Why not stay at home and work?" Once Archbishop Sudbury addressed a band in some such fashion, to the loudly expressed horror of those who listened; so that when Jack Cade struck off his head (1381) he was judged rightly served. In the early years when the martyrdom of St. Thomas was fresh in all men's minds one great Pilgrim had gone the Winchester way; a man so great that during Becket's life he was Becket's master, and even in Becket's own eyes would have seemed much greater than any mere priest,—that Pilgrim was Henry II.

Does it seem strange then that the road was called *the* Pilgrims' Way?

To-day, the fame of the way or its fragments is in one respect so great that it tends in popular fancy to obliterate the other routes. Many have a vague idea that every Pilgrim who went to the shrine went this route. The truth is quite the opposite, I think this was by far the least important. It was neither the way by which great folk nor the multitude went. Some took it naturally, for it suited them, but the vast majority followed the London Road. Along this Pilgrims' Way there are few traces of the Pilgrims. In following the road from London we have seen how frequent, how almost incessant, is the line of hospitals and shrines, and houses and places directly connected with the cult of St. Thomas. There is nothing of that on any other road. The writers on this route " pray in aid " desperate expedients to magnify its importance, but all their conjectures do not get beyond a "perhaps". Thus fairs were held over all England, and so at the towns near the route—which indeed avoids the towns themselves. Remember the two festivals of St. Thomas every year. The day of his martyrdom was 29 December. and the Translation of the Relics on 7 July, so that if a fair happened six or seven weeks before or after either of those dates it was put down to the crowd going or returning. Again, parish churches on the way are called Pilgrims' churches, why I know not! Words are curiously twisted; nay! you smoke the sham archaic occasionally; now and again, a Pilgrims' house seems of later origin than the Pilgrimage, and only so called because it was built on the Pilgrims' Way!

No doubt there are memorials of St. Thomas on it, but he was worshipped all over England; nay! as we have seen in Scotland, and in fact in all Christendom, so that the wonder would be were it otherwise. After every legitimate deduction something remains, but it is wonderfully little, and both from that and the historical fact that the names of well-known characters are wanting, I conclude that, though undoubtedly this was a Pilgrims' way, it was only so in a minor sense; I propose, however, to give it some brief consideration and examine such relics connected with the Pilgrimage as it can show forth.

The Pilgrims' Way generally followed the track of the old road, but it did not do so rigidly or slavishly. Considerations to which the old travellers were not subject deflected it from time to time; here it went south to visit a shrine, there it went north to pass nearer a town, and so forth. Mr. Belloc in the *Old Road* professes to trace the way, that is the original way from Winchester to Canterbury; he does so with amazing confidence, for he is nothing if not cocksure. It is scarce likely that he is in every case successful, but he tramped the route himself, trespassing, and using boats and so forth in a most amusing manner. He makes out a very good case, and is not the less trustworthy because he writes exceeding well. He points out the deviations and perhaps the areas of most value, also, as it is the old road he is tracing, he has no temptation to drag in forced references to the Pilgrims, nor is he compelled to twist the facts to magnify the importance of a Pilgrim route. Mrs. Ady has written a very well-known work on *The Pilgrims' Way*, but she is obsessed by the idea of making everything fit into the theory which seems to me untenable that this was the main route to the shrine. Now it is a certain fact that many Pilgrims made part of their journey by water. Some thus travelled from London to Gravesend, whilst others from the north side of the Thames crossed over at the ferry here. All this is sure enough, but it is ridiculous to suppose that having done this they proceeded across country until they struck the Winchester route; to do so, they needs must cross twice the direct route from London to Canterbury, which undoubtedly dividing at Dartford, only united again at Strood, before crossing the Medway into Rochester. This may have been done for some special purpose in one or two cases, but it is impossible to believe it common practice. Finally, Mr. Albert Wray in his *Canterbury Pilgrimages* has reconstructed, so to speak, the actual adventures of a party of Pilgrims by the ancient road. He has filled in the details from authentic sources, and has achieved an interesting and instructive narrative.

CHAPTER XVIII

THE WINCHESTER ROAD (*continued*)

St. Swithun — The Fame of Winchester — Its Sights and Shows — Its Memorials of St. Thomas—The Banks of the Itchin—Legend of the Tichborne Dole—An Early Adventure of Edward I—Problem of the Hog's Back—Through the Villages—The Pilgrim, the Beggar, and the Robber—St. Catherine's and St. Martha's—From the Wey to the Mole—Reigate and the Heights Above It—The Kent Border.

WE start our present journey from Winchester as a common meeting-place. It was hallowed by the memory of St. Swithun, whose name is ludicrously connected in the modern mind with excessive rainfall. He was Bishop of Winchester between 852 and 862 when he died in the odour of sanctity and good works. He was buried by his own directions outside of and to the north of the Cathedral as the least favoured spot in the precincts. His fame ever growing in the century after his death, he was duly canonised, and his relics translated to a shrine within the fane. The date fixed for this was 15 July, but it was delayed by excessive rains supposed to signify the humble protest of the modest Saint against those posthumous honours. We know how precious an asset such relics were, the monks would not be denied, and at length had him safely housed in the sacred building. Hence the legend that if it rain on 15 July it will rain for forty days after. The shrine attained to great renown, as many miracles were wrought thereat. When we read of the Pilgrims' door by which the pious travellers were admitted to the north transept, and the Guestan Hall where they were entertained, and the rations that were served out, we must picture them as Pilgrims of St. Swithun, not of St. Thomas. Obviously there was nothing to prevent those who began with St. Swithun and Winchester, or some less famous Saint and more distant locality, finishing with St. Thomas and Canterbury.

Winchester, as we all know, is a very ancient and a very famous city. Till the time of Henry II it might count itself capital of England. Afterwards London asserted its supremacy, so that our Babylon rose with the Canterbury Pilgrimage. Most of us have wandered through the ancient city on the Itchin, have admired its Cathedral, have taken the traveller's dole of bread and beer at the Hospital of St. Cross, though we had to go a mile beyond its walls for this. We have lamented the brutal destruction of Hyde Abbey, a destruction that did not spare the sacred dust of Alfred the Great, a destruction scarce atoned for by the splendid statue of that monarch which now adorns the town! We have gazed on the Round Table suspended in the Castle Hall; a sham antique, it is true, but so old as to be in itself a genuine curio. Winchester is, in short, wellnigh as fascinating as Canterbury, but here I deal only with the St. Thomas legend.

The Cathedral Library contains a life of St. Thomas written in medieval Latin. Among much else it tells the story of a monk imprisoned in Hyde Monastery, who having escaped by help of our Saint, forthwith proceeded to Canterbury where he offered up the reins of his fetters with a suitable inscription, which you believe said some cutting things about his ecclesiastical superiors. Probably his imprisonment was deserved, but that only shows the value of our Saint's helping hand. In Winchester College, for which all succeeding generations have thanked William of Wykeham, there is still preserved an MS. containing the legend of St. Thomas, deposited here by the founder, who held our Saint in special reverence. In the Church of St. Cross there was a chapel dedicated to Thomas, on the walls whereof are the remains of frescoes depicting scenes in his life. In the early English Church of St. John the Baptist, there was on the north side of the altar a representation of the martyrdom. The chapel of the castle was dedicated to St. Thomas the Martyr. A church dedicated to St. Thomas is still one of the parish churches of Winchester, true it is a modern building, but it replaces a much older edifice dating from about the reign of Richard I, which was pulled down in 1846.

In this connection, I may note, there was also a chapel to St. Thomas in Portsmouth, but then he was venerated all over the kingdom. Winchester, like Canterbury, was at one time crowded with churches; here, as at Canterbury, their number has been continually reduced, though according to our modern ideas the survivors are sufficiently plentiful. The memorials of St. Thomas do not strike you as excessive; there is nothing in any of them specially connected with the passing Pilgrim.

The Pilgrim setting out on his journey of a hundred and twenty miles would leave Winchester by the North Gate. He would pass by Hyde Abbey, of which there are now but shadowy remains, for some time following the course of the Itchin through Arlesford and so on to Alton. Of Arlesford it is only to be noted that it has been burned down an unconscionable number of times. All this country is historic ground, full of memories of old battles and old legends; here be two for sample. Near Arlesford is Tichborne Park, where abide the ancient family of Tichborne, most widely known in recent years from the strange story of the claimant, but the legend the Pilgrims heard was that of the Tichborne dole. In the time of Henry I, Sir Roger was the Tichborne in possession, a knight of like metal with that Earl of Coventry who taxed the ancient burghers almost to desperation till they were relieved by the Lady Godiva's quaint procession. Isabella, Lady Tichborne craved likewise a boon from her husband as she lay stricken beyond hope of cure—let him give her land sufficient to provide a dole of bread for the poor. Sir Roger thought that enough of his estate had already gone in charity, so he attempted to get rid of the request by an ill-timed practical joke. He seized a burning brand from the spacious hearth. He would give her all the soil which she could walk round while the brand was still aflame. To his wonder her will conquered her weakness; getting out of bed she crawled quite a long round, and then sank down exhausted and helpless. Hence the piece of ground named " Lady Tichborne's Crawles," and the dole of bread through the centuries, still distributed among the virtuous, deserving poor of those parts.

The scene of our other legend is farther on, in a dell, as it is somewhat vaguely put, between Alton and Farnham. When Edward I was as yet merely prince, he learned that one Adam Gurdon, a follower of Simon de Montfort, outlawed after the battle of Evesham, had established himself on the country-side, and was levying contributions on the enemy, in other words playing the part of an early highwayman. Edward sped thither from Winchester, sought and found Adam, to whom he suggested single combat; they went at it tooth and nail for ever so long. Pausing to breathe, Edward suggested to Adam that it would be better that he should surrender on terms, which no doubt it was, since the fight, whatever its immediate result, could scarce bring any good to the bold outlaw. The proposal being accepted the prince sent him off to Guildford to lay himself as captive at the feet of the Queen Mother, who was naturally much gratified at this proof of her son's prowess. Adam apparently gave a judicious version of the combat, at any rate he was high in Edward's favour ever after. Those stories are all very well, *c'est magnifique, mais c'est n'est pas la guerre*, or at any rate the Pilgrimage, and the only connection possible to establish between them is that such legends of the country-side were told to solace the tedium of the journey.

Between Arlesford and Alton the Pilgrims are supposed to have gone round Ropley, near which there is an ancient farm-house called "Pilgrims' Place," a faint indication that we are on the right track. After Alton, we follow the River Wey which we touch on and off till we reach Guildford. It is desperately suggested that the Wey was originally called the Way, because it ran by the Pilgrims' Way; as quaint an example of the far-fetched as you shall anywhere discover.

After Farnham is the beginning of that rise in the land called the Hog's Back, over which the main portion of the road between Farnham and Guildford now runs. Coming from Guildford you would naturally follow it, because having ascended the height you have a clear run down to Farnham, some five or six miles. The old road, and in this for the most part the Pilgrims followed it, adhered as usual to the hill slope to the south.

The parting of the ways is at Whiteway End, a mile or two east of Farnham. Hereby are the remains of the Cistercian Abbey of Waverley, which in its palmy days entertained such Pilgrims as passed by the gates. From here Scott derived the title-name for his romantic series of novels, though that is another pair of sleeves altogether. It is more relevant to mention that long after the Pilgrimage certain things came into being which did something to preserve the Old Way. When the world demanded better roads, turn-pikes arose; you had to pay if you used them, and many, for such is human nature, took special delight in dodging the collectors. The turnpike ran along the Hog's Back, and drovers and others preferred to turn to the right at Whiteways, and so escape the toll. It might or might not be convenient, but it was certainly cheaper. Mr. Belloc in discussing the causes of the preservation of the old road, treats this as of considerable importance. I think he makes too much of so modern and so temporary a phase. Another theory has been put forth as to the road here. It is suggested there were alternative routes, that the Pilgrims took the lower road in summer, and the higher in winter because it was drier. I think it more like that in those early days the summit of the Hog's Back was left severely alone.

Here we go by the low road, that is at Whiteways we take the right hand, and pass through Seal, Puttenham, and Compton, a delightful series of villages. Compton has been justly described as " exquisite ". You come on suggestive names. There is Beggar's Corner and Robber or Roamer's Moor, and a manor house of some three centuries named Shoelands which (thus Mrs. Ady) " is said to take its name from the word 'Shool,' which in some dialects is the same meaning as to beg ". Let us for the sake of argument grant the etymology, and even the Roamer, though it is probably the archaic local pronunciation of robber, but then what has all this to do with the Pilgrims? The beggar is not altogether an unknown figure even in our own enlightened day. In the times of which we speak he was the common object of the sea and every other shore, he was encouraged rather than repressed, and if many Pilgrims begged so did every manner of wayfarer. I should be grieved to think of our Pilgrims as robbers; we have always had the robber with us; then he was very inadequately repressed. We do not require to turn to Shakespeare's *Henry IV* or the traditions of Gad's Hill to learn that he considered Pilgrims fair game, but not more so than any other traveller. Of old times he specially affected heaths and woods and moors, and "Shoelands," at the best, cannot prove more than "Beggar's Corner".

As you get near Guildford, you come to St. Catherine's Hill, surmounted by the picturesque ruins of St. Catherine's Chapel; you cross the Wey, which you are now preparing to leave by St. Catherine's, otherwise the Pilgrims' Ferry, and on the other side is St. Martha's, which likewise picturesquely crowns *its* hill. These two chapels are the most striking things about Guildford, delightful town though it be, for they touch all the land round with the spell of dignified ancient romance and devotion. If they were not in the first place due to the Pilgrimage, that at least contributed to their support and upkeep. To win a summit and pray at the shrine on the top, whether that be penance or pleasure, was the very thing to attract the Pilgrim mind.

St. Catherine's Hill was of old known as Drake Hill. Hereon was a heathen temple with an altar devoted to the worship of the sun. It was the wise practice of the early Church to fix the shrines of the new faith on the sacred ground of the old, so it purified and sanctified the soil, it transferred the feeling of devotion already existing to a more worthy object. St. Catherine's has long been ruinous, but you will find it worth while to climb to the top—for its prospect, still more for its memories. As for St. Martha's, that also was a ruin and a very complete one, since, as we know from numerous prints, there was extremely little of it left standing. It was "restored" or practically rebuilt in 1848, and service is now held there at frequent intervals. In the old church a new chancel was built for the use of Pilgrims and consecrated to St. Thomas in 1186; also in the neighbourhood memorials connected with the Saint or his Pilgrims are not rare. Thus at East Clandon a church was built and dedicated to St. Thomas. Guildford itself had a pest-house at the top of Spital Street called St. Thomas's Hospital. Also on St. Catherine's Hill a fair was held for five days in September. Shalford, to which you cross by St. Catherine's Ferry, had also its fair in August expressly called Becket's fair. Moreover Chantry Woods, by St. Martha's, has at least an ecclesiastical sound!

To the Wey succeeds the Mole, which the road crossed near Burford Bridge past Dorking. I once deemed the way between Guildford and Dorking the prettiest in England, but of late years it is too much built on and there is the ever-increasing motor traffic. The Pilgrims' road, which winds along the hillside, is still remote, secluded, lovely. At Burford there are memories of a Pilgrim's Chapel, also Paternoster Lane and Friary Meadows are places alleged of this neighbourhood, thus hinting at Church and it may be Pilgrim affairs. Of the more modern associations of Burford Bridge, of "Nelson and his Emma," George Meredith, R. L. S., it would certainly be irrelevant and perhaps profane to speak; but one literary association may be permitted. John Bunyan, as travelling tinker, perambulated the country between here and Guildford. Various houses or their sites are even yet pointed out as places of his occasional abode. It has been ingeniously suggested that the name of his great work may have been inspired by the thoughts of his own steps on the Pilgrims' Way; assuredly it is not difficult to find local parallels for "Vanity Fair," "The Slough of Despond" and the "Delectable Mountains".

At Reigate the road passes high above the town, in fact is carried by a bridge over the London Way very near the top of Reigate Hill. If you have ascended or descended that summit you have noticed the suspension bridge. Perhaps your first impression was like my own, that it was a connecting link between private grounds dissevered by the road. In fact the London Way once went right over the hill, at the top, where it was cut by this ancient track. The cutting was made about a century ago to ease the steepness of the ascent for tender-footed wayfarers, whilst the bridge preserved the line of the crossway.

When the Pilgrims descended on Reigate, as no doubt they did for rest and food, they found a chapel to St. Thomas right in the middle of the street. We know it was a curious medieval practice to stick down chapels in this fashion. Perhaps you have wondered why the Town Hall is at Reigate placed in like manner. It more or less conveniently occupies the site of the Chapel. The way proceeds through Gatton Park, where we do not follow it, nor can we narrate the history of the ancient borough, such a cockshy for reformers. Its much-famed rottenness is at least of quite respectable antiquity, almost going back to the days of the Pilgrimage, since the records *temp.* 1541 bear witness that Sir Roger Copley, Knight, being in that year burgess and only inhabitant of the borough and town of Gatton, elected two M.P.'s for said borough and town in effect to represent himself! A little way on is Merstham, and here there was once wall-paintings on the church representing the death of St. Thomas, but they vanished as the result of a tolerably modern restoration. There is still a Pilgrim's Lane. Near Godstone there is Palmer's Wood, and Oxted parish has its St. Thomas's well. At Titsey there is a farm-house called Pilgrim's Lodge, but here as elsewhere the name may very well be a late one, the house so named not for that it entertained Pilgrims but because it was built on the way whereform they had vanished! The road once ran through Chevening Park, for which presumption it was extinguished by an Act of Parliament in the eighteenth century, a time when old commons and old ways were devoured wholesale. We are now in Kent, wherein we move to changes of scenes.

CHAPTER XIX

THE WINCHESTER ROAD (*concluded*)

Otford and its Palace—Legends of St. Thomas—The Nightingale Goes and Comes—St. Edith's Well at Kemsing—A Characteristic Piece of the Way—The Wrotham Hills—Solitude of the Byways—The Holy Land of Old Britain—Megalithic Monuments—Addington and Trottiscliffe—The Stones at Coldrum—The Long Line of Trees—Kits Coity House—" A Field of Antiquity "—The Last Stand against the Invader—Treasure Hunting—Along the Pilgrims' Way—A Night Encampment—The Ford over the Medway—Boxley Abbey and its " Sotelties "—Pennenden Heath—The Wonder of Charing Church—Exquisite Chilham—The Fort in Bigberry Wood—Cut-Throat Lane.

WE are now in the valley of the Darent, which river at an earlier stage of our subject, but at a later of its course, we passed at Dartford. The first place of importance is Otford; here was a Palace of the Archbishops of Canterbury of which there are still some remains; we shall meet others at Wrotham and Charing. In their time, they were sufficiently important. The name Palace is a little confusing. No doubt the old-time Archbishop of Canterbury was a mighty person, but what did he do with such superfluity of Palaces throughout Kent and elsewhere? The explanation is that he possessed a number of manors; the Manor House was also his. Because it was the house of a bishop it was called "palace". When he went from Lambeth to Canterbury he could lodge each evening, himself and his retainers, in his own house or palace. I doubt if he reserved a place for wandering Pilgrims. He had an official connection with these; also some of the Archbishops at least provided hostelries for their entertainment. I find no recognised or even asserted right they had to be his guests.

Otford was a favourite with St. Thomas. Two legends of him hang about it, one an example of the monkish, the other of the popular. A spring of water is still called St. Thomas's Well. Finding the place ill-supplied with that necessary fluid, he benevolently struck the ground with his staff, a spring forthwith welled forth and continues there to this day—that is monkish. The other shows him bent over his book in study or devotion; he is unseasonably disturbed by the strains of a nightingale from a near thicket, whereupon he banishes this particular bird from Otford. According to Lambard in his entertaining *Perambulation of Kent*, it returned after the end of the Pilgrimage. I fear it is like to be banished again by the continual increase of population. Philomela is driven farther back year by year!

At Kemsing, by the way, there is another well; this is St. Edith's. The water had miraculous power. Some averred it conquered barrenness, others that it relieved sore eyes, but no one tries it for either nowadays. The well was set in order some time ago after a long period of neglect. It is built about with what you might easily mistake for a shrine were you not aware that such things are now gone from our land. Alas, it again looked a little forlorn and neglected when I stopped by its waters about a year ago!

Wrotham is the next landmark. Mr. Belloc has pointed out that the tract between Otford and Wrotham is an excellent example of the changes to which the original way is subject. From Otford to near Kemsing it is recognised highway and has that quite commonplace air which the road of daily traffic needs must have. Then it continues on towards Wrotham on the bend of the hillside, whilst below it through Kemsing, Heaverham, St. Clere, and so on to Yaldham the modern road runs a little way down. At Yaldham the old road parts company with the new; it goes straight on whilst the other bends to the right and enters Wrotham just below the village.

On one occasion I followed the old way in muddy weather. It got worse and worse and at last became a footway between thick hedges. It is characteristic of the most disused parts that the hedges almost touch, and you have to force your way through as if your path were to the castle of the Sleeping Beauty. Ah, but you tread a way, not one, but many centuries old. Sure, there is something inspiring in the thought! As you get near Wrotham the suburbs, which every little village in Kent seems now taking to itself, become thicker and thicker, and the path becomes quite clear, well trodden, and fairly broad. Then you cross the high-road between Wrotham and London, some way above Wrotham, and a little after the highway from Wrotham to Gravesend and proceed farther on the slope of the hill. So you advance into the valley of the Medway. You have found the walk between Otford and Wrotham on the slope of the chalk hills very charming; if you mount those hills by any of the numerous side roads, you discover new scenes of beauty at every step. Even in crowded Kent the land on the heights is almost deserted and you may travel a mile or two without meeting a human being. Of late there is a change. Wealthy people have built huge mansions in one valley after another, and the process is likely to go on in the years to come.

The district we are now entering is bounded, roughly speaking, by a continuation of the chalk hills to the north-east, until these reach the Medway, to the west by the road to Wrotham and Wrotham Heath, to the south by the way to Maidstone, and to the east by the road from Maidstone towards Rochester; or you might more generally describe it as the space marked out by the Wrotham Hills stretching between Wrotham and the Medway in an irregular semi-circle, to which the road between Wrotham and Maidstone supplies a chord. That space is the Holy Land of Old Britain; here were the temples of her gods, the graves of her chiefs, the scene of her last struggle against the Saxon. Most of this you dimly guess for the monuments are prehistoric. We have not their original authentic names. It will always be matter of controversy what in reality they are, what in reality they mean; it is but some ten miles long from east to west, and three from north to south, little changed in essentials for centuries. I set down some jottings of a day's wandering, enriched, however, with experience of many other days.

I first made for Addington, as quaint and neat a little village as you will find in all Kent. So it will seem if you take a humble seat on the bench of the ancient village inn—"The Angel," to wit. Before you is the Green set round with old houses buried in their gardens and their flowers. The children must be at school for there is no sound save the rustle of the leaves in the great elm, and the soft cooing of the doves from the roofs. To the left is a gateway to a park, by which is a superb peacock, spreading the glittering honours of his tail in the sunlight, profoundly assured that he is monarch of all he surveys.

The park with its turf and its trees is fit casket for one of the stately homes of England and the ancient church that stands beside it, but it holds something still more rare, precious, and antique, for if you proceed through its gates you soon come on your right to that confused mass of huge stones known as the Cromlech in Addington Warren, of which there are many old records. It is mentioned by Leland and Stow and Camden and Lambard and everybody who has written about Kent from the time of the Tudors downward, but then the old writers were just as much at sea as you are, for their theories and explanations are ingenious fantasies of the brain. What your eyes tell you is this. Here are twelve stones more or less, a few upright, others flat on the ground, others again tumbled down or bending over one another at various angles. It is as if huge giants had tossed them about in some wild pastime.

You leave the park to climb upwards and northwards towards the chalk hills where runs the Pilgrims' Way. Here is the village of Trottiscliffe. Trosley is the old local name preserved in the country dialect and on signboards. It is even more old-world than Addington, that latter has the gaiety and charm of the "merry England" of Elizabeth; here you might fancy yourself in an earlier Tudor reign. At the road whose corner is marked by a walnut tree you turn to the right. You pass Trosley Church mantled in ivy on the left, and mount a lonely road through the bare fields; a solitary oast-house is outlined against the sky on the near height. Beyond it you turn again towards the hills by a rude cart-track. Here is the farm of Coldrum, and here away from all abode of men is another heap of giant stones. Two stand erect on the brow of a small height. A friendly hand has thrust a billet of wood between, so that they fall not on one another. Perhaps the rest once stood on the height also, but before we have any note of them they had fallen down, and now lie in most admired disorder, covered with grass, thistles, meadow sweet, elderberry bushes, pink throstles—all the wild luxuriance of the fields. They are strange, uncouth, sombre, but with an alluring charm of their own. Lonely and mournful, they intimate not so much vanished lives as vanished races, the mystery of an utterly dead and gone world. It is the fairest spot in all Kent; rich, peaceful fields are around you, the chalk hills with their exquisite contours rise behind, part bare, part woodland. Just a little way above their base you note for miles the long line of trees that marks out the Pilgrims' Way.

I will not drag you from field to field in a hunt for other giant stones. You find some piled up by a lodge at the entrance of a country house, others lie among the woods on the hill, others again scattered at random in the fields. Those at Coldrum are the most striking. Six miles, almost in a straight line westward, is the well-known cromlech known as Kits Coity House in the woods above Aylesford—three huge upright stones and one laid on the top for cover. It is now guarded by a fence else perchance it were chipped away to nothing. I have seen Kits Coity House and Stonehenge ere either was fenced—the loss in dignity and impressiveness is almost incredible. In a field hard by are the stones called Countless, because however often you number them, the result must always be different. The legend is that all formed part of one great plan—an avenue lined with those mammoth blocks ran from Kits Coity House to Coldrum; it led to a rude temple or ancient place of burial.

Some have professed to trace this avenue through the Medway which runs by Aylesford. There is or was a ford, but since medieval times no one has used it, for the beautiful bridge has stood for centuries there, and though of late threatened with wanton destruction, the danger is for the time being warded off. Kent can still show this relic of a distant past. Beyond Kits Coity House, the chalk hills which have been broken by the river rise again in picturesque beauty, again their sides are rich with stones and mysterious chambers. Also an ancient chalk pit of great size makes a gash in their flanks that is seen from a great distance.

The Pilgrims' Way passes quite close to this famous cromlech; here too the speculative builder has of late set up his boards. The " Kits Coity House estate " may any day be marked out, and the place desecrated with a crowd of trim, smug villas. The name of this famous cromlech means, it is said, the Tomb in the Wood, but this is mere guess. It is the only one that has any name at all, since the others take the title from the place where they exist. Here is a " very field of antiquity," and the antiquity is not of one pattern. The Romans came and went, but they left their marks, remains of their homes, broken pieces of pottery, coins, are found in the fields. Here also they had cemeteries, for here are multitudes of their graves.

After their time, as we know, the Britons held out feebly against the Saxons, but they did show some fight, and here where lay the " ashes of their fathers and the temples of their gods," they made, as was natural, the most desperate stand. In 455 a last battle was fought at Aylesford. The leaders bear half mythical names—Hengist and Horsa for the Saxons, Vortigern for the Britons, but the stronger prevailed. " They fled like the wind," says the Saxon Chronicle gleefully. Both Horsa and Vortigern fell, and on a spot which the local antiquarian professes to identify, Hengist was acclaimed King of all Kent. Some would take Kits Coity House for the tomb of one leader, and the stones at Addington for that of the other, but this is guess-work.

The country folk are of course familiar with those stones, but I gathered nothing from their talk. They have solved very simply the purpose of excavations—it is a hunt for buried treasure. Once there was some digging at Addington. A local gamekeeper was pressed into the service of the explorers; he worked with lusty vigour till the close of day when he confessed to bitter disappointment. In a dream he had discovered a crock filled with gold, and now there was nothing! It is well for the peace of the country-side that nothing substantial has ever been found. Pity when the peasant neglects his garden and his cornfield for wild delvings among these mysterious stones.

Amidst so many antiques the Pilgrims' Way might seem comparatively modern until we remember that it marks the ancient road of the early folk.

I finished the day by tramping along that part of it that runs between Coldrum and Wrotham. A labourer directed me; he told me it was passable though I should find some trouble with my bicycle. However, I climbed up the slopes, and if the expedition was not without trouble it was instructive.

There was a house at the point of junction, a farm labourer's or gamekeeper's perhaps, and as the way was a road to this house it was fairly passable till I came to a path that descended to the plain below. After that it plainly served as a passage from field to field. Now and again a path to the right led straight up the hill.

A little farther on one of those paths ran both up and down, up to the "Vigo Inn," which stands at about the highest point of the hill, down to the village of Trottiscliffe. At this meeting of the ways once stood the "Kentish Drover's Inn," still marked on the maps though now a private house. I think it is called "Pilgrim's House" or some such name. The tenant or proprietor came out as I rested on the turf, and discussed the Pilgrims' Way with me. He was evidently an authority on the subject, so much so that I was minded to suggest that hospitality was the first duty of the keeper of a Pilgrim's house. Perhaps he was afraid of something of the kind, perhaps he had been thus caught on previous occasions. At any rate he took a somewhat abrupt leave and disappeared behind the gate of his dwelling which was incongruously kept fast closed!

I went on through the roughest way I had ever known; it was a very rustic wilderness, the trees met overhead, and kept it in shade, the grass was thick under foot, the clumps of briar hedges on either side touched, and 'twas hard to force a path. You would have sworn that no one had passed since the last Pilgrims save for one sign of human presence. Ever and again were traces of an old fire, the sign-mark of the temporary camp of wayfaring men. On such the settled rustic looks with little favour; right or wrong, he fears for his poultry-yard and his farm-yard; thus the wanderer seeks a lonely spot like this.

In the thickest of the waste as the twilight was fading I came upon a family so encamped. A young woman with black hair and black eyes, and cheeks so red as to seem splashed with paint, was bending over a cheerful wood fire that glowed bright against the coming darkness. The evening meal was toward; her companion was stretched at his ease on the grass, smoking. He greeted me with a certain woodland courtesy—something about the weather, I think, that engrossing topic to the wanderer. The camping gipsy, I note, always addresses the passer-by. In his theory he thus disarms suspicion and hostility. A good way off, as the road wound up a height, I caught the gleam of the fire and felt a little envious of this night camp under the summer stars. Then as I turned the shoulder of the hill, fair and square before me rose the church tower of Wrotham, and the Pilgrim's track passed into the King's highway.

I have already discussed the way before Wrotham, and the piece to Coldrum I have taken in the reverse order. I follow it now till it joins the road by the side of the Medway, where it exactly struck that river and how a ford was found are points keenly debated. At Lower Halling there is said to exist the remains of a Pilgrim's chapel. At least the lancet-shaped windows are yet extant in certain cottages. Here, too, was an undoubted ford; there was another at Cuxton farther down, and at Snodland farther up. Mr. Belloc discusses at length the claims of each, and decides in favour of Snodland as against the others, including Aylesford, but he is little concerned with the Pilgrims. He is following the ancient track he calls the *Old Road*. To the Pilgrims different conditions apply. They were bent for Canterbury, and one assumes wished to get there with as little trouble as possible. Hard to see why they should have forded the river at all! Cuxton is only three miles from Rochester and Rochester was on the main Pilgrim track. Also since Roman times there has been a bridge there, always in existence at any rate during the days of the Pilgrimage. A great many of them surely, if they followed the track so far, would here bend away to the left.

But they were set on praying at some particular shrine! Claims have been made for Boxley, but Boxley could not compare with Rochester as a centre of devout interest. Again, they might have turned to the right, crossed the river by the old medieval bridge at Aylesford, and so have gone on to Maidstone or joined again the old road. You undoubtedly find that old road across the river near Kits Coity House, continuing its course on the slope of the hill. The megalithic masses were of prime interest to the prehistoric folk. They were erected by the road or the road ran near them; that seems inevitable. The Pilgrims passed among them or some of them, and it would be of deep interest to know how they regarded them. We seem to have no memorial at all of what Catholic and medieval England thought of such things. Perhaps they excited as little curiosity as the natural features of the route, the hills and the fields and the woods were accepted as something in the order of nature, or did they appear as the monstrous creation of demons wherefrom the pious would avert their eyes and thoughts? All the mind of the time was absorbed by the Church, by mystic dreams, doctrines of the faith, the search for and worship of relics, by anything but prehistoric antiquities; at any rate if they gazed and wondered no echo has come down to us.

Boxley is to-day a pleasant village on the hills above Maidstone. There are still some remains of the famous Cistercian Abbey which formerly flourished there. It had at least two prodigies fit for the adoration of the pious wayfarer; moreover as the place lay directly on his route he must often have visited the "sotelties". One was a small image of St. Rumbold. The sinless in thought or deed raised it with ease, the wicked tugged at it in vain for it would not budge an inch. The Reformers were very scornful; they averred the monks by some simple mechanical contrivance fixed or released the image at will. Favour or cash, not virtue, was plainly stated as the efficient cause. Rumbold himself was a royal youth of Saxon origin, who only lived three days. He proclaimed himself a Christian the moment of his birth; he spent his short life in explaining the mysteries of the Trinity to his thick-witted countrymen. Sure the most atrocious specimen of the infant prig ever presented to the attention of the world. How pleased you are that the fates gave him an end so speedy!

The second wonder was the famous Rood of Grace. The lips and eyes of the figure moved upon occasion; it had a very miraculous history for which I have no space. A somewhat similar explanation was given of its movements. Henry VIII's Commissioners exhibited the marvel in the Market Place at Maidstone, making great play of the rude devices, but then Henry VIII's Commissioners were employed to spy out the very worst things in the religious houses. Their professions seem to us every whit as odious as those on the other side. They had little to say against the Abbot himself, but his predecessors must, they averred, "have pleasured much in odoriferous savours," since they had converted the corn and grain rents of the monastery into " Gilliflowers and Roses ". I fancy this was "writ ironical". Nominal rents of roses and gilliflowers are not uncommon in old records; if the ancient Abbots converted the substantial into the fanciful, no doubt they had good consideration for so doing. The Commissioners are mighty wrathful since the final loss fell on the Crown or its nominees. A touch of letters hangs round the ruins of Boxley; it was from the grounds of the Abbey that Tennyson chose these charming pictures which serve for prologue to the *Princess*.

Between Boxley and Maidstone lies Pennenden Heath. Here was the great open-air meeting-place of the Kentish folk for centuries. Thus here was held the famous Council of 1076 when Lanfranc recovered for the Church great part of its possessions from that royal and episcopal robber Odo of Bayeux. Here appeared in a wagon drawn by oxen the aged and learned prelate Agelric of Chester to aid, with wellnigh his last breath, the cause of the Church by his intimate knowledge of Saxon law and custom. I found one inscription on this famous soil, it was to a Maidstone alderman who had helped to preserve part as a public park. A Maidstone man I met on it informed me "they used to hang people there," which seems the sum of local tradition on the subject.

Detling succeeds. Here Mr. Cave-Brown, the late vicar, avers was a resting-house for Pilgrims of which some slender fragments are extant. I do not think he makes his point quite clear, though he has carefully collected every scrap of historical information possible. Detling has lurked obscure through the ages. A local proverb avers it "barren in soil, fertile in twins". It nestles close to the lower slope of steep Detling Hill—ancient, sequestered, beautiful, you leave it with a sigh of longing. Boxley had its name from box trees, Hollingbourne from its hollies. By it the way is clear, and so on to Lenham and Charing, where a substantial fragment remains of the ancient palace. Vortigern gave the place, they say, to the early British Church, at least it possesses a charter old as Alfred the Great, but to the pious Pilgrim all was nothing compared with the choice curiosity here on show, the block, to wit, whereon John the Baptist was beheaded, brought from the Holy Land by Richard the Lion Heart! It, as you foresee, is long vanished. You now climb steep Charing Hill, to which succeeds a descent through wooded scenery of almost fairy beauty. At the bottom where the road from Ashford joins this way, stands on a modest hill exquisite Chilham.

The authorities trace the Pilgrims' Way among these roads through Eastwell Park, Boughton Aluph, and Godmersham and then on to the platform of Chilham Castle. I once remarked on the size of Chilham Church to the incumbent who was good enough to show me over. It is obviously out of all proportion to the number, past or present, of the folk of the district; he gave me the doubtful, but not rare, explanation that it was planned to accommodate passing Pilgrim crowds. It may be so, but remember the idea of your old-time church builder was to make the house of God as large and as splendid as he could. Of all the historical and other interest that lie hid in Chilham I must not here speak. It is to my fancy the gem of village Kent, with a wealth of ancient houses and noble trees and fair ways, and it is singular in this, there is no new suburb ringing it round. No week passed, I was told on the spot, but some one applied for ground on which to rear a more or less elegant villa, but no permission was given, and for the present at least this haunt of ancient beauty is unspoiled.

After Chilham the way, I think, gets a good deal

confused. If you follow along the bank of the Stour you are little more than five miles from the Sacred City. Indeed some time ago you caught a glimpse of the Angel Tower.

The many converging ways crowd close to one another and there are numerous by-paths connecting them, but it is certain enough that the old road must have gone through Bigberry Wood, where it cuts straight through the ancient earthwork of the fort that is still discernible there, a fort perhaps as old as the road itself. Then as I take it you proceed by a road through hop-fields finally degenerating into a suburban way, flanked by small houses and the backs and gardens of larger villas. One Sunday morning strolling along it I asked what was it called from two pert damsels tripping forward in all the sacred finery of the serving-maid. "Cut-Throat Lane" was, as I expected, the prompt answer, strange, but not altogether singular! The local authorities have left the place anonymous not daring to give the proper title, not as yet venturing to ticket it "Oxford Road" or "Clifton Vale" or something else threadbare and commonplace. A few minutes afterwards I turned round St. Dunstan's Church and was again before the West Gate of Canterbury.

CHAPTER XX

A NOTE ON OTHER PLACES AND ROUTES

"All Roads lead to Rome"—Maidstone and Canterbury—Pilgrim Traces—An Old Bridge—The Cult of St. Thomas at Maidstone—The Port of Dover—A Strange Monopoly—The Housing of Pilgrims—The Murder of Thomas de la Hale—Objections to Canonisation—The Chapels in Dover Castle—Stray Memorials of St. Thomas throughout Kent.

I HAVE now described in some detail the chief ways to Canterbury followed by the Pilgrims, but "all roads lead to Rome". Every important city is the centre of a network of paths. Canterbury is so now, it was so then. Through each of its seven gates Pilgrims entered, but only where the human stream ran deep has it left marks we trace to-day. I do not pretend to be absolutely exhaustive. I will content myself then with a reference to one or two chief places not already dealt with in this connection.

I take Maidstone first. The road by which Maidstone is entered from the west runs mainly on the low ground between two ranges of hills. It is very ancient. Most probably in early times it avoided that town, since there was no bridge there. Diverging it crossed the Medway at Aylesford; then went by Pennenden Heath on to Lenham, where presumably it fell into the present way and so on to Charing. From that point it has been sufficiently discussed.

Maidstone Bridge was built about 1327. If this date is correct the time was the primacy of John of Stratford, one of the great prelates. Most of the early building in Maidstone was done under the influence of the Archbishops for the manor belonged to them. They constructed well for the bridge remained as it was till 1808. The roadway was only nineteen feet, but in that year eighteen feet were added. In 1879 the present bridge was built. The old, which stood a little to the south, was thereupon removed. It was a trick of the time, as we have seen, to build churches on gates and houses on bridges. Old Maidstone Bridge was thus furnished. Perhaps they served as defensive fortifications, assuredly space was not lacking in other directions. Even in the days of the ford, devotees must have passed by Maidstone, for in 1260 Archbishop Boniface founded the hospital called Newark for poor Pilgrims. It was dedicated to St. Peter and St. Paul, and stood on the west side of the Medway. It was held by a master and brethren and had a revenue of £5 6s. 0d. per annum. However great the then purchasing power of money this was not a rich foundation.

In 1395 Archbishop Courtenay merged the hospital in the College of All Saints, Maidstone, of which we have substantial remains. At the Reformation all passed into the Royal hands, and then speedily out again, but not to the Church. In our own day the relics, one is glad to learn, are dedicated to the public use. The Archbishops had here from 1348 one of their favourite palaces, but that went with the rest. Newark was dedicated, though apparently in a subsidiary sense, to St. Thomas of Canterbury as well as to the two apostles mentioned. The small chapel of the hospital lingered on to our own time though it was put to all manner of secular uses. In 1836 it was restored, and opened for religious worship in July, 1837.

The principal church of All Saints was used for divine service right through the various changes. Here was a chapel containing an altar to St. Thomas where a chantry was endowed in 1406 by Archbishop Arundel; the appointed priest was to say masses for the welfare of Kings and Archbishops and some humbler

OLD PALACE, MAIDSTONE.

folk. He had £6 13s. 4d. secured to him from the tithes at Northfleet. All this shows what we might expect—the passage of a certain but not large number of Pilgrims.

I turn to Dover, ancient and famous, as all the world knows, its castle a Roman stronghold; a port ever in use for embarkation and disembarkation by travellers. It is connected with Canterbury by an old Roman road, a branch of the Watling Street called *Alba Via*, and moving along this, we call up a long procession of all sorts and conditions of men from Kings downward, shadowy forms passing to and fro over Barham Downs and in and out this ancient Cinque Port. The medieval citizen, grasping as is the merchant's habit, not content with the natural advantage the vicinity to the Continent gave him, made every effort to secure a close monopoly of the traffic. In the golden days of St. Thomas's shrine Pilgrims must have made a large proportion of the incoming travellers, but there were also many shrines on the Continent or still farther afield—"Ferne halwes kouthe in sondriy londes," as Chaucer puts it. Now if your Pilgrim went abroad it usually meant that he had some money in his pocket, and was worth the careful attention of shipmen and boatmen as well as innkeepers, for the richer sort were not content with the plain fare that charity provided. We have abundance of contemporary record to show that the various classes who live by travellers preyed upon them just as much then as they have ever done since.

The folk of Dover procured a royal charter confirmed by Parliament, providing that "no Pilgrim was to pass out of the realm except from Dover under the penalty of imprisonment for one year". This was an extreme measure, but how could it be effective? It did not try to regulate where Pilgrims were to land in England since that were wellnigh impossible. For their going how could you punish them after they were gone? Dover in the time of the Pilgrimage had Sandwich to compete with, even then it was important. For special provision there was a *Maison Dieu* which was erected in the reign of King John by Hubert de Burgh, Earl of Kent and Constable of Dover Castle, besides much else. It was a big hall with kitchen attached, where Pilgrims had free board and lodging for the space of fourteen days. In later years the scope of the charity widened, soldiers returning from the war, destitute or disabled, being here entertained. In our own day the corporation recovered and restored the hall, which is now adorned with portraits of more or less local celebrities.

Of the other religious houses in the town I will only mention the priory of St. Martin le Grand, where there was some provision for Pilgrims as well as at the house of St. Martin and St. Mary Newark. There is a curiously instructive story connected with the latter. In 1295 the French raided the place and found therein but one monk, Thomas de la Hale, to wit. He was old and had a great reputation for sanctity; he had refused to flee with the others, and though threatened with instant death if he did not discover the treasure of the house, remained silent. He was cruelly murdered. The French were presently expelled. The prior with his monks returned and hailed Thomas as saint. Soon the "Martyr of Dover" acquired a far-spread reputation. Pilgrims flocked to his tomb; there were frequent miracles, as many as five dead folk were restored to life. Richard II tried to get him canonised. Adrian VII, favourably impressed, issued a bull directing an inquiry. Unfortunately one of the chief members of the Commission was the prior of Christ Church, Canterbury. What was to become of *his* shrine if a new and captivating saint of the name of Thomas, moreover, were to divert one of the Pilgrim streams just where it began to flow? You are not surprised that interest languished, and presently the memory of the blessed Thomas disappears into obscurity, though there was an altar to him in his own house. In the keep of Dover Castle there was a species of double chapel or two chapels one above the other; the lower being dedicated to St. Andrew and the upper to St. Thomas of Canterbury. These are distinct from the ancient and famous church of St. Mary in the castle itself. I should also note that there was a hospital for lepers outside the town dedicated as usual to St. Bartholomew, but we know that such a place was in use for many who were not Pilgrims.

Of the road between Dover and Canterbury I will say no more. On the way we pass over Barham Downs, some four miles long. Here great armies have met and other assemblages have been held from time to time, but they have no connection with the Pilgrimage, so we leave them unchronicled.

It is not worth while to speculate where else Pilgrims may have landed on the Kentish coast. Folkestone, for instance, is ancient, also on the hills above it we have St. Thomas's Well, but such are scattered over the district; if any passed that way they have left no certain record. I shall not pursue these minute inquiries further.

CHAPTER XXI

A PILGRIM OF TO-DAY. LONDON TO DARTFORD

The Start—Over London Bridge—The White Tower—Southwark Cathedral—"The Moral Gower"—The Boro' High Street—"The Old Tabard"—Talbot Yard—The Old Kent Road—The Pilgrims Revived—"The Thomas à Becket"—"Admirals All"—Blackheath Hill—A Wayside Well—Some Quaint Names and Old Houses—Dartford.

THIS is an account of a present-day Pilgrimage to Canterbury along the main route from London.

I began my journey at the fit season of the year,

Whan that Aprille with his schowres swoote
The drought of Marche hath perced to the roote,

but seasons, save for change of temperature, pass comparatively unnoticed in London. In walking across London Bridge I discovered nothing of the pleasantness of spring save a certain softness in the air. It was the slack time of the day; the morning flow into the City was over, the evening ebb homeward had not begun, yet the traffic tide ran strong enough. There was a constant stream of vehicles, cabs, motors, vans, lorries, and so forth, and sufficient pedestrians to make a respectable crowd. Some loafers were gazing idly over the parapet watching the endless business of the Pool, others were tossing crumbs to the seamews. This last is one of the most characteristic sights of modern London, not unpleasing either, since the birds show every confidence in the rough folk that nourish them from their own scanty store. The chief object was the Tower, of which the White Tower is so prominent a feature. Were the old-time Pilgrim to pass over the Bridge to-day, this is the one single thing he would recognise. It was there ere he came, it is there now that he is gone.

Do you grasp how absolutely old London has perished? Places keep the same names, institutions are still in active life, but how changed every material form! The Great Fire is answerable for much, but not for everything. I know not what a Pilgrim would recognise on the south or Surrey side of the water. There right in front of me at the end of the bridge on the right hand was Southwark Cathedral or St. Saviour's as it was formerly called. There *are* pieces of old work about it; yet so much rebuilding and restoration, judicious or no, has gone on through the centuries that it must have looked quite other in bygone years. Even its tower, square, strong, unyielding, as it looks to-day, had seemed quite strange.

I went in to look at the monument of "the moral Gower". I suppose the effigy has some touch of the original. It is that of a man with a long lugubrious face, a kind of face that would move Chaucer to scoff though not unkindly, as he did at his friend. A tomb and figure like this enable you in some sort to touch the past; it was something to bridge over the long, dim centuries. The ancient church is full of other objects of interest. There is the stone effigy of a knight, older than Chaucer's time, but who "prefers to remain anonymous". There is the Harvard Chapel in memory of the founder of Harvard University, who was baptised here, but then that was as recent as 1607, and there is also a stained-glass window, dedicated as late as 1906, to Henry Sacheverell, D.D. (1674-1724), whose claim to renown rests on a sermon of such pronounced Jacobitism, that he was thought worth the dignity of impeachment before the House of Lords. Odd that any one considers him worth memorial at this time of day!

And so outside and along the Borough High Street, a busy yet dreary third-rate London artery, not now famous for its inns, nor even for its railway receiving offices, though they abound—since such things do not confer renown. The name of a yard here and there wakes an old memory. Thus 59 is the White Hart Inn Yard, but there is no "White Hart" Inn.

I fixed my "Tabard" with the greatest ease on the east side of the way. Its number is 85, it is designed "the old Tabard," and is at the corner of Talbot Yard which as we know is a corruption of Tabard. An inscription bears that it was rebuilt in 1875, but it is simply an ordinary public-house or inn. It was plastered with placards, turned with some quaintness of phrase, lauding its own meats and drinks. "Davis delivers digestive dinners daily"; here and elsewhere alliteration added its artful aid as strongly as in the master's works, and the words might be an up-to-date rendering of Chaucer's commendation of that very house—"And wel we weren esed atte beste". From the further statement that the beers were from the Cannon Brewery, you inferred it a "tied" house. The second and third floors had little, ornamental balconies obviously *not* copied from the old historic inn. I ventured into the eating room and had a repast, at least passable and extremely cheap. The room was decorated with ordinary advertisements of blends of whiskies and brands of cigars, but there was not even the cheapest print of Chaucer or his Pilgrims, nothing to remind that this bore the name and was on the site of the most famous inn in all England! It was a little odd, for one knows how keen proprietors of such places are to use everything that may add to the attractions of the place and draw customers. The obvious inference was that the frequenters had no possible interest in such things. "What did you 'ave?" said the barmaid, perhaps I ought to say the tappestere for the

A PILGRIM OF TO-DAY

sake of local colour. Those were the only words spoken to me, and in the hurry of midday traffic I could not commence a roving inquiry. Let Mr. Davis prosper as he deserves, at least he makes no traffic out of Chaucer's shadow.

I walked down the adjacent Talbot Yard. I found part rebuilding and part given over to hop factors; the whole absolutely commonplace and lacking in interest. Even "the passionate pilgrim" from America altogether neglects the "Old Tabard" and the Talbot Yard. Can you wonder? If you poke about in corners you find even in the Borough High Street interesting touches of antiquity. A little way before the "Tabard" you note the George Inn Yard, No. 77, inside whereof is the "George" Hotel on the right hand, as charming an old house as you could wish to see. There are two rows of wooden balconies on the second and third floors from which rooms open, all neatly kept, albeit some two or three centuries old and probably reproducing the style of an earlier date. It features the "Tabard" of your fancy; you regret it is not the "Tabard" in fact. Yet the completeness of the change is some comfort; how horrible had you found this modern "pub" masquerading as the old inn of romantic memories! But you wish the old name had gone with the rest.

Inns keep, even in such places, their catch names. I noted in the Borough High Street the sign of the "Blue Eyed Maid," perhaps a too flattering compliment to the damsels of the locality!

Leaving the Borough High Street I sought out the corner of Union Street and Red Cross Street to find if anything remained of that unconsecrated "single woman's churchyard" of tragic and sordid memories called the *Cross Bones* since it had "an emblem of the name over the gateway". I found no trace, but what I imagine to be the site had been converted into an open space with walks and seats where children were at play. Indeed a happy transformation!

I gained the Old Kent Road by Tabard Street, a modern thoroughfare to the left at St. George's Church. The street used to be known for its brush makers and its rag and rope merchants. Some were still to the fore, but fried fish shops and cheap lodging-houses were much in evidence. A great part was in process of reconstruction; perhaps something more noble may arise from the ashes. On the left was Camelot Street, which smacked of Arthurian romance, but was as dingy a hole as could be imagined. Then I turned into the Old Kent Road which is broad and lively at any rate. Here opposite the " Bricklayers Arms " was a Carnegie library given to Southwark in 1907-8. It is adorned with two mosaics which represent Chaucer and the Canterbury Pilgrims in the courtyard of the " Tabard," and at the prize feast, promised for the return, though Chaucer has left its joys untold. Thus the memory of the Pilgrims is in some sort preserved on the very route they took.

On the other side of the way my glance fell on an inn with a curious rococo or even rakish style of architecture quaintly termed the " World turned Upside down ! " and so I passed on " Unto the waterynge of seint Thomas ".

Alas for this place with its long and famous history, of which there remains no local memory! The brook or spring has clean vanished, if it still runs it must be in a drain-pipe. It is said to be at the second milestone, but even that has gone or I missed it, spite all my care, but one sign remains, to wit a large public-house at the corner of Albany Road called the " Thomas à Becket ". It is the lineal descendant of the original ale-house which stood there in the days of the Pilgrimage. I went inside to take a glass of that London ale commemorated by the master; the place was empty for the moment, so I ventured to inquire of the young lady (I will not repeat the feeble witticism of "tappestere") the origin of the name of that house; she stared and amiably replied that she had not the least idea. That was an end of the matter, and I departed neither a sadder nor a wiser man. To prevent a possible mistake I note that just opposite is the Maze Pond Baptist Church. An inscription tells that it dates from 1876 but was founded in 1692. I presume it was removed there from the original site, for Maze Pond has no connection with St. Thomas à Waterings, but was in Tooley Street which we passed just as we crossed London Bridge. Of late the London County Council have inscribed houses where famous men have spent some part of their lives. An extension of the system might be urged. This was an important historic locality on the edge of old-time London, and a few words of lettering to that effect were here assuredly in place.

The Old Kent Road is very long, containing, indeed, a thousand numbers, but I found nothing in it to help my present purpose. I must say the same of the New Cross Road which continues the way to Deptford. The ornate font of Deptford Town Hall is worth a glance, adorned as it is with four well-cut stone figures of English worthies, "Admirals All," which stand out in bold relief, but the earliest is, I think, Drake, and even Elizabethan times are too late for us. Deptford Bridge runs level with the road, but it is open to right and left, so you see on the right a patch of green and various pieces of broken pottery in the ooze of the Ravensbourne when the tide is out. On the left side towards Deptford creek the view is obstructed by the huge and ever-growing mills of the Robinson Company. In a street on the right hand is a monstrous, plain, but not ugly edifice called "Carrington House," a County Council hostelry, which accommodates 800 men at the reasonable charge of sixpence per day. They give you everything but food, and that you can purchase at reasonable rates. There are reading rooms, smoking rooms, and so forth. The guests are not Pilgrims, save in the sense we all are, but toilers, yet there are obvious points of resemblance between this and the Pilgrim hospices, though the accommodation would have seemed luxurious to the ancient wayfarers.

I turned up Blackheath Road, and so on to the Hill and Blackheath itself. A few minutes in an historic spot tell you more than much reading. It is an elevated tableland, imposing by its size, with a view all round, now mainly of houses, the very place for an encampment or a meeting, or a great ceremony, though the only campers there that evening were a party of boy scouts. I followed the road by the wall of Greenwich Park. The glimpse through the open gate was inviting in the sunset, but I had other business on hand, so worked round into the old Dover road. I asked a humorous individual if that was right for Dartford. He contemplated me with mirthful pity, " You've a tidy hill to climb ". " Shooter's Hill? " I queried; " Yes, and the way is mainly uphill." If he meant what he said, it is an illustration of a fact familiar to all who are interested in human testimony, to wit—its singular lack of accuracy. The rise is nothing to speak of, and once at the top the road to Dartford is mostly a descent. The hill is pleasant enough with fine trees and fine houses, and a bit of common or open space rigidly preserved. There are ale-houses—one quaintly termed the " Fox under the Hill "—as plentiful as in the old times, and hospitals at least as frequent as the vanished lazar houses. Human needs and cravings are the same in all ages, a trite but irresistible reflection. On the ascent I passed what looked like a wayside shrine or chapel, perhaps because my mind was filled with thoughts of other days. However, it was a memorial well, horribly scrawled over by irreverent passers-by. The inscription was a famous line of Browning: "Write me down as one who loved his fellowmen". It seemed irrelevant and even ironical!

There was a fine prospect from the hill-top. A great fire glowed at some distance; all round sparkled thousands of lesser lights; behind, green, fresh, dim, alluring, lay the pleasant fields and hills of Kent, but not through them was my way, for I was tied down by the very conditions of my journey to the main route, which was one endless suburban street, though the names of sections were sufficiently quaint and rural, "Shoulder of Mutton Green," "Bellgrove," "Welling". I recall Welling, a Cockney paradise, the bourne of the beanfeaster; there he went and thence he returned "much bemused in beer," noisy and jovial. It was some way out in the country, when the means of transit were the lumbering car, drawn by the slow horse. Nowadays your beanfeaster, tearing along in the specially chartered motor-bus, contemns the one-time village, save as a temporary halt. Beyond it are Crook Log and Bexley Heath, though the "heath" is but a memory. Crayford is merely suburban. Among the modern villas I noted two very old houses, wayside taverns from time immemorial, and still to the fore: the first was "Earl Guy of Warwick," the other the "Fox and Hounds," better known as "Ye Olde Crooked Log," both on the right hand, and spite the sham antiquity in the title of the latter, they were very interesting relics. I was heartily glad to step down the hill into Dartford, where at length the suburbs begin to lose themselves in the country. And at the "Bull" Inn, at least you are in one of those ancient posting houses which recall vanished modes of travel and old-time arrangements, for you step from your bedroom on to a gallery that runs round the courtyard as was the case in the "Tabard" whence you have come, and the "Chequers of the Hope" towards which you are progressing.

CHAPTER XXII

A PILGRIM OF TO-DAY (*continued*). DARTFORD TO ROCHESTER

The Church at Dartford—The Priest's Chamber—A Pleasant Retreat—Houses by the River—The Parting of the Ways—A Roadside Adventure—Beautiful Stone Church—Epitaphs, Quaint and Otherwise—Prospect of the Thames—Churches on the Route—Roadside Inns—Up Gad's Hill—The Dickens Country—Dartford Brent Again—A Genuine Bit of Watling Street—The Noontide Halt—Round by Singlewell—Wisdom, if you Wait—The Well of St. Thomas—Swanscombe Church—Clapper-napper's Hole at Last—The Story of its Ruin—Junction of the Roads.

I WAS not interested in the bustling activities of modern Dartford, so I got me forthwith to the church, where I could dream myself back to earlier days. I found it stuck out into the roadway most abruptly; however the roadway gracefully gives way, so the difficulty of passage is readily solved. Inside I first visited "Thomas à Becket's Chapel," whereof the name alone reminds of our saint. Long ago it was swept bare of any vestige of him. Henry VIII had seen to *that*. I gazed at the mural painting or fresco on the wall where St. George appears vigorously pounding a mighty Dragon; it looked quite clean and new, had recently been touched up, I suppose, for it is seventy years since they found it under the whitewash. My guide then took me up a narrow stair, hollowed out of the thickness of the wall, assuredly the most narrow and awkward stair I had ever climbed, but it was too short to make the journey dark or painful, and the discomfort was genuinely medieval. I value the twinges such things give me, when I wax sentimental over the days of the Pilgrimage! I then remember how much better off we are!

Between that narrow way and the modern lift, what a development there is in the means of rising from the surface!

Above is the Priest Chamber, a fair-sized room with two slits in the wall through which you look into the church. "If you was down there and I was up here," said my guide, "I could see you but you couldn't see me," and he explained that the priest peered through the squint to play a sort of one-sided hy-spy with the congregation as well as the clergy. "But why?" I queried. Like most of his kind he was not able to answer.

The thing could scarce be long done in secret, for wind of the squint would soon get about the parish. Also what was there to spy? Perhaps the congregation were possessed by an uncomfortable feeling that they were watched by an unseen observer, and the feeling might pass for religious awe! For the rest you are shown a tomb of a German printer with an inscription in old-time German, a rare thing in an English church, and some old brasses. The church is right by the Dart, and the huge square tower, they say, was raised to guard the passage in time of need; it looked admirably fit!

My wandering in Dartford was desultory. I did not explore Priory Road to seek out the scanty remains of the once great religious house, nor did I hap on Spital Street, whose name smacks of antiquity. Coming down the hill I noted with interest the Asylum Houses with the inscription setting forth the "very ancient Charity," begun and voluntarily continued for several generations by the Horsemans of Horseman's Place in this parish; even as restored it dates from 1579. A modest yet venerable foundation! Behind is a green secluded garden where the elderly inmates take their ease of an evening. This was on the right hand side of the road; on the left was the casual ward, where the modern Pilgrim of the road is put up perhaps as materially comfortable as his predecessors, but with no respect or reverence at all. A notice plainly informed the vagrant, an he entered, he must stay for two nights—why, one can only guess!

A few quaint houses linger by the river; one is built on piles under which the water gurgles and swirls. Perhaps it retains some feature of the ancient hospital that was thus edified, but the poor old houses have not been well treated,—they looked battered and out of repair; also the parts restored are done in the roughest fashion of our time. Just before you reach the church there is a narrow way called, I think, Battlow Lane. At the entrance is the most charming old house possible, with an overhanging story, quaint windows, spacious rooms. A brass plate bore the names " Shadbolt and Scales, Architects and Surveyors". Shadbolt has a good old Saxon ring about it, and as for John o' Scales, is he not famed in a ballad? Dartford Bridge is level with the road and only worth mention for that here is a pleasant view with the river in the foreground. I climbed up East Hill, for the name of St. Edmund is no longer in use, yet there is still St. Edmund's Cemetery, I think not now used for burial. For that you must seek the modern ground higher up, but the old, bounded by an ancient brick wall, is a pleasant spot when you have climbed up to it, quiet and secluded, as befits the resting-place of old-time Dartford. It has been a place of tombs since the most distant record.

When you gain on the top the historic ground of Dartford Brent, you are only in another street, for small houses are rising, thick as weeds. Here the road to Rochester parts in two, only to reunite at Strood Hill. I " did " both, and first swung round towards Gravesend. I had trifled away much of the forenoon and felt myself all of a sudden tired and hungry. Now I hold it perfect felicity to eat and rest in the open air. Alas, in the modern English country how difficult to find a piece of vacant grass to serve for couch or even seat! Everything is so confined, bounded, walled in. Here was a piece of fairly green sward abutting on the highway, yet of easy access, ready for the builder, but not yet entirely spoiled. There I took my modest meal, and was dozing sweetly over a grateful pipe, when a voice broke in, "Do you know you're a-trespassin'?" I protested that I could not possibly be doing any harm, that there was no notice given to the stranger, but the man, a short, stout, bull-necked fellow of the bailiff class, kept on in strong Kentish accent, "I don't say you're a-doin' harm, but you know you're a-doin' wrong, you know you're a-trespassin'". There was no use arguing; I curtly told him I should depart when I had finished my pipe, and that he must be quiet—a reply which seemed to astound him, for he stood staring with open mouth until I presently took myself off.

I soothed my shattered nerves by a visit to Stone Church, which stands a little back from the road on the other side of the way. It was empty and restful, a dream of medieval beauty, full of graceful lines and carving, an old-world gem in uncouth setting. A huge chalk pit in active operation was at your feet, you looked right down into it from over the churchyard; within a stone's throw were some half-dozen great black chimneys, lazily smoking, for it was a Sunday—houses of all sorts were thick around, the river to the north itself seemed as populous as the land. The churchyard was unusually crowded; also local poets had done their poor best on all manner of monument. One verse was almost epigrammatic:—

> I miss thee when the morning dawns,
> I miss thee when the night returns,
> I miss thee here, I miss thee there,
> Dear wife, I miss thee everywhere.

—almost but not quite, and I preferred the bald simplicity of another record which told in unadorned prose, how a promising youth had fallen off a steam trawler and was drowned, to the great grief of all who knew him. Stone Castle I altogether missed; probably it is swallowed in some modern mansion house.

Views of the river enliven part of this road—and at Northfleet you have a very pretty picture indeed. The barges with their red sails give a touch of picturesque, for the Thames is never without its barges. Here I fell into a trap. The long road stretched before me adorned with an endless succession of standards to carry the overhead wires for the tramways. I tried to dodge Gravesend altogether and floundered in a succession of green lanes and raw suburbs. I did come through finally somewhere about Milton Church, which I knew by the huge dial over the porch. A few yards farther, on the left side of the highway, I noticed a small, interesting-looking chapel. It was enclosed within a high wall, the gate was barred, and the ground about it seemed vacant. I asked passers-by what it was; most were indifferent and said they did not know, others were vague and useless. One hazarded the guess that it was a private chapel, attached to a fair-sized mansion which stood near. At last I chanced on a better informed person; even then he did not remember the name at first till I suggested Denton (St. Giles' Denton), which undoubtedly it was. He said service was held in it, once or twice a year, by the incumbent of Milton either for the sake of some neighbouring landowner whose church-going must be of a very intermittent character, or else just to keep it open. Then the houses ceasing, there was some stretch of fields on both sides of the way. Chalk Church stood solitary and imposing in the evening light. It is in a tuft of trees on a hill; the cottages that once hemmed it round are clean vanished.

I went by inns at frequent intervals. The motor

had brought some of the prosperity of the old coaching days along this main road. Each dubbed itself "half-way house"! I suppose between Rochester and Gravesend, but it might be between Chatham and Milton or Strood and Northfleet, or anywhere else. It was a barefaced suggestion to the thirsty traveller. Then I toiled up a long ascent to Gad's Hill, still crowned with woods as in the days of the robbers. Alas! the woods are threatened—"the Gad's Hill Park Estate" is in course of development, a large part of the hill was already planned for streets, and the axe had been busy among the trees. A little wooden estate office obtrusively shows itself at the side of the road. At the top the "Sir John Falstaff" Inn recalls in name at least the most famous traveller the hill ever had. Just opposite, as all the world knows, is the house where Charles Dickens stayed so long and wrote so much and where he laid down his pen for ever. The road we are traversing is in the very heart of the Dickens country, for we are descending on Rochester and a little over is Cobham and our destination is Canterbury. It is impossible to move about here without recognising how fresh and green the memory of him and his works remains. The common decoration of the rooms everywhere were reproductions of the well-known face and the well-known characters from the well-known novels. Mr. Pickwick is almost the *genius loci*. The house and the trees in front seemed strangely familiar; they are kept unchanged with pious care by the present tenant, a retired Indian lawyer. Some one had named the adjacent cottage Dingley Dell, which it assuredly was not.

As I went down the other side of Gad's Hill a prominent obelisk on the left slope, among the brushwood, caught my eye. "What was it?" I asked the cottager who sat smoking in his garden. He professed profound ignorance, and might be excused, for I found out afterwards from the exact Murray, it was in memory of a

A PILGRIM OF TO-DAY

Rochester auctioneer who had made a local reputation the better part of a century ago. A little more climbing and the windmill came in sight to the left hand of the road, that picturesque landmark so superb for scenic effect. Now the spires of Rochester, its Castles and Prisons, the Medway, the ships in the estuary, and the rising hill on the other side were before me, and presently half down the descent at the "Coach and Horses" Inn I came on the junction with the other way which I had yet to travel.

On the morrow I was again at Dartford Brent. Here taking the right hand way I followed as best I could the ancient Roman Watling Street. At this spot, if anywhere, it is as near as possible in its original condition. It is straight and narrow, going up hill and down dale with most uncompromising directness. In some parts the aboriginal Britons must have left the heads of all their arrows, for I never saw such a large and varied assortment of flints. Under the surely well-founded apprehension that no bicycle tyre could live in such a sea, I dismounted and walked. There was one compensation, I left the growing houses behind and progressed through the pleasant country. Even there it was hard to pick out a convenient place for the midday halt, where in the language of *Canticles* I could make my flocks to rest at noon! One ideal spot I did find; it was an old chalk quarry lined with a patch of particularly fine virgin grass. Here a party of gipsies were in possession, "seized as of fee". They were blithely carousing though I know not on what. Pursuing my way I had to put up with much less exquisite accommodation at the edge of a field.

Watling Street had one great advantage, it was impossible to mistake it, therefore as long as the highway remained identical therewith everything was well. Then all of a sudden my Roman guide went off by itself looking more ancient and venerable than ever!

There was a post at the point, but it was significantly silent in the direction of the old road. According to the map it went past Clapper-napper's Hole, and right on to Singlewell, where I was bound. Yet I feared it would land me either in a field or a wood, for it has been broken in many places. A youth digging in a garden at hand said it went to Gravesend, a place I was particularly anxious to avoid. He told me that the way to Singlewell was the second to the right and the first to the left and the second on the right again, which somewhat complicated direction turned out absolutely correct, for at last the name of Singlewell appeared on a sign-post! The way though less Roman had a good deal of ups and downs. Beyond a turning marked by the " Old Gatehouse " Inn, I saw a country dame with a basket addressing every passer-by. "They say," she began, as I came within earshot. Perhaps she had an appropriate rustic aphorism for each wayfarer, but neither I nor any one else tarried to listen.

At Singlewell I refreshed myself at the " Shinglewell Tea Gardens," where I rejoiced to see the ancient spelling so well preserved, though I did not find the well which gave the place its name, but every one knew the well of St. Thomas. It is charmingly placed under an oak tree in a little valley by the wood. A miniature lake is close at hand, or perhaps I should call it a pond. There was a modern antique tea-house just behind which at least possessed a most lovely garden. The fitness of things seemed to call for a draw-well, but in fact there was an ungainly wooden pump on the rim whereof was printed in very legible letters the dire warning, " This water is not fit for drinking". I am sure no reflection on St. Thomas was intended; the fluid, I suppose, filtered through from the pond, stagnant at times. I continued through pleasant Cobham Woods and was soon again in sight of Rochester and the Medway. Presently I touched the " Coach and Horses " and stood once more on the main track.

I must add, to complete these notes, my exploration of Watling Street, beginning at the point where it left the ordinary road. It kept its genuine character for a little and then shrunk into a mere footpath. The way was through a pleasant wood, where the footpath divided again and again though it was easy to see which was the chief. Alas! the district had been acquired by a Portland Cement Company, for the soil, it seems, is highly suitable for their purpose. They had succeeded in closing many leafy ways; one notice magnanimously stated that, not needing the ground at present, they were content to let the public use it; only the wayfarer must remember that he was on sufferance! It was a Sunday forenoon. I was not far from the populous road that connects Dartford and Gravesend, perhaps this accounted for the multitude strolling in this woodland. Then the road ran between wire fencing. Watling Street thus fenced assumed a dismally pathetic aspect. I remembered how the landlord at Singlewell had addressed me. " Sir, you now stand on the Watling Street." Some touch of distinction you observe still attached to this far-off relic of ancient Rome, though it were unreasonable to expect a cement company to concern itself about such things; but then, was this Watling Street after all? I could not tell!

Presently I found myself in Swanscombe, which is now mainly a collection of villas with some new workmen's houses. Even the church did not impress me much, perhaps because it was raining, and my thoughts were elsewhere, but at least there was the Saxon window in the tower and other Saxon bits dating from the time of Edward the Confessor, and so more ancient than the Pilgrimage itself.

I now set hard to work to find out Clapper-napper's

Hole. It was in a wood behind the church, Murray averred, and was famous in local folk-lore. The first people I asked had never heard of it, finally a young man told me he had been there some years ago ; it was nearly filled up and lay in a wood by a field more than a mile away on a footpath towards Betsham. The footpath, though it meant a long push of the cycle, was a pleasant one, by the side of a wood, and with a broad prospect of fair fields. " Just before the stile at Betsham," had directed my informant. Well ! There was the stile and beyond it were the houses of the village, but where was the Hole ? Stepping back a few paces along the path which had just left the wood, I gazed anxiously around. Ah ! there was a notice board. " No road this way ; trespassers will be prosecuted." There seemed no reason for its existence till I remembered these words of ancient wisdom. " Did you ever see that notice except where there *was* a road that way ? " I crept round by the wood and there in a corner among the trees was a little hollow in the earth. Alas ! all that was now left of this famous Danes' hole. I turned away disappointed and doubtful.

Just at the stile I encountered a labouring man about fifty-six, as he said, who had lived in the village since a boy. Yes ! It *was* Clapper-napper's Hole ! but the cement company for which he himself worked had made many changes ; they had grubbed up a piece of adjacent woodland and had filled up the hole with debris ! A piece of wretched vandalism, but " 'tis their nature to ". My friend remembered when the Hole was a great and spacious vault or chamber made, as he thought, to contain carts and horses ! The folk-lore, you see, had little of magic interest. I told him the ancient legend of the Danes. He was much interested and very appreciative. Then the talk wandered off into the evil doings of the cement company. He said one most beautiful path in the woods, a favourite of rustic lovers, had been cruelly shut down. Its offence was that it led nowhere, but meandered about at its own sweet will! What better could a woodland path do? Of course the law says otherwise, but if you are inclined to follow Mr. Bumble and call the law "a hass," you have the higher authority of Sir John Falstaff, who would have it nothing less than " Old Father Antic ".

I have already said enough on the way from Betsham or near it to Rochester, so we will again convey ourselves to that city.

CHAPTER XXIII

A PILGRIM OF TO-DAY (*continued*). ROCHESTER TO SITTINGBOURNE

The Suburbs of Rochester—The New Bridge—Provident City Fathers—The Town Wall—Rochester Cathedral—Desolate Shrines and Beautiful Gardens—The Grim Old Castle—A Bunch of Hospitals—Chatham Hill—Memories of Latter Day Saints—Rainham and Newington—On the Road at Night—Time's Whirligig at Schamel—The Modern Growth of Legends—Sittingbourne High Street.

I SPENT the night at the " Royal Crown," hard by Rochester Bridge. A famous inn it is with a long history, which nothing of to-day's appearance intimates. I took the tram to Frindsbury. I found it, spite of a few old houses, a dreary suburb—an old windmill on the height the only notable object. A certain number of windmills are sprinkled over Strood and Rochester, preserved for scenic effect, I suppose, for I never saw one working. The best thing in Strood is the view of the Medway. When the tide is full it is a pretty picture. The barges beating up or down make a gallant show; pleasure boats skim gaily along, and the hills on either side form an agreeable background, but Strood itself is as dreary as Frindsbury. I looked at the site of Newark opposite North Street, a little way towards the bridge, but the houses told nothing. The "Angel Inn" was sufficiently in evidence at the corner of North Street where it had lately been rebuilt, and was of a commonplace, not to say dingy type, though the name and the site are equally ancient.

I crossed the bridge back into Rochester. There near the " Crown " are the remains of the Bridge Chapel, carefully preserved and guarded. And next them the Bridge House had been rebuilt, also an inscription informed you what the ruins were, and that the old bridge—that is the one *before* the last—had crossed the river from that point. The new bridge had just been opened, and that is the newest of all, for the last one only endured about sixty years, so quickly have our wants increased. A bystander explained that the additional height and shape of the arches allowed barges to pass under much more readily than of old. The bridge looked very spic and span and grand with its paint and gilt and stone lions.

The Rochester Corporation have ticketed the objects of interest so liberally that he who strolls may read, thus even the passing stranger gets to know the most important features of the city in a pleasant and easy fashion. The ancient Undercrofts beneath the houses in the High Street are indicated, likewise the dwelling where Charles II put up when he returned from exile as well as another house where his less fortunate brother spent his last night in England ere he went as exile from our shores to which neither he nor his race were ever to be restored. Then again at the turning of Free School Lane you are directed both up and down to view a part of the moat and a very considerable and massive chunk of the city wall. This is, I suppose, the oldest visible thing in the city. Yet the Roman bricks in the mass stand firm and strong as when they first came from the builder. A bastion to the north, stern and firm, transports you for a moment to another world older than the days of the Pilgrimage.

Not far off is Eastgate House which the inevitable placard informs you is the " Westgate House " of the *Pickwick Papers* and the " Nuns House " of *Edwin Drood*. It is now the Corporation Museum. The quaint old rooms are admirable setting for the quaint old contents whereof most are local; you are not wearied with irrelevant matter. There is a Dickens room devoted to relics of the novelist. You may admire the genius of Dickens, and yet think that he occupies almost too great a place in Rochester, for something about him meets you at every turn, yet, if the relics are to be collected anywhere, it were well it should be in this place, the nearest city to his home, the city that he loved so well, about which he has written so much. You go out from the quaint gardens into the street to find, a little way eastward, the house raised to fulfil the charitable purposes of Richard Watts, Esquire. The Corporation have not ticketed this because the quaint little front is sufficiently inscribed already with a full account of its purposes and history. *The Tale of the Seven Poor Travellers* preserves its memory not so much perhaps as that clause from the founder's will, intimating his hatred to proctors, who along with rogues he banished the precincts. In this very town are more ancient foundations to which the world pays no heed. Why should he thus detest proctors is a mysterious and fascinating riddle. There are various solutions; none is satisfactory, and I think that, after all, the simplest is the best; that for some reason, peculiar to himself, he held in peculiar horror this peculiar type, partly clerical, partly legal, not seldom endowed with the ugly vices of both callings.

The Cathedral and the Castle stand each on a moderate height, the one above the other, widely conspicuous from road or rail. As they look to-day so they always looked. Add the fragments of wall and a few odd bits here and there, and you have a quite satisfactory medieval picture. You will wisely ignore such modern rubbish as cumbers the ground and chokes the landscape near and far. I gained the Cathedral by St. William's Gate, at least by the anonymous passage next to the old post office, which I suppose is on the site since it is the next approach eastward from the Gatehouse. The Corporation had for once omitted to affix their usual instructive inscription. It is a narrow way between modern brick walls. The glorious west door was wide open; a ray of sunlight, coloured from stained windows, fell on the floor, yet all was chill and desolate for neither priest nor people was visible, even the casual visitor was absent; no active centre this of life and thought, but something shoved to one side from the busy pressure, the absorbing interest of to-day.

A little later I went the regular round of the sights. I was most interested in the vacant chapel where once stood the shrine of St. William of Perth, totally bare now of any vestige of that old-time saint or his cult, for the slab once part and now sole remaining part of the shrine has been put somewhere else in the great church. Amid the tombs and effigies of so many bishops I lingered by that of Gundulf, though here the effigy, if it ever existed, is long gone. Even if he built not the Keep of Rochester, at least he had a finger in the pie, if I may use so irreverent an expression. A great man and a great builder; you cannot forget him for his work is all around you.

After the West Porch I duly paid my meed of praise to the chapter-house door, for these are the two architectural glories of the place, and there were quaint remains of mural decorations and the other endless wonders time has heaped together through centuries. The rough Cromwellian soldiers who destroyed over thirty brasses forgot to take away all their guns and coats, which very things are now themselves show items! Then I paced after my guide into the crypt, " the finest in England ". I ventured to hint something about Canterbury. " Canterbury larger, but not so fine," was the answer in a tone that silenced discussion. It was large and clean and dry, and bare; no mouldy smell now said our mentor with a reference to *Edwin Drood*. He told how the late Dean Hole had devoted to cleansing and restoring the proceeds of an American lecturing Pilgrimage. "How proud the Americans will be!" said an enthusiastic young lady, apparently a native of the place, who had just then come into the crypt; yet the altars that once adorned it were all gone and it stood as bare of everything as a temple of some extinct faith on the bank of the Nile! It was a relief to come out again to the sunlight. There was a gate leading to private ground. An elderly gentleman, in academic cap and gown, with a courteous wave of the hand invited us to inspect, whereupon we timidly peeped into the most exquisite of gardens. Over three centuries ago when the old order of things cracked up, and the monks were sent packing, the priory was adapted to what were then modern dwellings for the new cathedral dignitaries. How altogether charming these sequestered nooks where the old walls contrast with the fresh foliage of the opening year! Even the modern houses are some centuries old.

From the Cathedral I passed to the Castle, where I loitered away the afternoon in the garden until its trim walks became rather crowded, for it is the favourite promenade of the place. It is almost too formal and trim a garden, but the tower, even to-day, looks grim and savage enough, with its walls twelve feet thick and its massive strength. Its hundred or so empty windows gaze on you as the sightless and eyeless sockets of a body that had suffered cruel evils, but it is all an ancient, wellnigh forgotten story. The doves cooed softly in the ruins. Children played in the trim garden, and from the terrace you looked down on the peaceful traffic of the Medway. Strolling again towards the gateway I refreshed myself in the "fifteenth century tea-room".

On leaving the town I climbed Star Hill, and passed St. Catherine's Hospital, and St. Bartholomew's a

ROCHESTER CASTLE

little farther on. Both are modern brick, and would scarce excite your attention though they have a long history, the first being the foundation, transported from Eastgate, of the pious old innkeeper of the " Crown," Simon Potyn. Just at the back of St. Catherine's runs Delce Lane or Road, memorable as the scene of the murder of the pious William. His hospital stands a full mile and a half along this road. I tramped through the meanest and rawest part of the town, to find at the end a brick building useful and beneficent, but without distinction.

I now set myself to climb dreary Chatham Hill, crowded with bare houses, and with its bird's-eye views of long streets of bare houses. At the top on the left hand are the remains of Jezreel's Tower, wherefrom the Latter-day Saints were to rise to the heavens. I remember it a huge imposing building with windows and galleries, a sort of local Coliseum, but it has been sadly pulled to pieces in recent years. I think it was forfeited for non-payment of ground rent. The sect went to pieces almost as quickly as it arose, and the brick which was of especially good quality was disposed of when most convenient. A farrier of that persuasion had a workshop at the top of the hill some twenty years ago. He exhibited for sign the flying scroll and crawling characters that looked like Sanscrit, but were, perhaps, only ornamental flourishes. There is still a forge, but it bears the unromantic name of McNally, and there are no mystic signs at all. Upward I went my weary way even as my old-time predecessors, whose ancient groans and curses I heartily re-echoed. But I gained the top at last and was speedily at Rainham.

Rainham church tower stood out square, massive, imposing, but the shades of night were fast falling, so I drove past through a long straggling street, beyond the gas-lamps, and into the open country. The road continued switchback with great hopfields and orchards on either side, and frequent knots of houses. As the darkness thickened the way was lit up by the flashing lights of swift-moving motors. With a thrill of excitement I saw each approach ; it seemed to bear straight down on me, and I could do nothing but keep as near the footpath as possible, then I entered a circle of glaring light that made everything swim round. A roar and a motion as of passing winds, and I was safe on the other side. Scarce had I time to recover before there was again the swift-moving light in the distance, and the whole thing had to be gone over again ! I suppose it looks more dangerous than it is, for they see you if you don't see them, also one must assume that they take necessary precautions, but no length of experience can make cycling nowadays, along a main road on a moonless night, aught but a severe nervous trial. Though the most patent this was not the only danger of the country; it was Saturday, when the rustics throng into the villages, returning at all hours and in all conditions. The local matron has a habit of pushing a perambulator before her, of course it is not lighted, also she shows no preference for one side of the road more than another. Her nerves are not easily disturbed, apparently motors are no terror, and if they are not what else can be ? These small incidents of the way were quite sufficient to drive the thoughts of other days out of my head, but there was nothing special on view. Newington Church is a little off the main path, and for that time I gave it the go-by.

At Key Street you enter once more a long tract of houses, for it is practically now joined to Sittingbourne which lies a mile farther on. Between Key Street and Sittingbourne were the two chapels of Dental and Schamel. There is still a Dental farm, and as we have seen a modern Dental villa, but the name Schamel seemed to have perished utterly. However, a house was built there of late whose proprietor, casting about for a title, bethought him of "Schamel House". Then the place was acquired by the Roman Catholic Church. There a Sisterhood of Nuns have set up a school, taking, no doubt, some proper and pious satisfaction in the fact that their Church has in a measure got back its own, and that after so many changes the service that does not change is there again. But such names are rather literary than traditional. Victor Hugo was entranced when he heard a peasant girl singing one of his finest ballads as a folk-song, just as if it had been a traditional lay of the country. So if you wander in Kent or elsewhere to gather information at cottage doors, you must not assume that what you get is tradition at all. Here Canon Scott Robertson delved down into the history of the local past. He wrote and lectured on the subject, so that the country awoke to consciousness of its old-time history. One effect was the revival of old names, also some scraps of information are very widespread. Do not assume that what you hear has arisen from the soil, it has often filtered down from the more educated classes above.

I found the High Street of Sittingbourne crowded; it is a great neighbourhood for the making of bricks. To those who have been hard at work all the week, it seems pleasant to stand idle, to say a few words and to visit at frequent intervals one of the numerous alehouses. It is not all so stupid and senseless as it looks. Like my Pilgrims I was proceeding by small stages, so here I made my halt for the night.

CHAPTER XXIV

A PILGRIM OF TO-DAY (*concluded*). ON TO CANTERBURY

Roadside Inquiries—The Intelligent Rustic—Queen's Court at Ospringe—A Quiet Nook—Brenley Corner—Another Parting of the Ways—A Village Parliament—A Woodland Ramble—Roads, Ancient and Modern—By the Waters of the Stour—Back to Brenley Corner—Up Boughton Hill—At Harbledown—The Prospect of Canterbury—Through the West Gate.

SITTINGBOURNE church is a huge structure, too big you think for the country population of an earlier day, at least sufficiently spacious to hold such, from the now crowded district, as retain the church-going habit of their fathers. I noted the fair, beautiful, carved niche no longer filled by that statue of the Virgin which no pious Pilgrim passed without some meed of adoration.

The west end of the town is no longer called Swanstree, but there is a house called Swanstree Lodge, hard by Snips Hill, which has revived the old name. The country continued more open, and to the right was practically untouched, but the villages were frequent and always growing. I was soon in Bapchild to which Radfield and Green Street succeeded, each with a fair measure of old houses, though none, I think, that date from the Pilgrimage. Mr. Littledale gives precise directions where lie the scanty ruins of Stone Chapel. I followed them as carefully as I could, but could see nothing of the "broken walls of flint," which perhaps were hid in a wood by the stream, but it is twenty years since he wrote, and they may have quite disappeared. I forgot to put the question to a countryman I met on the road, who identified at once the

Beacon Hill and "Judd's Folly". The flat ground between is called Syndale Bottom, also Syndale House is close at hand, though then hid by the luxurious summer growth. I regretted afterward that I had not asked this intelligent rustic other points. It is only such a person who works in the fields, is daily in contact with the earth itself, that knows the ancient and minute names of places. I suppose he has occasion to distinguish one from the other. The casual tramp never professes to understand anything beyond the next town, and the shopkeeper or clerk or gentlemen of that kidney out for a stroll are equally ignorant. I had proof of this a little later in the day, after I had left Ospringe.

Here I inspected the *Maison Dieu*, as it is inscribed, which one can fairly believe is part of the old hospital as well as the equally old house beside. I turned to view Ospringe church, and on the way to it, just off the High Road, I came in Queen's Court to a very delightful piece of old-world Kent. A fairly broad and beautifully clear though shallow stream takes the place of roadway. On either side is a row of small, extremely old houses, with that quaint, projecting first story and little lattice windows which you recognise as the regular type of the ancient Kentish dwelling. One, perhaps, because it was thatched, seemed quainter than the others; it was twisted and shrunken with age, and, alas! was untenanted, as indeed were not a few of those picturesque abodes. Was it but the folly of the moment that made this thatched house so peculiarly delightful? There it stood in profound quiet, with the clear water rippling before its door; you had a choice of either world. A few hundred yards farther on, you were among the green fields and quiet ways of the genuine unspoiled countryside. A little backward set you in the turmoil of the London Road with its motors, nay its motor-buses; quite close at hand the busy town of Faversham, with its main line of railway. But few would follow the narrow path between the water and your door, or disturb the quiet of your ancient house! I presently found the water came from a sufficiently large mill-pond that was running Thames-ward, after having done its duty by a quaint, wooden mill. Still a little farther on, and there was the church, large, and with a large graveyard around it. No doubt much of it was old, but it looked quite new, owing, I assume, to necessary restoration. Just behind it, down by the stream, was a curious-looking little building of flint walls of uncertain age, which excited my curiosity. A man, having the appearance of a prosperous farmer, coming round from behind speedily satisfied me. It was there the bier for funerals was stored, also part of it was used for a very ordinary purpose indeed. I regained the High Road by following the other side of the stream, thus passing opposite the thatched house which from that point of view looked, if possible, even more attractive. If ever I revisit Queen's Court it will be with hesitation. I may have lost my appreciative mood, it may have lost its attractive aspect. It may have suffered an ignominious end under the hands of the common builder!

My next point was Brenley Corner, as to the which the passers-by expressed a curious ignorance. The Chapel House, just before, I easily found, but it was a mere modern villa, possessing only the interest of the name. The point about Brenley Corner is that some have held that by this way ran the old London Road. I have already given reasons against this theory, and everything I found that day confirmed my former opinion; however, it was an escape from the dusty highway, moreover the attempt thus to gain Canterbury had an alluring touch of adventure. I had to go by Boughton church and the village of South Street; I overshot the Corner and was only set aright by another intelligent rustic. As Mr. J. M. Cooper is

A PILGRIM OF TO-DAY

the advocate for this route, I followed his directions as closely as possible. I easily gained Boughton church, very charmingly placed amid small green hills, not restored, closely locked, its graveyard covered with long grass, and full of hillocks of the ancient type, all which gave it a certain quaintness. It is called Boughton-under-Blean, plain all around were huge remnants of the ancient wood. Numerous ways branched off, but there was a plentiful supply of guide-posts. I had no difficulty in picking out South Street, which was not of the least interest when found.

I must now pass between Fishpond Wood and College Wood. Two boys told me I was to go straight on; not content I summoned the natives round me and held a sort of rustic parliament. I found nobody knew anything of the places mentioned, save that there were fishponds in one of the woods. A lady suggested I had better go right on to the top of the hill where some cottagers would be found who had lived there all their lives, and must know. On I went, when presently the way divided right and left, with sign-posts indicating roads that led into two main ways to Canterbury, but plain before me was a wood and through that wood up the hill ran a path ancient and steep, evidently little used. This I followed, found the cottage and interviewed an antique woodman. There were many paths visible, but he pointed out one, assuring me it was possible to work round to Canterbury that way! Perhaps it was! I went along the path, if path it could be called, for it was absolutely the worst I have ever known. The ruts were several feet deep, miniature chasms in fact. I cannot understand how they ever were made. I suppose great trees had been cut down and dragged along, or carted along, in wet weather. Fortunately it was dry or I had stuck helpless.

Such must have been not seldom the medieval roadway whereupon the traveller must of necessity have sought the open country on either side, but if he were on horse, and the way as here was through a wood, what then? Frankly, I cannot tell; he may have floundered through or retreating, crept round the wood, but then to creep round the Blean!

How long I wandered I cannot quite say, paths diverged to the right and left so that I soon felt hopelessly at sea. The note of the cuckoo from a near thicket had to me a note of distinct personal mockery! Taking the most passable road I blindly stuck thereto! It dwindled to a footpath, then ran through a garden of a house and immediately thereafter discharged me on a highway, quite close, I am sure, to the point where I had entered this bewildering thicket—not trackless, but only too full of tracks! I gave up the search for Hatch Green Wood and the Old Pilgrims' Way and various other places through which I was to proceed and was content to go through Old Wives Lees, and so into the Ashford Road and then by the pleasant waters of the Stour. Without diverging I gained Canterbury by the ancient Wincheap Gate, and could only comfort myself by the trite reflection that the Pilgrims must have entered the sacred city by every gate and every way, and so by this gate and this way as well, if not as frequently as by any other.

I am the last to deny the attraction of those woodland paths in which I wandered that Sunday afternoon. Had fate permitted, I had gladly spent many days in exploring them, one after the other, till I had conquered the maze. The great difficulty is to avoid falling into the London Road or the Ashford Road which at that distance from the end are only two or three miles apart. On a moderately sized map you can see how it is possible to twist about, so as to get to the city without impinging on either, but I cannot see any reason why the great body of Pilgrims should turn and double in this fashion.

A PILGRIM OF TO-DAY

I take up the main road again at Brenley Corner. The ascent of Boughton Hill is a little trying, the main part of modern Boughton lies about the lower part thereof. The thick wood in the background is a relief to the eye; indeed this is the most agreeable of all the numerous heights on the road to London. I plodded steadily up; not even the tragic memory of Sir William Courtenay inducing me to turn to the left into Bosenden Wood, where he was shot by the soldiers on 31 May, 1838, or picturesque Herne Hill churchyard, where he was buried. He preached a sort of crude socialism and perhaps the "Canterbury Fanatic," as he was called, was not altogether a charlatan. I do not wonder that the rough folk heard him gladly. In the tradition of the district, as reported to me by an old man whose father had listened to him, he was singularly eloquent and persuasive. The secret of his success was that he brought to the peasant and woodman the gift of hope; a gleam of fancy and romance brightened for a little their dull lives. If he was in fact anything of a genuine well-wisher of the poor, it would have gratified him to know that he had not lived or died in vain. The outbreak had so many strange features that it called widespread attention to the folk of the Blean. The Church awoke to its duty. Schools were established and the Blean is now as well ordered and commonplace as the rest of this district.

Dunkirk looks modern as was only to be expected; you pass from it, descend a little, and top a minor height, whence you first see Canterbury Cathedral and its Angel Tower. Then you descend the hill towards Harbledown, where I turned aside to visit the hospital. Inmates do not come out now to meet the passing stranger as they did in the days of Erasmus, but you enter to purchase a ticket, whereupon a brother, or sister, shows you over. Of the guide as of the poet, it may be truly said *nascitur non fit*. Thus I have experienced a various fate. One brother rolled off the story with quaintness and unction, how the place was built "a puppus for lepards" by Lanfranc after the conquest, how these same "lepards" took part in the service by looking through the "squint," and so forth.

Be not critical or sceptical in such places; far better wrap yourself in the old-world atmosphere, no difficult thing in that old church, with its ancient oak seats, its touch of old fresco on the wall, and the old yew tree, which stands outside in the ancient churchyard. Then you are shown in turn the old dishes, and the skewers, and the mazer bowls, and the famous alms-box; you touch the antique crystal; you hear the quaint regulations of management; you are told of the dole of firewood given to each inmate, I dare say, since the place was first founded; you go out into the little gardens and pass to the fellowship farm and so you draw near to the Black Prince's Well which bubbles out just behind; you listen again to the dubious legend that connects its history with the last illness of that ancient English hero. The water as I saw it lay clear and pure though amidst somewhat peculiar surroundings. The sister who was my last guide assured me that it was excellent for the cure of sore eyes, but it had not been cleared out for twelve years; before that time she had constantly used it herself. She was an old woman and had been there through many seasons. She spoke of the twelve years as if it were last week, and why not? after all, what are twelve years in the centuries of still life in Harbledown?

I set myself to the last hill, and then there was Canterbury. In fact, as houses go, there is no break nowadays between the city and Harbledown. From this hill you have the most impressive view of the Cathedral. In the clear light of a summer evening the whole gigantic bulk stands out so far above the city

A PILGRIM OF TO-DAY

that it seems to have no relation thereto; the tallest houses are mushroom growths round its base. But above that the Angel Tower soars to an incredible height; you are impressed with awe as at something marvellous. Truly said Erasmus that the very aspect far off *intuentibus incutiat religionem*.

The London Road turns a sharp angle round St. Dunstan's Church. I strolled inside, and finding a reasonably intelligent official of some sort, was shown over. Every old church collects to itself in time a number of minor curiosities, each with a more or less romantic history. The great memory was of Henry II fresh from his journey, preparing himself for his memorable penance at St. Thomas's tomb. I was duly shown the chapel which seemed a very suitable spot for the preparation, though cross-grained historians stoutly deny it was in this special part of the building. There were the usual leper myths to which I paid little heed. The quaint communion table dates from Puritan times, and I suppose the two chairs near it are of the same period. With bated breath my guide told me that £500 each had been offered for the chairs. It was more interesting to gaze on the chapel of the Roper family, though it is now seated and looked disappointingly commonplace. Outside, right before me, was the West Gate. I crept reverently under its ancient walls, and so entered the goal of my Pilgrimage, the ancient and still sacred city of Canterbury.

CHAPTER XXV

TO-DAY AT CANTERBURY

The Best of the City—The Old World Charm—Medieval Remains—Gates, Vanished and Existing—The Cathedral—Its Overpowering Effect—The Service Therein—The Regular Round—Talks with a Verger—Memories of St. Thomas —Old-Time Customs—St. Augustine's Past and Present—St. Pancras' and St. Martin's—The Lesser Churches and their Yards—The Greyfriars and the Blackfriars—Modern and Ancient Creeds—St. John's Hospital—Ivy Lane—In the Museums—The West Gate Again—Farewell to Canterbury.

A BEAUTIFUL place has often one rare spot where its whole splendour flowers forth into perfect excellence. Prepared by a succession of choice passages, the last touch completes as it crowns anything. I am not sure that this is true of Canterbury; it has much on a high level, it lacks yet this climax. My own preference halts between the prospect of the city wall from Lady Wootton's Green with the ancient gateway of St. Augustine's for background, and that part of the precincts where from the Green Court you look at the Cathedral across the ruins of the Priory with the Norman Staircase behind.

Canterbury gains little from its site; on every side you see it ringed with low hills, ever and again you meet the slow river trickling through the plain, admirable enough to set off the glories which old-world art has there raised, but it is on these the city depends for its attraction. Its enchantment again is altogether medieval; unless you feel the spell of those mystic ages of faith, and the strange, to us wellnigh incredible atmosphere that hung round them, what glamour has Canterbury for you? Yet it is not a medieval city, but a city of medieval remains. There is none such in

CANTERBURY FROM THE NORTH-WEST

England to compare with (say) Bruges or Rothenburg. We have got on too well; things had to be changed and altered and destroyed for hard, practical needs, not so much here as elsewhere, fortunately, not so much here as at Edinburgh, for instance, where the device of a New Town has only to a trifling extent saved the quaint character of the old. Here the remains are so splendid and frequent that they sometimes give you the illusion of the city as perfectly medieval.

As you walk through the streets you note how strenuous is now the conservation of the past; it was not always so; here, as elsewhere, there was once a fury of vandalism; the most obvious loss was the old city gates, which are all gone, save the West Gate, and even that is now an ornamental summit, for the highway runs round as well as under it. A notice, familiar to all who have ever been in Canterbury, ordains you to enter the city through, but to leave by passing round it. It were mere obstruction, did it not serve to regulate and divide the traffic at a busy spot. We have pictures of the vanished gates; they were quaintly beautiful, not merely in themselves, but in their surroundings, but the subject is painful to all who love Canterbury; here I am concerned with to-day's aspects.

Of ancient remains, the most impressive is the Cathedral, ancient and modern too, such is the continuity of English life. Service in it has never failed, even, I think, in the time of the Commonwealth. In the city it dominates everything. You never for an instant forget it, as you wander here and there, for the great tower comes sudden on your sight at street turnings, from near and distant ways, holding the imagination captive, filling the mind, destroying the impression of everything else. You repeat again the words of Erasmus, *ut procul etiam intuentibus incutiat religionem*. Then you enter and there falls upon you the spell of the great church. Does it seem bare and cold?

Do you recall it built for more gorgeous rites and to hold relics, which even the most pious of the now worshippers would scornfully cast forth? Again there is the question of your individual taste. I at least have never felt the sober and decent ritual of the Anglican service with its restrained and measured dignity touched to finer issues.

I recall one Christmas celebration. The Archbishop was on his throne, the dignified clergy in their stalls, the scene faintly touched with colour as the winter's morning sun pierced through the painted windows, while the exquisite music rose and fell in a stream of melody, through "the long drawn aisle and fretted vault"; I heard the Dean preach a singularly eloquent sermon. He faced with a certain sad courage the later prospects of the Church, he recognised that it was pushed more and more impatiently aside, as a thing almost irrelevant to modern life; an interesting survival of ancient modes of thought, with perhaps some strains of truth at the bottom of its creeds, but how much exactly the world was far too busy to inquire, a thing excellent for ceremonial purposes, but for the rest! He showed how from his point of view the Church was again to win what it had lost, or was fast losing; yet no one looking round would have thought the faith decadent. There was a crowded and attentive congregation. The Archbishop was then in residence, and was present at every service that I saw; he did his part in serving the communion to those who came forward. The days are past when an Archbishop of Canterbury was enthroned by proxy, scarce deeming it worth while ever to visit his own cathedral city. "Ah!" says the mocker, "because the Church then felt itself secure, and is only awakening at the sense of danger," but we are treading perilous paths, and I return to my own impressions.

I went the round of the Cathedral, trotting obediently

after the verger who, fortunately for his flock, was in a leisurely mood, since it was the winter and the tourist was rare. Also he was just about to lay down his duties after half a century's service and was playfully reminiscent. At Cardinal Morton's tomb, which is in the crypt, he worked off a carefully prepared joke wherewith he had been in obvious labour for some minutes. He related for the thousandth and second time the story of "Morton's fork"; how if a noble was ostentatious, he taxed him as one able to throw gold by the windows, whilst if he made a poor show, he taxed him as one whose secret money-bags were over-plenished by rigid economy, and so either way he got supplies for his royal master the first Tudor, "a sort of early War Chancellor," he chuckled with a grin, and what could we do but smile, whatever our politics, in respectful appreciation? The crypt looked bare and cold notwithstanding its many wonders, as must look the crypts of our modern cathedrals wanting as they do the decorated altars and the burning lamps. Above we duly inspected the tomb of the Black Prince, the steps and places in the pavement worn by the knees of generations of Pilgrims and the vacant space where once stood the gorgeous shrine of St. Thomas.

It was 29 December, the anniversary of the Martyrdom. I had chosen it for my visit, but there was no mention of it till I reminded the verger. "Bless me, so it is," said he, whereupon he was careful to recall the fact several times to the attention of visitors especially as we went through the Martyrdom, were shown the very spot where St. Thomas fell, and walked out through the very door into the cloisters through which he entered the Cathedral, only a few minutes before the agony of his death struggle. We were mere casual visitors, for of Pilgrims to the shrine there were none. Your modern Catholic does go there, it is only fair to state, in considerable numbers, but he goes prosaically by train, marches from the station to the little Roman Catholic church of St. Thomas which is in Burgate just outside the precincts, and thence to the Cathedral. Perhaps you will think it worth while to look in at the church as I did if only to note the ingenious reproduction of the shrine to be found therein. Also he selects the second of the festivals, that is the Feast of the Translation of the Relics on 7 July for observance. This you will remember was also the favourite day of the old-world Pilgrim and for the same reason, because it is in the pleasant summer time.

In talk with the visitors the verger rambled on as to old observances in the precincts. The gates were locked and a register kept of those who entered at untimely hours, but, he observed with a chuckle, there were ways of evading the rules. Also the time o' night and the state of the weather were still called out at intervals through the dark in this preserved spot of old-world England. "Ah!" said one of our band whose night's lodging had been hard by, "that's what awakened me so often last night! What a voice he has!" "I believe he was what was called the bos'un on board ship," replied the verger. That stentorian bawl must be a sore trial to the new-comer or visitor in the precincts, but the canons minor or other with their spouses, being seasoned, sleep only the sounder for it all. I have wandered often in the precincts content to find them a bewildering dream of beauty, for I lack the skill to reconstruct from these fragments a perfect picture of the ancient priory.

Perhaps you will take St. Augustine's after Christ Church for the historical reason that it was once of almost equal importance; you know it has been reconstructed as a missionary college, but the place is only interesting for its past; the decay had gone too far. Here you have the antique mingled with the sham antique and the quite modern in an incongruous jumble.

Part is under the hands of the excavator and reminded me somewhat of the Roman Forum as it appeared the only time I had ever seen it. They have dug out wonderful medieval relics. The Cemetery Gate and the Great Gateway are gems of their kind, the scanty walls and even the bare space of St. Pancras' have their own interest, but as a whole I found St. Augustine's depressing. You recall that after the Reformation the place went to rack and ruin, until in the first half of the last century part was used as farm, part as tea-gardens, and part as public-house, also you are told with pious horror that in the ancient hall was held a carnival of dancing and merriment. After all the old monks were, or tradition lies, upon occasion a jovial crew. To revel in the very scenes of antique entertainment, among the battered relics of the past, were piquantly delightful! The days of the tea-garden and the public-house possess an unholy attraction for me which I unblushingly confess, but those days are now numbered with the past, are gone as irrevocably as the monks themselves and the relics they cherished!

They say St. Pancras' was originally the site of a heathen temple, and though the remains be of the scantiest you can look out and touch the Roman bricks in the structure and so link on to a remoter past. Perhaps St. Pancras' is even older than St. Martin's, but then the one is gone whilst the other remains, and of a surety so old is St. Martin's that it makes you dizzy to consider the centuries of its being. It carries the true smack of antiquity, it is small and twisted, as if shrivelled up with age; it dates, you are told, from Roman Christian Britain, also Romans and Saxons and Normans have in turn occupied and left visible marks of their occupation. There is endless discussion about the font; you may believe if you like that in this very urn King Ethelbert was baptised by St. Augustine. The person appointed to show the church rattled off its wonders in a curious mechanical manner after the fashion of a talking machine; you paid threepence and the figure worked and spoke. When interrupted and questioned, he responded in the slow drawl of vernacular Kentish, but presently resumed his mechanical strain. And so Queen Bertha came through the postern gate of Queeningate to this very spot to worship, and her yet heathen husband came through the same way to sacrifice to his gods in the temple that stood on the bare site you have just seen where later was the Christian church of St. Pancras'. How strange to think of it all as you stand there!

The minor churches of Canterbury have their own interest. There are some dozen or so, many being those of united parishes. Thus St. Margaret's is now the church of three, St. George's has two. I went through them all and found all of interest, but I have no space for them here. Each bore traces of a present active life, even if the reduction in their number can only mean that the worshippers are less though the population be more. Those that stood in the middle of the street or over the gates have long since been cleared away or moved elsewhere. At St. George's, the crowded graveyard stands right on the main thoroughfare. It is set round with houses and there are public paths through it in various directions. Of course they don't bury there now. All is trim and neat, and you can look at the crumbling stones with tender and respectful interest. It seemed a kindly thought to set the place of the dead among the abodes of the living, so they were not shut out and forgotten but retained a posthumous share in the life of the day.

The past is very obvious in Canterbury. The Cathedral, the West Gate, the Hospital of St. Thomas, at the King's Bridge over the Stour, parts of the city wall, the old Castle neatly kept though in the service of a Gas Company and used for the base purposes of a coal store, the Dane-John, are things pressed on your attention, impossible to reject. Nevertheless you must seek the choicest morsels, the liver wings of the place, so to speak, in the back-ways and the by-ways. Of these first must come the Greyfriars.

I left the main street near Kingsbridge by a narrow path to gardens, running northward; here was an inscription on a door:—

Ye waye to ye Graye Friars ruins.

The sham medieval touch laid on by the profuse use of " ye " is sufficiently irritating, but save for a vulgar placard now and again there was nothing to annoy. The Stour making a bend, forms the quaintly named, quaint looking, altogether delightful Island of Bynnewith. Here the Franciscans with excellent taste of old time made their home. It is now a garden full of ancient fragments; here a wall, there an arch, again a piece of buttress. There also built over the river is a perfect quaint old house which arches support on the stream. It dates from the thirteenth century, and though it looks its age is still sufficiently strong. There was no one to open the ancient gate, but perhaps the view of the bare inside had but destroyed the exquisite impression of the exterior. After the monks were driven forth, the place was the property of the Lovelace family, who were great folks in Canterbury in a day that is itself now dim and distant, and here for a little abode the cavalier poet Richard Lovelace, who has enriched our language with at least one charming lyric. I looked at the house from various points of view and strolled and loitered in the shady ways of the garden, discovering some quaint bit or prospect at every turn. None demanded toll. At last I went as I came nursing the quaint reflection that I alone of that day had trod untaxed the sacred soil of Bynnewith!

The remains of the Blackfriars are reached by a road a little to the west of Kingsbridge, but in a southward and so opposite direction. There is a perfect view of the chief building from one of the ancient bridges over the Stour. It looked not unlike Greyfriars, but it is built at the side of and not over the stream; it is not secluded enough for a show place, is reached by a bridge of its own, is in private hands and is now, I think, a furniture store. I sought no nearer access, for I saw what was best from the not distant bridge. The chapel still stands on the other side of the river. Since the Dominicans went forth, it had a strange later-day history, being used in turn by Baptists and Unitarians. In the last days of 1913 I saw it half ruinous, placarded with bills which vaunted its antiquarian and historical interest as inducements to the purchaser. I peeped at it some months afterwards. It had been patched up in some rude fashion, though what is its present use I know not.

As I wandered to and fro I passed various dissenting places of worship always mean, ugly, insignificant. Perhaps they were oppressed by the Church, perhaps they showed badly against their surroundings, I cannot tell. In a low part of King Street I noted two massive stone pillars at the end of a short avenue; the enclosure round was neglected and forlorn; this was the Jews' Synagogue, it was plainly not in regular use; next to it was an ale-house, and next to that again an old disused burial ground with two forlorn tombstones, the inscriptions whereon were quite illegible. I thought it might be an ancient Jewish place of sepulchre, but believe it really belongs to the parish of St. Alphege, the church of which is hard by. Here was the borough of Staplegate, the first ground given by Ethelbert to Augustine for a place of residence, and here, at every corner of the squalid ways, the Angel Steeple discovered itself towering upwards in ineffable majesty, gaining rather than losing in grandeur from its contrast to the mean paths I was treading.

I spent some time in hunting out the various hospitals. In Stour Street I passed Jewry Lane where was of old the quarter of that ancient people. This was on the left; the Poor Priests' Hospital on the right is a hospital but in name. The building like the Greyfriars and the Blackfriars dates from the thirteenth century or even earlier, but the chapel is now a dwelling house and the hall a furniture store. A quaint irony of circumstance has kept the bell, which bears the very respectable date of 1373, still hanging in the turret. When such places were dissolved the bell was usually the first thing to go. A little farther on, and of not much later date, is the ancient foundation of Maynard's Hospital, still fulfilling its early purpose as haven of refuge for poor old folk. I did not try to enter or penetrate into the garden that lay behind.

One hospital I went over with some care, that was St. John's, which stands on the left side of Northgate Street a little way past the site of the old North Gate. It is one of the most enticing things in Canterbury both in itself and for its history. Founded by Lanfranc, it still subsists on his endowment. You enter by a noble fourteenth-century archway. Shutting out to-day you call up much that was noblest, much that was merely common, in medieval England, but all quaint and interesting. A garrulous aged brother tottered in front mumbling the oft-repeated tale, but still with a certain relish for he spoke of his own home. Many of the houses are modern, but the hall and kitchen are very ancient indeed. In the one we were shown a wealth of old-world implements: candlesticks, plates, drinking cups, salt cellars, a collecting box, and the ancient accounts of the hospital. The spit in the kitchen might have held an ox, assuredly the fire-place was big enough to roast it. The chapel is in keeping, and the font looks even older than the one at St. Martin's. Here and there in the grounds there are large masses of ancient masonry, some prop a shed, others stand alone as at ease after long service. On the other side of the street is Jesus Hospital, quaint and curious enough, but only some three centuries old. Being in a critical mood after St. John's, you are disposed to disdain it as a parvenu or mere mushroom growth.

There is something to attract you in every street in Canterbury, and there is no end to the hunt for old houses. You will often be in Mercery Lane, which to the stranger is the very navel of the town. Since old time it has been the favourite approach to the Cathedral from the main street. The entrancing Christ Church Gate closes it at one end. There is the memory of that famous house, "The Chequers of the Hope," also it was the great mart as it has always been for memorials of the city. Thus, though "The Chequers" has vanished, there is sufficient of the medieval street left to make it pleasant to loiter there. Ivy Lane is a much humbler and less well-known thoroughfare, in fact it is perhaps necessary to mention that it runs between Lower Bridge Street and Chantry Lane; I never failed to turn into it as I passed, for its wealth of quaint and curious cottages, whose first folk may have seen the last days of the Pilgrimage. The old type of Tudor houses were after this pattern. I saw the road complete at Christmas, 1913, six months later half was gone, and most of the rest shut up, waiting the housebreaker. Such things are inevitable; you cannot put Canterbury under a glass case and preserve it, if you could; I do not pretend it would be altogether worth while. The new houses, however, were, of necessity, sufficiently new, but was it also of necessity that they were so terribly ugly? Not even three centuries could tone them down into comeliness, but the centuries will never have the chance; they were not built to last a third of the time.

There is a Corporation Museum where I spent an agreeable forenoon in converse with the most courteous of keepers, who showed me a wealth of material illustrating old times in the city, but I got still more satisfaction from the curious little collection which is housed in the turrets of the West Gate. It contains few objects, but they are native to the spot, and bring before you vividly some phases of the past. There is the prison, and the strait and narrow condemned cell from which you ascended to the gallows, suspended over the gate. So miserable is this cell that many a man must have taken that step with some alacrity! Here is kept a deep-toned curfew bell, old pistols, and old irons. Here was a bicycle or tricycle without gearing, without tires, with quite a rudimentary brake. It gave an impression of antiquity like last year's newspaper, something more hopelessly out of date than the Roman vases in the town museum. Finally I climbed a narrow stair and took one last, long look at the town that lay at my feet; the Angel Steeple that soared above me, the river that wound through the plain, the ring of hills set about the city, and then I climbed down again, and passing out of the gate and round St. Dunstan's, set my face towards London.

INDEX

A.

Acre, 35, 57.
Addington, 201, 220, 223.
Ady, Mrs., 206, 213.
Agincourt, 63, 119.
Alexander III, Pope, 5, 18, 19, 22, 39.
Alfred, King, 204, 209, 229.
Alphege, St., 9, 13, 90, 142, 280.
Angel Steeple, The, 128, 149, 156, 230, 269, 271, 280, 281, 283.
Anselm, St., 90, 146, 151-3.
Arthur, King, 204.
Ash-next-Sandwich, 178, 179, 186.
Audrey the Ferryman, 58-60.
Augustine, St., 115, 141-4, 150, 277.
Augustine's Abbey, 143-5, 164, 174, 176, 272, 276, 277.
Aylesford, 190, 222, 223, 226, 231.

B.

Bailly, Harry, 65, 66, 75, 76, 78-80, 87, 88, 90, 91.
Ball, John, 96.
Bapchild, 119, 120, 264.
Barham Downs, 233, 235.
Bartholomew, St., 105, 110, 183, 235, 260.
Becket's Crown, 39, 44, 153, 169, 170.
Becket, Gilbert, or à Becket, 2, 3, 36.
— Thomas, or à Becket, *see* Thomas, St., of Canterbury.
Belloc, Hilaire, Mr., 201, 206, 213, 218, 225, 226.
Benedict, Abbot, 25, 26, 42.
Bermondsey Abbey, 59.
Bertha, Queen, 139, 143, 278.
Betsham, 104, 254, 255.
Bexley Heath, 92, 243.
Black Prince, The, 39, 154-6, 172, 175, 275.
Black Prince's Well, The, 129, 134, 135, 270.
Blackheath, 88, 89, 91, 92, 242.
Blean, The Forest of the, 126, 127, 133, 267-9.
"Blue Dick," 135, 155.
Boughton Hill, 127, 128, 269.
Boughton-under-Blean, 83, 126, 127, 266, 267.
Boxley, 113, 115, 226-8.
Boys' *History of Sandwich*, 184, 185.
Brenley Corner, 126, 266, 269.
Broc, De, 7, 8, 10, 11, 17, 193.
Browning, Robert, 243.
Bunyan, John, 215.

C.

Cade, Jack, 60, 92, 204.
Cæsar, Julius, 89, 114, 126, 136, 137.
Canterbury, 1, 6-10, 13, 17, 19, 21, 25, 27-34, 38, 40-3, 46, 50, 52, 54, 56, 65, 68, 81-7, 89, 90, 100, 102, 105, 113, 115, 117, 119, 122, 126, 127, 130-3, 135-48, 155, 163-7, 175, 176, 186-91, 193, 194, 197-9, 200-2, 204, 206, 207, 209, 210, 217, 226, 230-6, 250, 259, 266-83.
— Cathedral, 5, 7-9, 11, 13-5, 21, 22, 25, 38-43, 82, 90, 128, 139, 142, 143, 149-74, 182, 269, 270, 273-6, 278.
Canterbury Tales, The, 37, 56, 76, 80, 83, 84, 99.
Cathedral precincts, 157-9, 164, 165, 272.
Chalk, 102, 249.
Chapel of London Bridge, 35, 61, 62.
Charing, 217, 229, 231.
Charles II, 122, 257.
Chatham Hill, 111, 112, 261.
Chaucer, 37, 50, 52, 56, 58, 65-8, 70-84, 98, 99, 116, 129, 168, 233, 237-40.
— Philippa, 72.
Chaucer's children, 72.
"Chequers of the Hope," The, 81, 164, 165, 244, 282.
Chilham, 229.
Chillenden, Prior, 152, 164, 165.
Clapper-napper's Hole, 105, 252-4.
Clarembald, 10, 145.
Cnut, 90.
Coldrum, 201, 221, 222, 224, 225.
Colet, Dean, 132-4, 173.
Columba, St., 53, 145.
Compleynt to his Purs, 73.
Constantinople, 53.
Constitutions of Clarendon, 5, 19.
Cooper, Mr. J. M., 83, 126, 127, 266.
Courtenay, Archbishop, 172, 193-4, 232.
Cranmer, Archbishop, 43, 45, 147, 194.

Crayford, 93, 243.
Cromwell, Thomas, 43.
Crusades, 49.
Crypt, The, of Canterbury Cathedral, 14, 20, 26, 32, 39, 150, 153-5, 160, 168, 169, 259, 275.

D.

Danes, The, 90, 95, 105, 146, 150, 254.
Dante, 77, 78.
Darent, The, 94, 217.
Dartford, 85, 86, 93-7, 119, 207, 217, 242-5, 247, 253.
Dartford Brent, 95, 98, 103, 247, 251, 253.
Delce, 109, 261.
Dental, 116, 262.
Denton, 102, 249.
Deptford, 83, 85-9, 91, 241.
Dethe of Blaunche the Duchesse, 76.
Detling, 115, 228.
Dickens, Charles, 79, 250, 258.
Doomsday Book, 94, 126, 127.
Dover, 30, 139, 183, 187, 233-5, 242.
Dreams, 31.
Dunkirk, 127, 128, 269.
Dunstan, St., 145, 160.
Dunstan's, St., Church, Canterbury, 20, 135, 160, 161, 230, 271, 283.

E.

Edmund, St., King and Martyr, 95, 247.
Edward I, 41, 53, 107, 117, 140, 211.
— II, 101.
— III, 66, 71, 95.
— IV, 123, 147, 167.
— VI, 184.
— the Confessor, 253.
Elizabeth, Queen, 89, 91, 101, 103, 154.
Erasmus, 50, 56, 101, 127, 132, 133, 167, 172, 173.
Ethelbert, 115, 139, 140, 142, 143, 150, 163, 277, 278.

F.

Faversham, 82, 83, 118, 122-5, 265.
Fisher, Cardinal, 61, 100, 101, 124.
Four-Went-Way, The, 115.
Frindsbury, 105, 106, 256.
Furnivall, Dr., 98.

G.

Gad's Hill, 102, 103, 128, 213, 250.
Gaunt, John of, 72, 73.
Gilbert de Glanville, Bishop, 105, 106, 109.
Goldstone II, Prior, 152, 156, 164, 173.
Golf, 185, 186.
Gower, 78, 237.

Gravesend, 98-101, 103, 206, 219, 247, 249, 250, 253.
Greenwich, 83, 86-91, 242.
Gregory the Great, Pope, 141.
Grim, Edward, 12, 13.
Guildford, 211, 212, 214, 215.
Guilton, 178.
Gundulf, Bishop, 108, 110, 111, 259.

H.

Harbledown, 20, 81, 83, 84, 105, 128-34, 269, 270.
Hasted, 92, 102, 104, 114, 120, 122, 126.
Hengist, 193, 223.
Henry II, 3-9, 17-21, 36, 41, 43, 53, 113, 125, 131, 160, 175, 204, 209, 271.
— III, 66, 94, 117, 123.
— IV, 73, 74, 95, 102, 172, 213.
— V, 63, 92, 119.
— VI, 95, 96, 147.
— VII, 89.
— VIII, 1, 43, 45, 67, 88, 89, 91, 92, 100, 101, 117, 118, 124, 155, 156, 171, 194, 198, 227, 245.
Hoccleve, Thomas, 74, 75.
Holy Land, The, 18, 49, 50, 53, 54, 109.
Horsa, 223.
Hous of Fame, The, 76.

I.

Inns, 63-5, 79, 93, 110, 119, 164, 165, 177, 178, 185, 238-42, 244, 249, 250, 256.
Itchin, The, 209, 210.

J.

James II, 257.
John, King, 116, 118, 193, 194, 234.
— — of France, 117, 155, 175.
"Judd's Folly," 121, 122, 265.

K.

Key Street, 114-6, 126, 262.
Kits Coity House, 201, 222, 223, 226.
Knaresborough Castle, 17.
Knights Templars, The, 95, 96.
— The, 8-19, 145, 166-9, 193.

L.

Lambard, 104, 106, 107, 218, 220.
Lambeth, 43, 157, 217.
Lanfranc, 90, 128, 129, 146, 150-2, 281.
Langton, Stephen, 40, 146, 147.
Legende of Good Women, 76, 78.
Leland, John, 198, 220.
Leper Houses, 20, 105, 110, 118, 123, 126, 128, 129-35, 214, 215, 235, 242, 265, 269, 270.
Lindhard, Bishop, 139.

INDEX

London, 2, 3, 7, **35**, 36, 56-8, 63, 68, 70-2, 74, 77, 85, 89, 90, 92, 93, 96, 99, 100, 102, 111, 112, 115, 119, 123, 137, 139, 145, 161, 205-7, 209, 219, 236-8, 240, 241, 265, 266, 268, 269, 271, 283.
— Bridge, 8, 35, 57, 58, 60-3, 88, 101, 108, 155, 161, 236, 237.
Louis VII, King of France, 41, 171.
Lourdes, 55.
Lymne, 10, 137, 187, 190, 195-9.

M.

Maidstone, 115, 219, 220, 226-8, 231-3.
Main Route, The, 56-69, 85-135.
Manciple's Tale, The, 129.
Marlow, Christopher, 89.
Martin's, St., Canterbury, 138, 139, 142, 176, 277, 278, 282.
Martyrdom, The, Canterbury Cathedral, 12, 20, 38, 42, 43, 151, 167, 275.
Mary, Queen, 46, 91, 95, 171, 174.
Medway, The, 106-8, 207, 219, 222, 225, 226, 231, 232, 251-3, 256, 260.
Megalithic Remains, 201, 220-4, 226, 227.
Mercer's Chapel, The, 2.
Middle Ages, Character of the, 17, 47, 48, 50, 51, 77, 79, 85-8, 99, 126, 140, 146, 147, 151, 181, 213, 226, 227, 272.
Miller's Tale, The, 78.
Milton, 100-2, 249, 250.
Miracles, 22-34, 113.
Mole, The, 215.
Monk's Tale, The, 78.
More, Sir Thomas, 50, 61, 100, 101, 161.

N.

Newington, 112-4, 262.
Northfleet, 104, 233, 249, 250.

O.

Ospringe, 82, 83, 119, 121-4, 265.
Otford, 217-9.
Ovid, 77.

P.

Pancras', St., Canterbury, 138, 140, 142, 143, 277, 278.
Paris, 3, 57.
Parlement of Foules, The, 76.
Paul III, Pope, 44.
Paul's, St., London, 90.
Paulinus, St., 108, 109.
Pennenden Heath, 228, 231.
Peter Colchurch, 60, 62.
Petrarch, 72, 77.
Pilgrim Houses, 52, 53, 63-7, 93-5, 99, 106, 110, 116, 117, 119, 123, 124, 161, 163-5, 176, 183-5, 205, 208, 212, 216, 217, 224, **228**, 232-4, 278.

Pilgrim of To-day, A, **236**-71.
Pilgrims and Pilgrimages, 1, 20, 21, 26-34, 40-3, 46-58, 60-70, 72, 73, 80-2, 84, 85, 87-9, 91-5, 98-128, 132, 135, 154, 160, 177, 181, 182, 184, 185, 198, 200, 204-22, 224-37, 240, 242, 253, 261, 263, 264, **275**, 276, **282**.
Pilgrims' signs, 51, 52, 93, 165, **166**.
— Way, The, 20, 200-30.
Plague, The, 29, 95, 123.
Pole, Cardinal, 45, 46.
Pollard, Mr., 83.
Portsmouth, 210.
Potyn, Simon, 110, 261.
Prologue to the Canterbury Tales, 37, 66, 77, 79, 83.

R.

Rainham, 112, 261.
Raleigh, Sir Walter, 55.
Ravensbourne, The, 88, 89, 241.
Reculver, 137, 142, 180.
Reeves Tale, The, 78, 87.
Reformation, The, 43, 45, 54, 88, 94, 99, 115, 121, 126, 130, 143, 147, 152, 158, 183, 232.
Regale, The, 41, **42**, 171.
Reigate, 215, 216.
Relics, 14, 37, 38, 42, 43, 62, 132, 133, 144, 153, 168-70, 173, 174, 208, 227, 229.
Richard I, 175, 229.
— II, 66, 73, 74, 96, 234.
Richborough, 137, 176, 179-82, 196, 203.
Rime of Sir Thopas, The, 75.
Rochester, 33, 68, 82, 83, 92, 98-100, 102, 105, 106, 108-11, 119, 121, 122, 124, 207, 219, 226, 247, 250-2, 255-61.
Rome, 3, 18, 38, 45, 49, 109, 141, 145, 150, 170, 181, 231, 252.
Romney Marsh, 196.
Roper Family, The, 161, 271.
Rumbold, St., 115, 227.

S.

Saltwood Castle, 7-9, 17, 187, 191-5.
Sandwich, 6, 87, 175-86, 234.
Schamel, 116-8, 262, 263.
Scott, 79, 212.
Scott Robertson, Canon, 117, 263.
Shakespeare, 66, 79, 80, 102, 137, 213.
Sheppey, Isle of, 113, 115, 120.
Shooter's Hill, 92, 93, 102, 128, 242.
Shoulder of Mutton Pond, 93.
Singlewell, 104, 252, 253.
Sittingbourne, 83, 115-9, 262-4.
Skeat, Mr., 83, 84.
Smith, C. R., 198.
Southfleet, 104.
Southampton, 20, 200, 204.

Southwark, 56, 60, 63, 65, 67, 68, 80, 83, 84, 93, 237.
Spenser, 84.
Stanley, Dean, 35, 45, 73, 82, 129, 152.
Stephen, King, 127.
Stigand, Archbishop, 145, 146.
Stone, 99, 248, 249.
Stone Street, 10, 187-91, 195, 196, 198, 203.
Stour, The, 137, 163, 175, 179, 181, 230, 266, 278-80, 283.
Stow, 44, 220.
Straw, Jack, 92, 96.
Strood, 7, 98, 103, 105-7, 110, 207, 247, 250, 256.
St. Thomas à Waterings, 68, 83, 85, 105, 240, 241.
St. Thomas's Hospital, 36, 67.
Studfall Castle, 196, 198.
Stukeley, Dr., 198.
Sudbury, Archbishop, 147, 162, 204.
Swale, The, 115, 118, 120, 142.
Swanscombe, 104, 253.
Swanstree, 118, 264.
Swithun, St., 204, 208, 209.

T.

"Tabard, The," 56, 58, 64-6, 80, 83, 165, 238-40, 244.
Tale of Beryn, The, 81, 82, 168, 172.
"Tavern Sentiment, The," 79, 80.
Tennyson, 12, 40, 84, 228.
Thames, The, 57, 58, 88, 89, 100, 180, 201, 206, 249, 266.
Theobald, Archbishop, 3, 4.
Thomas, St., of Canterbury, 1, 19, 20, 52, 57, 58, 61, 68, 69, 83, 90, 95, 106, 107, 110, 112, 125, 135, 152-6, 160, 182, 201, 204, 209, 234; archbishop, 3, 5; chancellor, 3-5; canonisation, 22, 23, 53, 162; early years, 2, 3; exile, 5-7, 175; honours, 35, 36, 43, 44, 67, 94, 116, 124, 161, 163, 166, 174, 183, 184, 205, 209, 210, 214-6, 232, 235, 245, 271, 275; miracles of, 23-34, 45, 113, 145, 151, 167, 218; murder of, 9-16, 21, 129, 145, 148, 151, 187, 193, 205, 275; relics of, 38, 39, 43, 45, 110, 132, 133, 167-74; return of, 6-8, 175; shrine of, 1, 39, 41-4, 46, 81, 102, 154, 156, 160-74, 233, 234, 275, 276; translation of, 39-41, 43, 147, 153, 162, 205, 276; wells, dedicated to, 21, 24, 29, 33, 68, 104, 105, 172, 218, 235, 252.
Tichbourne, 210, 211.
Tong Castle, 120.
Troilus and Cressida, 76.
Trottiscliffe, 221, 224.

V.

Verona, 38, 54.
Virgil, 77.
Vortigern, 223, 229.

W.

Walworth, Sir William, 96.
Warham, Archbishop, 147, 173.
Watling Street, 98, 103, 104, 107, 137, 233, 251, 253.
Wat Tyler, 92, 96, 97.
Welling, 92, 243.
West Gate, Canterbury, 20, 135, 147, 148, 160-2, 185, 230, 271, 273, 278, 283.
Westminster, 22, 63, 73, 74, 76, 119, 140, 141, 155.
Wey, The, 214, 215.
William of Canterbury, 25.
—— Perth, St., 107-10, 258, 259, 261.
—— Sens, 151.
William the Conqueror, 53, 104, 105.
—— Englishman, 151, 153.
—— Lion, King, 20, 21, 36.
Willis, Professor, 157.
Winchelsea, 87, 176.
Winchester, 7, 28, 90, 200-2, 204, 206, 208-11.
— Road, The, 200-30.
Wingham, 177, 178.
Wrotham, 217-20, 224, 225.
Wycliffe, 45, 50.

DATE DUE